Attack on the Scheldt

Attack on the Scheldt

The Struggle for Antwerp 1944

GRAHAM A. THOMAS

Pen & Sword
MILITARY

First published in Great Britain in 2017 by
Pen and Sword Military
an imprint of
Pen and Sword Books Ltd
47 Church Street
Barnsley
South Yorkshire S70 2AS

ISBN 978 147385 067 5

A CIP record for this book is available from the British Library

Printed and bound in England
by TJ International Ltd, Padstow, Cornwall

Typeset in Ehrhardt by Chic Graphics

Pen & Sword Books Ltd incorporates the imprints of
Pen & Sword Archaeology, Atlas, Aviation, Battleground, Discovery,
Family History, History, Maritime, Military, Naval, Politics, Railways,
Select, Social History, Transport, True Crime, Claymore Press,
Frontline Books, Leo Cooper, Praetorian Press, Remember When,
Seaforth Publishing and Wharncliffe.

For a complete list of Pen and Sword titles please contact
Pen and Sword Books Limited
47 Church Street, Barnsley, South Yorkshire, S70 2AS, England
E-mail: enquiries@pen-and-sword.co.uk
Website: www.pen-and-sword.co.uk

Contents

Author's Note

In history it is fairly easy to speculate about what might have happened if so and so had done this or that. Histories of the Second World War are full of that kind of look back where the historian has made speculative theories about what could have happened had things been different. These theories are based on the historian's research and so have some validity. But they are still speculation.

My purpose in writing this book is to detail the gruelling, ferocious fighting in terrible conditions that the Allies had to undertake in order to clear the Scheldt Estuary of the German Fifteenth Army encamped on the south shore of the estuary, on South Beveland and on Walcheren Island. In September 1944 the Allies captured Antwerp. The city's port facilities were intact and therefore could be used by the Allies to bring in supplies, men and materiel so they could continue to take the fight to the Germans.

However, in order to get to Antwerp Allied shipping would have to navigate the Scheldt Estuary and the northern shore of the estuary encompassed South Beveland and part of Walcheren Island. All along this shoreline the Germans had built gun emplacements pointing into the estuary ready to blast any ship from the water. Indeed, the whole of the coastal area of Walcheren Island was ringed by a dyke and in that dyke the Germans had constructed concrete gun emplacements and bunkers. The island was a fortress. For the Allies to use the port facilities at Antwerp this fortress needed to be captured and put out of action.

Where the speculation comes in is regarding the delay between the capture of Antwerp and the battles to clear the south and north shores of the Scheldt. Why did the Allies stall? The German Fifteenth Army was in a shambles after the Allies broke free from the constraints of the Normandy beachhead and British armour rolled virtually unopposed across Belgium as far as Antwerp before they finally stopped. Behind them came the infantry, mopping up any corners of German resistance that the tanks hadn't dealt with. The Germans were stunned by the speed of the British advance and, initially, they were unable to mount an effective defence against the advancing Allies. So the question that many have asked over the years is why didn't the British take advantage of the German collapse? Why did they allow the entire German Fifteenth Army to slip through their hands, regroup, reorganise and prepare such difficult defensive positions that the operations to clear the Scheldt would prove to be possibly the most difficult of the entire war?

Scholars and historians will likely have different answers and different interpretations for the reasons why the Allies stopped at Antwerp. Montgomery wanted to concentrate on Operation Market Garden, the ill-fated assault across the Rhine at Arnhem, the British had run out of fuel and were waiting for supplies to catch up with their armour and so forth. Antwerp was captured by the Allies in the first few days of September 1944 and operations to clear the Scheldt did not begin until a month later.

There is no doubt that there was a clash of personalities between Montgomery and Eisenhower or between Montgomery and Patton. Some of the blame for the delay can be levelled at the inertia created by the clashes between these men and other senior officers, British and American. While my research seems to put most of the blame onto Field Marshal Viscount Bernard Law Montgomery's shoulders, I don't believe that is entirely the case. Montgomery wanted a quick end to the war. He believed that crossing the Rhine at Arnhem and then pushing across the northern plains of Germany to Berlin with a large enough force would give the Germans a hammer blow from which they could not recover. However, one could say that the motives behind Montgomery's decision could be because he wanted the glory of entering Berlin first. It has been well documented that Patton was a glory seeker and, to some degree, so was Montgomery as were other Allied generals. But does it really matter?

Personally, I don't believe it does. That's why my reasons for writing this book are not to point fingers but to document the hard, bitter fighting the Allies had to go through to defeat the Germans in the Scheldt area. From the start of operations it took the Allies eighty-five days to clear the Scheldt and be able to use the port facilities at Antwerp. Those eighty-five days saw some of the worst fighting of the war. It was an inch by inch, foot by foot, yard by yard hard slog through thick mud, oozing slime, deep water in virtually continuous rain against fierce, concentrated enemy fire. It was a fight that saw many German officers ferevently forcing their men to hold out to the very last man. It saw some of the more fanatical Germans shooting their own troops when they tried to surrender.

Much of the material for this book comes from reports written by Canadian military historians, military officers who were embedded with units and were able to document with a high degree of accuracy what went on. The battle to clear the Scheldt was a Canadian and British affair with support from other Allies including the 1st US Army. It was an Allied coalition of joint operations where the combined arms and services, land, air and sea, operated in conjunction with one another. Armour supported the infantry, air support was there when requested, weather permitting, and the Royal Navy provided bombardment support from the sea as the amphibious landings took place.

My reasons for writing this book were not to lay blame or look at 'what ifs' but to document these operations as best I could so readers can get an understanding of all-out war. We've seen war glorified in films and in books as well but what is written in these pages are the facts as they were taken down by the people there. The Canadian historians attached to their units were very meticulous in what they documented, the British much less so. The British did not have historians in every unit and what they would have recorded came after the battles, based on eye witnesses, on debriefings and so forth. So these are the facts as closely as we can get them. My hope is that the reader in this early part of the twenty-first century gains a deeper understanding of full-scale war. I believe we should all know this so that we never have to go through this again. Hopefully, the next time politicians want to get involved in a war, readers will be able to cite this book along with many others, and say, never, ever again.

Graham A. Thomas
Warminster, 2017

Maps

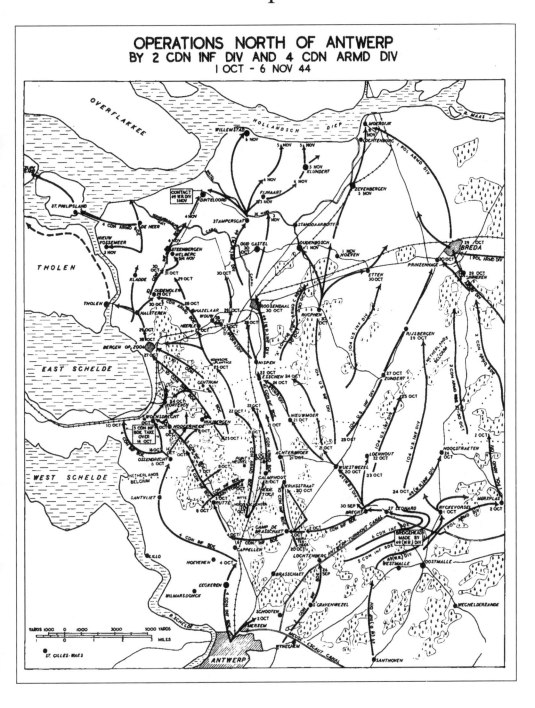

OPERATIONS NORTH OF ANTWERP
BY 2 CDN INF DIV AND 4 CDN ARMD DIV
1 OCT - 6 NOV 44

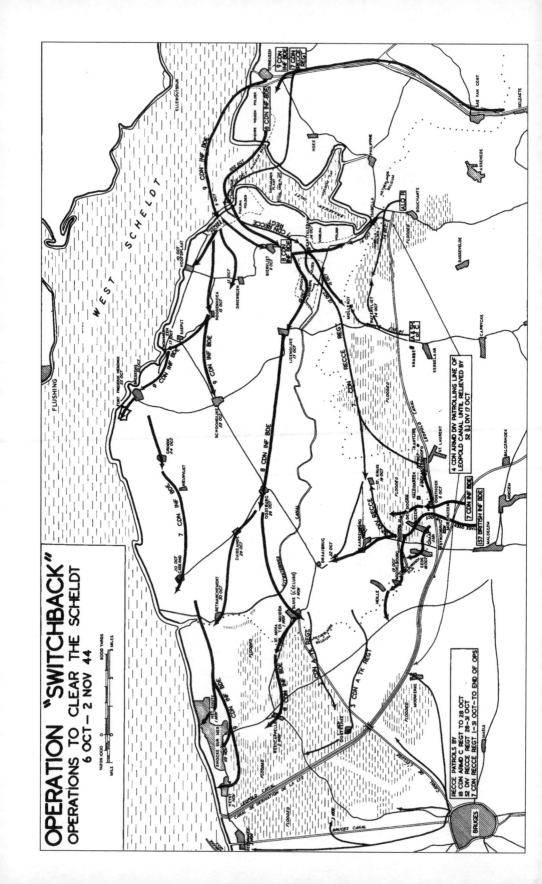

OPERATION "SWITCHBACK"
OPERATIONS TO CLEAR THE SCHELDT
6 OCT – 2 NOV 44

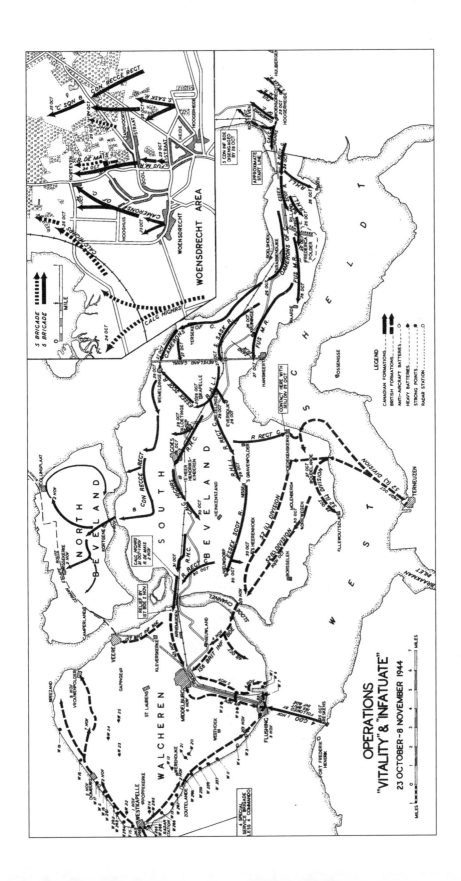

OPERATIONS
"VITALITY" & "INFATUATE"
23 OCTOBER - 8 NOVEMBER 1944

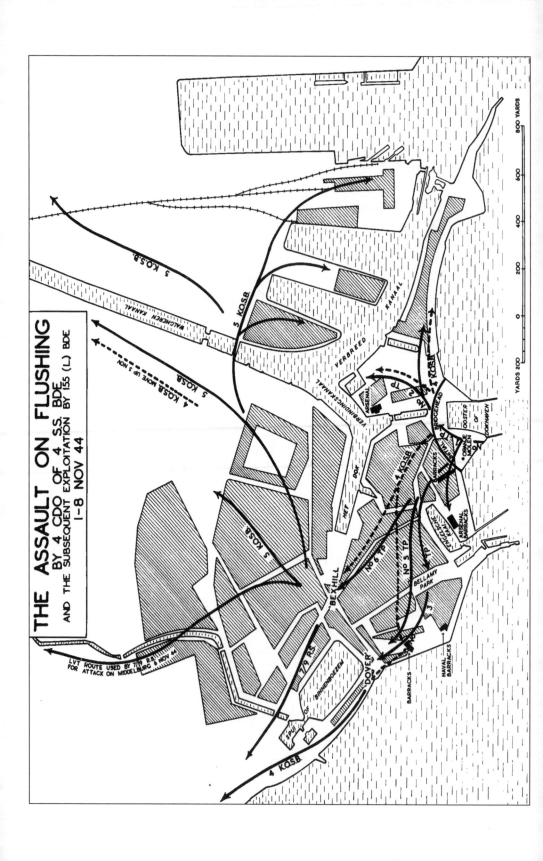

THE ASSAULT ON FLUSHING
BY 4 CDO OF 4 S.S. BDE
AND THE SUBSEQUENT EXPLOITATION BY 155 (L) BDE
1-8 NOV 44

Part 1

First Moves

Chapter 1

Clash of the Titans

The Allies captured the huge port of Antwerp on 4 September 1944. Surprisingly, when the 11th Armoured Division rolled in the port facilities were intact. Yet, instead of getting the vital port up and running as soon as possible, which meant clearing the Scheldt Estuary of the entrenched enemy positions, it took the Allies eighty-five days before the first convoy sailed into the port of Antwerp and began unloading supplies vital to the Allied march into Germany.

Why it took so long is a subject that has been, and likely will be, controversial. That Field Marshal Montgomery prevaricated on mounting operations to clear the Scheldt has been well documented by historians and scholars. The key reasons come down to the personalities of the three main Allied commanders, Field Marshal Montgomery, US General George Patton and Supreme Allied Commander General Eisenhower.

Antwerp was the second largest port in Europe and 'the only port equipped to sustain an army of two million men'.[1] Indeed, the number of men under arms for the Allies doubled by the time the Rhine was reached. Antwerp was the only port suitable for sustaining such an enormous army. Antwerp was the gateway to victory, the key that turned the lock and opened the door for the Allied advance to Berlin. It meant that the route across the northern plain of Germany was now open to the Allies with all roads ultimately leading to Berlin.

Before the 11th Armoured Division arrived in Antwerp the Belgian Resistance forces had fought to protect the port facilities from the retreating Germans and the damage they would have caused. In complete disarray and panic, the German forces could have been mopped up quickly, their only escape route cut off. But this was not to be.

The German Fifteenth Army, under the command of General Gustav von Zangen, quickly regained its balance and conducted an orderly withdrawal. In its wake it left behind well-armed and trained garrisons to defend the Channel ports. In order to guard the approaches to the southern bank of the Scheldt the Germans set up a near impregnable line of defence along the Leopold Canal. To defend the entry into the South Beveland isthmus, von Zangen concentrated a large force in the area of Woensdrecht. On 6 September, the bulk of von Zangen's army began an orderly withdrawal north from Breskens, across the Scheldt Estuary to Flushing on Walcheren Island.

Despite constant air attacks by the Allies, von Zangen managed to withdraw 80,000 men, 600 guns and all their vehicles in just 2 weeks.[2] Von Zangen was able to achieve this successful retreat by day under the protection of the powerful artillery guns already embedded in concrete emplacements along the dykes on Walcheren and South Beveland. To avoid air attack, he continued the bulk of the withdrawal by night.

While the Germans escaped destruction and disaster, their withdrawal was very costly for the Allies. From 6 September 1944 to the German surrender on Walcheren Island on 28 November the total number of casualties, killed and wounded, amounted to more than 60,000, with over half of them being British and Canadian.[3]

The battle to clear the Scheldt was one of the worst the Allies had fought. For a start the weather was foul. It was a bitter 'winter deathtrap of the Dutch polder lands by men exposed not only to the weather but the direct fire of the enemy'.[4] This was especially true on Walcheren Island where much of the battles were fought in the oozing mud that clogged vehicles, tank tracks and made advancing extremely difficult.

At this point it should be emphasised that Walcheren Island, guarding the mouth of the Scheldt Estuary, bristled with some of the most powerful and heavily concentrated gun emplacements in existence. Against this island fortress, the Allies launched an amphibious assault by 4 Commando Brigade.

Eisenhower became Supreme Allied Commander of the Supreme Headquarters Allied Expeditionary Force (SHAEF) in January 1944. He took over as Supreme Commander in the field from Montgomery on 1 September and his first priority was to capture Antwerp and clear the Scheldt Estuary.

His first struggles, however, were with Allied leaders and officers on matters vital to the success of the Normandy invasion; he argued with Roosevelt over an essential agreement with de Gaulle to use French resistance forces in covert and sabotage operations against the Germans in advance of Overlord. Admiral Ernest J. King fought with Eisenhower over King's refusal to provide additional landing craft from the Pacific. He also insisted that the British give him exclusive command over all strategic air forces to facilitate Overlord, to the point of threatening to resign unless Churchill relented, as he did. Eisenhower then designed a bombing plan in France in advance of Overlord and argued with Churchill over the latter's concern with civilian casualties; de Gaulle interjected that the casualties were justified in shedding the yoke of the

Germans, and Eisenhower prevailed. He also had to skillfully manage to retain the services of the unruly George S. Patton.[5]

The urgency for this operation was sparked by the June gales that hit the Normandy beaches on 19 June, lasting four days and destroying the Mulberry harbour and the installations on the beaches. A better, more permanent solution needed to be found that would enable the Allies to land men and materiel on a continuous basis in order to supply the mainland armies. This steady flow of troops and materiel was kept going through ingenuity and hard work. However, in June the Allies were still very close to the beaches but by September they had pushed out by hundreds of miles. The supply lines grew longer and longer as the armies advanced and that meant the challenges of supplying and maintaining these armies became greater and greater. In September the gales struck again, adding to the difficulties of keeping the supply lines functioning. Antwerp had to be opened and opened soon.

However, six weeks after the actual port facilities at Antwerp had been captured a message was released by Headquarters 21st Army Group that the priority had changed and that the Army Group was going to head west to clear the Scheldt and get the port up and running. Yet, this announcement, issued on 18 October, was little more than hot air as much of the British Second Army was facing east and operationally committed elsewhere. It was the First Canadian Army that began operations to clear the Schedlt which ultimately led to the surrender by the Germans on Walcheren Island. But it would be a long and bloody slog that the Allies would pay dearly for and that could have been avoided.

In part, the slowdown along the front facing Germany was due to my decision to employ our greatest strength in the north to attain flanking bridgeheads across the lower Rhine beyond the main fortifications of the Siegfried Line. In view of the fact, however, that the main highway to Berlin, the plains and level fields of Northern Germany – lay beyond the Rhine in the north, and that the southern country was unsuitable for the desired rapid advance and continued exploitation by reason of its mountainous and forested terrain, my commanders and I were in full agreement as to the desirability of exerting our strongest pressure in the north. The attractive possibility of quickly turning the German north flank led me to approve the temporary delay in freeing the vital port of Antwerp, the seaward approaches to which were still in German hands.[6]

Before detailing Allied operations on Walcheren it is worth looking at what lead up to the decision to finally clear the Scheldt of enemy positions. For example, why did the Allies take so long in making that decision when they had already captured Antwerp?

First of all it is necessary to examine the period between August and September 1944 when the German armies in the Normandy sector were on the brink of total collapse. Allied commanders saw an opportunity to, what they thought would, end the war by Christmas by smashing through the disintegrating German defences and racing across France into Germany and straight to Berlin. Of course, these grandiose ideas did not take into account the logistical problems such quick thrusts would cause. 'It was a time when Army Group and army Commanders needed to have their feet firmly on the ground as never before.'[7]

> The quickest way to end the German war was not merely to have the free use of Antwerp, as some have alleged. It was to act quickly in the middle of August, using the success gained in Normandy as a spring-board for a hard blow which would finish off the Germans and at the same time give us the ports we needed on the northern flank.[8]

Allied planners had calculated that the end of the European war would come on 1 June 1945. In fact, the ceasefire was three weeks earlier, on 6 May 1945. Most of the objectives formulated under Operation Overlord were reached before their planned-for date had arrived. For example, the Allies reached the Seine on 20 August 1944 – that's D+75 days when it had been planned that the Allies would reach it in D+90 days, D-Day being 6 June 1944. What this means is that the Allies did not, and could not, have planned for the collapse of the German armies in Normandy. Instead of fighting an organised and determined enemy through France the Allies found themselves in mid-August confronting a situation for which they were wholly unprepared.

Faced with the collapsing enemy defences, Montgomery telegraphed the War Office with a bold plan. The telegram he sent on 18 August stated that the 'U.S Twelfth and British Twenty-First Army Groups should stay together as a solid mass of forty divisions' that would have massive firepower and be capable of sweeping aside anything that Hitler could throw in its path.[9] Montgomery believed that a quick march directly to Berlin with such a huge force would end the European war quickly.

However, the plan was flawed. Montgomery pushed it onto Eisenhower on 19 August, but things were moving so quickly on the front lines that his plan became obsolete. What was missing was the strategic integrity and logistical understanding. To make matters worse a rivalry was growing between the Americans and British, specifically US General Patton's Third Army and British General Dempsey's Second Army.

The fast-moving events on the front line derailed Montgomery's proposals. For example, the destruction of the German armies in the Mortain–Falaise gap was complete by 20 August. Patton's Third Army was racing across France and the speed with which the Allied armies were moving meant they were using 1 million gallons of petrol per day.[10] An astonishing figure! At the same time, in Paris, the resistance fighters mounted a fresh offensive against their oppressors that ultimately meant that the Allies would have to divert an army to liberate the city. The significance of this was not lost on the Allies. Liberating Paris meant feeding and supplying Paris as well as tying down an entire army to do so. Something Eisenhower as Supreme Commander did not want to do.[11] Indeed, it was estimated by Supreme Headquarters Allied Expeditionary Force (SHAEF) planners that Paris would need 4,000 tons of supplies a day, which, according to historian Gerald Rawling, was more than enough to keep seven divisions rolling.[12]

The reason for this is that supplies were extremely limited. The armies were basically forging ahead faster than they could be supplied. The roads from the Normandy beaches were battered and potholed. The logistics chain was stretched to the limit and what petrol was available was funnelled forward to the advancing armies. Indeed, in Normandy entire corps and divisions not involved in the convoys for supplying the forward armies were left standing still for want of transport and gasoline. Day and night the American Red Ball convoys drove the 350 miles from the Normandy beaches over the rough roads that had been torn and ripped from the thousands of tanks and armoured vehicles that used it on the way to the front lines.

In the end, the decision to bypass Paris was, ultimately, out of Eisenhower's hands. He had vowed not to bring politics into military decision-making but in this instance the decision to take Paris was a political one and could not be ignored. Eisenhower had many balls in the air and was constantly juggling the needs and desires of his subordinates, Montgomery in particular, as well as politicians such as Churchill and Rooseveldt, and many others, especially, in this case, Charles de Gaule, 'who was not prepared to see Paris by-passed by Allied troops and then subsequently liberated by a Communist-led resistance movement which would be unsympathetic to a Gaulist regime after the war'.[13] So, on 25 August 1944, Paris was taken by the Allies; and while British and American troops liberated the city, other Allied divisions raced on.

A lighting strike into the heart of Germany would mean a quick end to the European war as well as glory for the Allied commander that achieved it. This was Montgomery's idea but he also knew that for this to take place it would have to be at the expense of all the other Allied armies advancing towards Germany and ultimately Berlin. General George S. Patton, commanding the

US Third Army, was the one commander in the position to be able to do this and 'unless Montgomery could have Patton's army grounded his own hopes were in vain'.[14] 'The way Allied armour was tearing across northern France towards Belgium, Luxembourg and Lorraine, any other course, in the circumstances, would doubtless have been regarded as total madness.'[15] The visions of an end to the European war in the autumn of 1944 were just that, visions. The only way, according to R.W. Thompson writing in *Eighty-Five Days*, was for the port facilities at Antwerp to be captured and put into use as quickly as possible.

> The distances over which the Allied Armies had pursued the enemy had carried our fighting troops so far away from their bases of supply within the bridgehead in Normandy as to place our administrative services under very considerable strain. While this condition remained it would be impossible to sustain the momentum of the advance along the entire front and it had already become clear that the Germans, reorganizing with desperate efficiency and disposed to take their stand in rearguard actions of increasing bitterness might succeed in prolonging the defence of their own country through a winter campaign. Given better fortune, the further projection of our offensive by means of the airborne thrust across the Maas and Rhine might have deprived the enemy of any such opportunity. On the other hand, our early possession of the port of Antwerp, which had fallen into our hands so surprisingly without resistance, and so completely intact, had invited an immediate effort on the greatest scale to eliminate the enemy from the environs of the city and the shores of the estuary as a preliminary to making use of those ample docks and warehouses for the purposes of supply.[16]

That this alternative was rejected in favour of the attempt at crossing the Rhine before the Germans could recover sufficiently to develop the full defensive potentialities of their river constituted one of the most important decisions of the campaign. Yet, it accorded only partially with the ideas of Field Marshal Montgomery on how best to exploit the situation and bring the German war to an end. 'My own view, which I presented to the Supreme Commander', wrote Montgomery, 'was that one powerful full-blooded thrust across the Rhine and into the heart of Germany, backed by the whole of the resources of the Allied Armies, would be likely to achieve decisive results.'[17]

However, General Eisenhower was unwilling to accept the full implications of this reasoning, for he stated that:

Success in such a plan would have been, to my mind, dependent upon our ability to concentrate sufficient administrative resources, to ensure the maintenance of the momentum from the time we crossed the Seine. The project therefore involved calling upon the combined Allied resources in the widest sense; and could have entailed reverting sectors of the Allied Front to a purely static role.[18]

To demand that the Allied advance elsewhere be brought to a standstill was to ask too much, yet the possibilities of breaking into Germany swiftly by the north east were too promising to be denied. The main attack had been thrown into the assault on the river crossings; the American front continued, though more slowly, to close up towards the Rhine, and the allocation of resources for the opening of Antwerp was lower down the list or priorities. Momentarily, offence was more important than maintenance or logistics.

General Eisenhower states the consequences of this decision and declares his acceptance of full responsibility for making it:

In part, the slow-down along the front facing Germany was due to my decision to employ our greatest strength in the north to attain flanking bridgeheads across the lower Rhine beyond the main fortifications of the Siegfried Line. In view of the fact, however, that the main highway to Berlin – the plains and level fields of Northern Germany – lay beyond the Rhine in the north, and that the southern country was unsuitable for the desired rapid advance and continued exploitation by reason of its mountainous and forested terrain, my commanders and I were in full agreement as to the desirability of exerting our strongest pressure in the north. The attractive possibility of quickly turning the German north flank led me to approve the temporary delay in freeing the vital port of Antwerp, the seaward approaches to which were still in German hands. I took the full responsibility for this, and I believe that the possible and actual results warranted the calculated risk involved. Had our forces not pushed north and east to hold the line of the Maas and Waal well north of Antwerp, the port itself would have been in constant danger not only from a blow possibly synchronized with the later breakthrough in the Eifel but from independent attacks launched at close range from Holland.[19]

The plan to open the way to the Ruhr by the northern bridgeheads did not lessen the strain upon Allied extended supply lines. This forced the Allied High Command to divert attention and resources to an Allied main base at Antwerp, as General Eisenhower stated:

With the completion of the MARKET-GARDEN operation the Northern Group of Armies was instructed to undertake the opening of Antwerp as a matter of the 'first priority'. While the city and port installations had fallen virtually intact to 30 Corps on 4 September, the harbor had proved and was to continue to prove useless to us until the Scheldt Estuary had been cleared of mines and South Beveland and Walcheren Island, commanding the sea lane to the harbor, had been reduced. The operation to achieve this involved the employment of amphibious forces, and the joint naval, air, and ground force planning was immediately undertaken and worked out during the latter part of September and early October at the Headquarters of the Canadian First Army.[20]

Notes

1. R.W. Thompson, *The Eighty-Five Days, The Story of the Battle of the Scheldt*, Hutchinson & Co. Ltd, London, 1957, p. 19.

2. Ibid., p. 21.

3. Ibid.

4. Ibid.

5. Dwight D. Eisenhower, Wikipedia, last modified 6 June 2015, Creative Commons Attribution Share-Alike License.

6. Montgomery's quote taken from the 'Report by the Supreme Commander to the Combined Chiefs of Staff on the Operations in Europe of Allied Expeditionary Force, 6 June 1944 to 8 May 1945' (page numbers are those of edition published by the Superintendent of Documents, US Government Printing Office, Washington), p. 67.

7. Ibid., p. 22.

8. Bernard Law, Viscount Montgomery of Alamein, *Memoires*, Collins, London, 1958, p. 285.

9. See Thompson, *Eighty-Five Days*, p. 24.

10. Ibid.

11. This is according to Thompson.

12. Gerald Rawling, *Cinderella Operation, The Battle for Walcheren 1944*, Cassell Ltd, London, 1980, p. 14.

13. Ibid.

14. See Thompson, *Eighty-Five Days*, p. 25.

15. See Rawling, *Cinderella Operation*, p. 12.

16. Law, Viscount Montgomery of Alamein, *Memoires*, p. 285.

17. 'Report No. 188, Historical Section, Canadian Military Headquarters, Canadian Participation in the Operations in North-West Europe 1944', 7 April 1948.

18. Ibid., Normandy to the Baltic, p. 149.

19. 'Report by the Supreme Commander to the Combined Chiefs of Staff on the operations in Europe of the Allied Expeditionary Force , 6 June 1944 to 8 May 1945', pp. 67, 68.

20. Ibid., p. 68.

Chapter 2

The German Perspective

And what of the Germans? The accounts of battles, operations and wars are, usually, written by the winners, the vanquished rarely getting a mention, or if they do it is in an abstract sort of way. At this stage it is worth looking at the German perspective of the coming Allied operations to clear the Scheldt Estuary. Their outlook was quite different to that of the Allies.

One of the questions that is posed in this book is why did the Germans put up such a difficult, hard defence when at this late stage in the war most of the German generals probably knew the war could not be won by Germany. So why keep fighting? The cost to the Allies and the Germans in terms of men and materiel was very high. This is probably something we shall never really know for sure. What we do know is that Hitler ordered the Germans to fight to the last man. We know that von Rundstedt issued this same directive to his troops in the Scheldt. This order was passed down the line, from the high-ranking officer to the private soldier.

However, in many cases the Germans would not fight to the last man, but surrender to the advancing Allies. In other cases, fanatical German officers forced their men to keep fighting or face being shot if they tried to surrender. Many believed that their families back in Germany would be killed if they didn't keep on fighting.

The Germans knew they would be fighting a defensive battle. Also, they must have realised there was no way that they were going to win that battle. All they could do was stave off the inevitable collapse and surrender for as long as possible.

Prior to, and immediately after, the fall of Antwerp to the Allies on 4 September, Montgomery's attention was on Operation Market Garden, the ill-fated airborne assault on Arnhem. Approved by Eisenhower, the Supreme Allied Commander, Operation Market Garden was a compromise for Montgomery. As we have already seen, Montgomery wanted a massive force of forty divisions punching a narrow front across the northern part of Germany all the way to Berlin. He believed that the Germans had nothing that could stop such a massive force. To achieve this plan, US General George S. Patton, commanding the US 3rd Army, would have to stop where he was and the 1st Army, commanded by General Hodges, would have to come under the command of 21st Army Group, or Montgomery. However, Eisenhower wanted an advance across a much broader front and so the two men clashed. Days went by as they argued. Finally, Eisenhower approved Montgomery's plan for the assault on Arnhem but he would not sanction diverting much-needed supplies, ammunition and fuel away from Patton who was continuing to drive across France.[1]

History has recorded that Operation Market Garden, which took place from 17–25 September 1944, was a failure. Yet, for two weeks after this debacle Montgomery continued to order attacks on Arnhem 'in futile attempts to rescue the situation', giving precious supplies to the British 2nd Army while the Canadian 1st Army had to make do.[2]

On 9 October the situation exploded when British naval officers told Eisenhower that the Canadians had an acute shortage of ammunition and would not be able to move until 1 November. In a flash of anger, Eisenhower cabled Montgomery and demanded that he put his personal attention onto immediate operations to clear the Scheldt and get the port facilities at Antwerp up and running. According to Rawling, this cable from Eisenhower enraged Montgomery, who suspected the report about shortages of ammunition had come from the British Naval Commander-in-Chief at SHAEF, Admiral Ramsay. Monty's reply to Eisenhower stated in no uncertain terms that there was no shortage of ammunition and that the Canadians were, in fact, advancing.[3]

While the British were desperately trying to save the debacle of Operation Market Garden, and the bickering between Montgomery and Eisenhower continued, the Germans, specifically General Gustav von Zangen commanding the Fifteenth Army, took advantage of the breathing space and began re-organising and withdrawing. 'At the moment, however, the nearly sixty miles wide area between Antwerp and Maastricht lay almost undefended within Allied grasp. Moving up forces to the Albert Canal between the two cities might make it possible to stem or delay the enemy's advance.'[4]

The Germans had positioned powerful, strong garrisons in the Channel ports they still held, Le Havre, Dieppe, Boulogne, Calais and Dunkirk. To guard the approaches to the south bank of the West Scheldt, von Zangen set up a strong defensive line along the Leopold Canal that would be known by the Allies as the 'Breskens Pocket'.[5]

On the morning of 4 September Army Group B (German) gave orders to rush the bulk of the formation to Antwerp. At that time substantial elements of 347 Infantry Division were already returning from the northern outskirts of Brussels to Antwerp by rail. They were supposed to detrain at Antwerp and take part in defence under 719 Infantry Division, but the trains rolled on to Capelles (7 miles north of Antwerp). Army Group B had been anxious to defend the city. At 0915hrs it even demanded the use of every type of civilian vehicle to rush all available naval and air force fighters to the defence of Antwerp. But the British had moved very fast, the slow moving coastal divisions had been pulled out too late, and all chance of holding Antwerp had been lost.[6]

In the Woensdrecht area, von Zangen established another powerful defensive force to stop the Allies from entering South Beveland via its isthmus. The rest of his forces were moved across the Scheldt to Walcheren Island.

70 Infantry Division was placed directly under Fifteenth Army and set in motion from Walcheren to the area of Ghent to form a blocking line and screen off towards Antwerp. 67 and 86 Corps were withdrawing as planned. The advance party of Fifteenth Army Headquarters reached Walcheren and by the next day Army Headquarters would be complete at Middelburg. At 1800hrs Field Marshal von Rundstedt arrived at the Headquarters O.B. West, at Arenberg (near Coblenz), and resumed his former command as O.B. West and O.B. Army Group D. The opponent had used the day to close up and regroup his forces.[7]

When General von Zangen was taken prisoner in late 1944 he was interviewed by Major General D.C. Spry DSO, who commanded the Canadian 3rd Infantry Division. Von Zangen provided his perspective of the month of September 1944 during his interrogation. It was von Zangen who commanded the German forces on the southern shore of the Scheldt. This covered the area north of Antwerp up to the Leopold Canal and onto the port towns of Breskens and Terneuzen to Woensdrecht and beyond. He was in charge of the withdrawal of German forces behind the Leopold Canal that lead to the evacuation from Breskens across the Scheldt to Flushing on Walcheren Island. Therefore, his account is especially important in providing an overall look at the plight of the Germans during this crucial time. He thought the Allies had made a great strategic mistake when they failed to push northwards out of Antwerp immediately after they had captured the city. Indeed, von Zangen believed that if the Allies had taken the opportunity and covered the relatively short distance north, between Antwerp and up to the entrance to the Beveland isthmus, much of the German Fifteenth Army would have been trapped. He stated in his interview with Major General Spry that during the evacuation from Breskens to Flushing he and his staff were constantly worried that the Allies would, indeed, push north. '89 Corps at first regarded the operation as a forlorn hope and for once we do not read the usual protestations that everything would have gone well but for the interference of the High Command'.[8]

In the area north of Antwerp there was only one weak and untried German infantry division defending the area.

> Although von Zangen realized that the Allies were relatively weak in Antwerp, he felt that a greater effort should have been made to advance north. By the Allies not covering this distance of about fifteen miles, he was able to bring out 62,000 men and 580 guns. This force was thus able to take up positions south of the Maas and play an important part in frustrating the object of the Allied airborne landings at Eindhoven, Nijmegen and Arnhem.[9]

In his interview, von Zangen stated that the sudden fall of Antwerp had placed the Germans in a very awkward position because they had very few available troops in this region. Because of the scarcity of information on Allied progress, individual German officers had to act on their own initiative. One such officer was Lieutenant General Chill, commanding 85 Infantry Division. When he realised the Allies were approaching Brussels, on 2 September he positioned his division along the lines of the Escaut and Albert Canals through Henenthals to Hasselt. When Antwerp fell to the Allies on 4 September, Chill's troops, reinforced with German police, security troops and stragglers, held this thin line behind the canals. The following day, the German High Command, realising how precarious their line east of Antwerp was, ordered General Reinhardt, commanding 88 Corps, to move into the sector held by Chill. In addition, 719 Infantry Division was sent from Holland to bolster Reinhardt's force. After slowly making its way southwards, 719 managed to take up positions north and east of Antwerp. Reinhardt was able to hold the canals with this inexperienced and weak force while the Fifteenth Army made its escape to Walcheren Island. As the divisions made their appearance on the mainland they reassembled and then thickened the line being held by Reinhardt. During this period 88 Corps was under General Kurt Student's First Parachute Army.[10]

> With all hope gone for a breakout, and with pressure from the South increasing steadily, Fifteenth Army's situation had become precarious. Enemy spearheads were at Poperinghe, Ypres, Cruyshautem and Deynze. There was heavy fighting at Bevers and Eyne, German forces at Ghent had been thrown back to the northern outskirts of the city. Battle Group 226 Infantry Division had reached Dunkirk, 5 Sec Regiment

Boulogne. Further east First Parachute Army had assumed command in the Antwerp - Hasselt sector.[11]

Initially, von Zangen crossed to Walcheren Island with his troops during the evacuation but he soon returned to Breskens where he remained until he was captured.

When von Zangen left Walcheren he left two lastditch garrisons holding north and south of the Scheldt. He thereby deprived the Allies of the use of the port facilities in Antwerp until these garrisons were eliminated. Although Walcheren had been designated as a fortress long before the fall of Antwerp, von Zangen received his orders to hold south of the Scheldt only about 12 September. He therefore ordered 64 Infantry Division to defend to the last in the Breskens area, while 70 Infantry Division held Walcheren Island. In von Zangen's opinion the object of these fortress troops was two-fold. First, to deny port facilities and second, to hold down as many Allied troops as possible. Von Zangen claims he did not have any definite idea as to how long Walcheren would hold, but he did believe that it would last at least three to four weeks after a serious attack against it was begun.[12]

During his interview with Major General Spry von Zangen talked about the effect that Operation Market Garden had on the disposition of his forces and the difficulties he faced.

The air landings had placed the Army Group in a most precarious position, particularly so in the Eindhoven area, where First Parachute Army was under attack from north and south. The severity of this crisis, however, did not diminish Hitler's interest in the defence of the Scheldt estuary. Again he demanded that the entrance to the river be kept in German hands at all events.[13]

According to the author of *The Campaign In North West Europe, Information From German Sources, Part 3*, the German Naval Special Staff Knuth reported on 24 September that 86,100 men, 616 guns, 6,200 horses, 6,200 vehicles and 6,500 bicycles had been ferried from Terneuzen and Breskens across the Scheldt.[14] The report does not say exactly where this materiel was sent but one can assume that it was dispersed throughout South Beveland, North Beveland and Walcheren Island, as well as some of the smaller islands further up the Dutch coast beyond the Waal River. Those German defences left behind took up positions from Antwerp to the area north west of

Hertogenbosch. The 67 Infantry Corps was responsible for the area from Antwerp to Turnhout, while 88 Infantry Corps took over the rest of the Army area. The 67 Infantry Corps had under command 711, 346 and 29 Infantry Divisions, while 88 Infantry Corps was composed of 245, 59, 89 and 712 Infantry Divisions.

Of course, re-taking Antwerp was out of the question for the Germans. Von Zangen knew his force wasn't equal to the task and that there was very little chance of him being reinforced with any more troops.[15]

> The High Command order of 4 September had clothed the commander of Walcheren Island with the powers of a fortress commander. Instructions to such commanders were strict and simple. They were to hold out to the last. According to General von Zangen the High Command now designated Walcheren as 'Scheldt Fortress North', and the Breskens area north of the Leopold Canal as 'Scheldt Fortress South', and selected 70 Infantry Division to defend the former and 64 Infantry Division the latter. Neither Walcheren nor Breskens were fortresses in the strict sense of the word, of course, but they were called so to define and stress the concomitant obligations of the troops and commanders.[16]

So, as September 1944 came to a close, the Germans were defensively ready for whatever the Allies could throw at them. The flat waterlogged land, with dykes and canals acting as natural defensive barriers to any assault, led the Germans to believe they had every reason to feel they were secure. However, they would soon discover what the Allies were made of. October would prove to be a disaster for the Germans.

Having looked a little at the perspective of General Gustav von Zangen, as commander of the Fifteenth Army and the man responsible for the defences on the south shore of the West Scheldt, it is worth taking a look at another German point of view. This time, that perspective comes from Lieutenant General William Daser, commander of 70 Infantry Division and in charge of the German defenders on Walcheren Island. Interrogated after the war by the Allies, what follows is his viewpoint as recounted by the author of *The Campaign in North West Europe Information From German Sources, Part 3.*

Lieutenant General Daser knew the islands of Walcheren, South Beveland and North Beveland quite well. His first encounter with them was as commander of 165 Reserve Infantry Division, a post he took up in the winter of 1943. The First Battalion of 89 Festungs Stamm Regiment, made up of about 1,000 men either recovering from wounds or unfit for front-line duty, augmented his garrison on the island of Walcheren. In 1944, shortly after the

Normandy landings, Daser was given intelligence that another Allied landing might take place in the Antwerp area. The Normandy campaign was less than a week old when 165 Reserve Division began moving units out of their island positions to fight in France. Daser was then notified by High Command that his training division was to be given a new designation and the status of a fighting formation.

Daser's command was a curious one. The troops who made up 70 Infantry Division largely consisted of men with digestive problems severe enough to make them liabilities in their original units. The German High Command decided to concentrate all these sick men into special Magen (Stomach) battalions where their tasks could be made lighter and their feeding better supervised. By putting all the men with stomach problems into special battalions the Germans were able to ensure the original units from where the unfit men came from remained fighting fit, while treatment of the men in the stomach battalions continued apace in order to return them to a state of full fitness. That, at least, was the theory.

The original units of fit, healthy troops under Daser's command moved back across the Scheldt to fight in France. The invalids took their place. A dispirited General Daser soon realised that his command now consisted largely of men recovering from wounds in the stomach, or complaining of stomach ulcers or nursing stomachs that were abnormally sensitive or nervous. Daser managed to retain the original healthy staffs of his divisional and regimental headquarters, a few healthy engineers, a troop of normal artillerymen and a fit complement of company commanders. However, all of the platoon officers under his command were fellow invalids along with their men. This division was nicknamed the 'White Bread' division reflecting their dietary needs. Three regiments were created out of this motley division of invalids – 1018, 1019 and 1020, each of two battalions. They were supported by a fusilier battalion, their artillery regiment with three batteries of about twelve guns each along with their signalers and engineers. Outwardly, they could have been mistaken for a fighting division.[17]

What of Daser himself? The Canadian historian provides a small glimpse of the man's character in the report he wrote.

Daser was a well-meaning man from the Palatinate. He had shown little emotion in the earlier phases of the war and would show little on Walcheren. Quite likely, however, he received just as much or more co-operation from his tired dyspeptics than any driving Prussian could have obtained. How much longer better troops might have held out is hard to say. The main mistake of the German defence of Walcheren seems to have been faulty use of the artillery, which raises the question whether or not more competent infantry officers could and would have demanded the kind of artillery support that might have defeated the Westkapelle landings.[18]

While Daser had a certain amount of sympathy with the High Command's decision in creating a division like his own to provide a reasonable solution to a difficult administrative problem, he could not understand why this formation would be tasked with defending what was one of the most vital sectors in Europe – the approaches to the port of Antwerp.

He knew his division was of low fighting value, at least it appeared that way on paper, but he did not agree that even though Walcheren Island was in a part of Holland where there was an abundance of white bread, fresh vegetables, eggs and milk they should be defending the mouth of the Scheldt. Where Daser did agree with the High Command was that put into concrete defensive positions such as bunkers, pillboxes, gun emplacements and behind walls his 'stomach' men could probably fire a gun as well as any fit soldier.[19]

With millions of men under arms, and the incidence of gastric cases high, it was inevitable that ultimately there would be a veritable little army of stomach sufferers on the borderline of employability. For various medical and administrative reasons these men were gradually separated from other categories and bonded together in 'Stomach' companies and battalions. In step with the progressive deterioration of the manpower situation their leisured life comes soon to an end; at first they were used for light tasks, later for heavier tasks and finally for combat duty.[20]

Despite the disabilities of the troops in Daser's command they were not spared the rigours of full combat. In early September the fusiliers were ordered into Belgium, in the sector around Ghent, and in a single day they lost some 300 casualties.

On 9 September, Daser reported to von Zangen at Headquarters Fifteenth Army, which was at this time in Middelburg on Walcheren. Daser was yet to move into these headquarters and von Zangen was yet to move back across to Breskens. Indeed, it was at this meeting that von Zangen told Daser that he would have to transfer command to Walcheren Island. General von Zangen explained to Daser that 712 Infantry Division would be responsible for South Beveland while 64 Infantry Division would be defending the mainland behind the line of the Leopold Canal, the Breskens Pocket, while 70 Infantry Division would take on the responsibility of defending Walcheren itself.

As our Intelligence soon became aware, these three divisions were to be controlled by 89 Corps under General von Gilsa. Although the enemy's arrangements for defending the approaches to Antwerp were completed before the port had fallen, Daser corroborates the other evidence that the sudden capture of the city came as a complete surprise. The forces opposing our farther advance to the north had to be strengthened, and by the time that 70 Infantry Division returned to Walcheren, about 19 Sep, the original plan had been considerably modified. This meant that 712 Infantry Division having made its escape from Breskens to Flushing, had to be rushed out into Brabant, leaving the devoted 70 Infantry Division to defend both Walcheren and the two Bevelands.[21]

After a fortnight of bitter fighting on the mainland around Wettern and Laerne, Daser's 'stomach' troops were down by 700 men. In his interview, Daser related how, shortly after they landed on the mainland (prior to going back to Walcheren), he lost 1018 Infantry Regiment from his command as it was attached to 346 Infantry Division, 'then holding a sector from Lille to Merxem, and was never seen by Daser again'.[22] He was left with the uncomfortable realisation that he would be called upon to make a last-ditch stand on the island with what troops he had left.

During his interview, Daser was asked what he thought of the term 'Fortress Island', as it applied to Walcheren Island as a whole. His conception of fortress was a very limited area with sufficient supplies, ammunition, weapons, cement and so forth for enduring a lengthy siege. He thought that it initially referred to the port of Flushing on Walcheren because it had a moat and the anti-tank wall gave the town the resemblance of a proper fortress. However, von Zangen had designated the entire island as a fortress. He also referred to the area south of Scheldt in the same terms, which meant for Daser that the term no longer had any tactical meaning. Instead, it merely defined the area the Germans were going to use to make their final stand and fight to the last man and the end of their ammunition. Daser, therefore, had to fortify Walcheren in this way. 'There was sufficient ammunition to last for eight weeks, and food for six weeks, after the Isthmus had been sealed off. Daser estimated that his troops might be able to hold out for about four weeks against a direct attack.'[23]

As will be shown later in this book, it took the Allies a week to fight their way up the South Beveland isthmus to the causeway connecting the isthmus with Walcheren Island. On the sixth day after the Allied amphibious assault on the island itself, Daser surrendered the island and all his men. By that time, the vast majority of the island had been flooded by the RAF breeching the dykes that run around the coast of the island, essentially ringing it, keeping the interior of the island dry.

For late in the afternoon of 01 October the German Air Force strongpoint northeast of Domburg was bombed from the air and lost two major pieces of sea-searching and coast-watching radar equipment (one 'Mammut' and one 'Wurzburg Riese'). A much more serious development occurred on 03 October, when O.B. West recorded that two waves of Allied aircraft had carried out heavy bombing attacks on Walcheren and South Beveland and had succeeded in breeching the dyke on the south coast of Walcheren. There was now danger of flooding.

If the Germans counted on gaining valuable time by defending Walcheren gun by gun and ditch by ditch, they must have been sorely disappointed to see the inundations on the island grow from day to day until there was not enough dry land to put up any kind of effective defence. By 23 October all areas lying open to flooding were covered with water. A map showing the extent of the inundations at that time was submitted to the Naval Operations Staff early in November.[24]

However, for the Allies to get to the 'Fortress Island' they had to clear the south shore of the Scheldt, the Breskens coast, of German defenders. This would take four weeks of bitter, harsh fighting.

But while it is true that the small infantry forces on Walcheren could do little to protect the batteries, it is also true that larger forces would hardly have been able to postpone for long the elimination of artillery positions that were exposed to unhindered bombardment from the air, sea and land. The real strength and substance of the German defence of Walcheren was embodied in the various Naval Coast Artillery and Antiaircraft Batteries.[25]

In March 1944, the Germans laid down the policy for defending Walcheren Island and South and North Beveland. At that time Field Marshal Rommel believed that the Allied invasion had to be defended on the beaches and as such ordered that all coastal divisions were to be positioned within a 5km strip of the beaches along the coast in order to concentrate their defensive power. Essentially, all troops, reserves as well, were to be situated within this defensive zone. However, for Daser such a scheme was impractical because of the nature of the islands under his command so he asked for, and received, permission to modify his defences accordingly to fit in with the particular geographical conditions in this area. The dykes, for instance, and canals that permeate the region posed unique challenges.

On the island of Walcheren, Daser placed a 5km ring of troops that circled the island as per Rommel's instructions in March. On the western side of North

Beveland island, facing east, strongpoints were built, while on South Beveland on the southern and western coasts several field positions were dug. Some towns were designated as strongpoints such as Goes, which had defensive positions of gun emplacements, bunkers and so forth to give it all-around protection. The Beveland Canal, which cuts across the isthmus and having been designated as a second line of defence, had several defensive positions dug that faced eastwards. In order to protect against a land attack by the Allies striking from Woensdrecht or Bergen Op Zoom, another set of defensive positions was built at the very edge of the Beveland isthmus.[26]

In his interview as a prisoner of war Daser described to his Allied captors the way in which he deployed his troops:

> 1020 Infantry Brigade manned the Isthmus from Woensdrecht to the Beveland Canal; 2nd Battalion 89 Festungs Stamm along the southern coast of South Beveland facing the West Scheldt; 1st Battalion 1019 G.R. in the port of Flushing; 2nd Battalion 1019 G .R. along the eastern shore of Walcheren Island and defending the causeway between Walcheren and Beveland; 1st Battalion 89 Festungs Stamm along the northwest shore to Walcheren; 3rd Battalion 89 Festungs Stamm along the southwest shore of Walcheren.[27]

Daser also provided details of the flooding that resulted from the Allied bombing campaign on Walcheren:

> In the middle of October the concrete floodwall in the northwest corner of Flushing, and at the time the narrow dam one kilometer southwest of Fort Rammekens were destroyed, each with 500–600 aerial mines with time fuses. The flood surging in immediately inundated the areas in the vicinity of the gaps, later in a part of Flushing and the district as far as West and East Souburg and finally the whole area as far as the anti-tank ditch and wall.[28]

Daser gave information about the state of the German defences on Walcheren Island prior to the Allied amphibious assault. These details, highlighted in the appendix of the *The Campaign In NorthWest Europe, Information From German Sources, Part 3*, follow:

> In accordance with the principal combat mission: 'To repel any enemy attack from the West, and in particular in combination with the neighbouring division to the South to block the Scheldt Estuary and the port of Flushing', the west coast of Walcheren from Vrouwenpolder to

Fort Rammekens (both included) was built up 'fort-like' as far as possible – by a number of concrete strongpoints and resistance nests that were reinforced by field works. The northwest coast of North Beveland and the southwest coast of South Beveland were provided with field works sited in the main between individual minor strongpoints.

Organized for defence by field works were: facing east: the isthmus of Bath and a line about 3km east of the west coasts of North and South Beveland, facing both ways: the Walcheren Canal north of Middelburg, and the South Beveland Canal, for all-round defence: the town of Goes.

The northern limit of the 'Fortress Area Flushing' was a line of field works and individual bunkers connected by antitank ditches and walls.

a) Strongpoints:
On the main coastal points and in the rear area there were, accommodated in a series or group of concrete gun emplacements and bunkers, proof against shell fragments, and shell-proof against calibres up to 15 cm;
• all naval coast batteries (With the exception of the 22 cm battery east of Domburg),
• three heavy (15 cm) batteries and some of the light batteries of the Divisional artillery [while on the island],
• nearly all anti-landing guns, anti-tank guns, infantry guns and mortars at the coast,
• anti-tank weapons and heavy infantry weapons at the anti-tank ditch,
• crews of guns and heavy infantry weapons, observers, radio and telephone posts,
• Divisional command posts, the infantry and artillery regiments, the Senior Naval Officer, the naval coast artillery and flak unit, a part of the reserves, ammunition and food.

The walls of the bunkers were up to one metre thick, while the roofs were up to 2.5 metres. Some were covered with armour plates, many with revolving panzer cupolas, a great many were provided with panzer doors, all with heating and air conditioning installations and gas traps (air locks). All strong points were prepared for close and all-round defence by reinforced field works and were surrounded by wire entanglements and mine belts.

b) Resistance Nests:
Field fortification type resistance nests were established between individual strongpoints and at the other positions. The resistance nests were surrounded by ditches and provided with bunkers and machine gun positions, splinter-proofed with iron rails, wood, stones and earth.

c) Wire Obstacles:
All strongpoints and resistance nests, as well as entire batteries and individual positions for guns and heavy infantry weapons were encircled by wire 50 metres wide.

d) Off-shore Obstacles the Germans used:
At first individual pylons 20–30 cm thick, iron posts and rails were embedded, later on, only triangular jacks of 30 cm and thicker wood, rammed in and fastened together with iron clamps. Waterproof anti-tank mines, or grenades, were attached to the obstacles. As far as they were available, wire cables as broad as a finger were stretched between them. Concrete boxes loaded with mines or explosives were set up at different elevations from the ground.

e) Anti-tank Ditches and Anti-tank Wall:
Connecting up with existing water courses, a water ditch was dredged out from the coastal road from halfway between Flushing–Zoutelande via Koudekerke Klein Abeele (1.5 km south of Middelburg) towards Fort Rammeken. The ditch was 10 km long, 8–10 metres wide and 1.5–2 metres deep. Beginning at the end of the ditch, a concrete anti-tank wall, 1.3 km long, 2.5 metres high and 1.5 metres wide was erected.

f) Mine Obstacles:
Consisted of:
• mine belts around the individual strongpoints and resistance nests,
• lines of mines forward of the main line of resistance on the northwest and southwest coast of Walcheren,
• large fields of anti-tank and anti-personnel mines in the rear area, principally east of Westkapelle. They were fenced in and marked with warning signs,
• dummy mine fields on fairly large stretches of ground in the rear area.

g) Anti Landing Obstacles:
On all surfaces suitable for the descent of paratroops or air-landing troops, especially on Walcheren and South Beveland, strong tree trunks were dug in and pounded in firmly at intervals of 15 metres. They were between 15 cm and 30 cm thick, were inserted 1.5 metres below ground and protruded 3 metres above ground; some were wired and equipped with anti -personnel or improvised mines. The lumber for this was taken to some extent from the roads with several rows of trees right on the spot, but to a greater extent from the wooded areas south of Bergen op

Zoom and from outside of the divisional sector. They were moved in by rail, vehicle convoy and ship. In addition to this, the former airfield 2 km south of Middelburg was made unserviceable for landings by ditches and earth cast up.

The 'fort-type' installations (concrete constructions, anti-tank ditches and anti-tank wall) were created in accordance with a building programme of the Fortress Construction Staff at 89 Corps Headquarters under the direction and supervision of a Special Construction Staff of the Division by the Todt Organization and civilian construction firms. At the time of the invasion on 06 June 1944, the installations were 75% completed; by the time of the attack on the island group itself in October 1944 they had been completed.

All obstructions and field-type installations were built by the troops themselves. All mines were laid by engineers. The blocking and destruction of the ports and the preparatory work were the task of the Navy.[29]

These were the German defences the Allies would have to deal with when they began operations to clear the Scheldt. The Germans knew the Allies were coming and they were ready for them.

Notes

1. For greater detail on Operation Market Garden and the argument between Eisenhower and Montgomery see Rawling, *Cinderella Operation*, pp. 18–22.
2. Ibid., p. 23.
3. Ibid.
4. 'Report No. 69, The Campaign In NorthWest Europe, Information From German Sources', Part 3, 'German Defence Operations in the Sphere of First Canadian Army', 30 July 1954.
5. Walcheren Island, North and South Beveland split the Scheldt Estuary in two. The West Scheldt has for its southern shore the continent with the ports of Breskens and Terneuzen, while the north shore of the West Scheldt is South Beveland and Walcheren.
6. 'Report No. 69, The Campaign In NorthWest Europe, Information From German Sources', Part 3.
7. Ibid.
8. 'Report No. 188, Historical Section, Canadian Military Headquarters', Part IV, 'Clearing the Scheldt Estuary', April 1948.
9. 'Special Interrogation Report, General Gustav von Zangen', p. 3, cited in 'Report No. 188'. It is interesting to note that this report states that 62,000 German troops came out of the fighting around Antwerp whereas other sources, as has been shown earlier, cite much higher numbers.
10. 'Special Interrogation Report, General Gustav von Zangen', p. 3.
11. See 'Report No. 69, The Campaign In NorthWest Europe, Information From German Sources', Part 3.

12. Ibid., p. 4.
13. Ibid., p. 30.
14. Ibid., p. 32.
15. Ibid., p. 4.
16. Ibid.
17. 'Special Interrogation Report, Lt-Gen Wilhelm Daser', pp. 3, 4, cited in 'Report No. 188'.
18. See 'Report No. 69, The Campaign In NorthWest Europe, Information From German Sources', Part 3, p. 32.
19. See 'Special Interrogation Report, Lt-Gen Wilhelm Daser', p. 4.
20. See 'Report No. 69, The Campaign In NorthWest Europe, Information From German Sources', Part 3, p. 32.
21. See 'Report No. 188, Historical Section, Canadian Military Headquarters', Part IV, April 1948.
22. 'Special Interrogation Report, Lt-Gen Wilhelm Daser', p. 5.
23. Ibid.
24. See 'Report No. 69, The Campaign In NorthWest Europe, Information From German Sources', Part 3, pp. 86–7.
25. Ibid., p. 32.
26. See 'Special Interrogation Report, Lt-Gen Wilhelm Daser', pp. 5, 6.
27. Ibid, p. 6.
28. Ibid., p. 23.
29. See 'Report No. 69, The Campaign In NorthWest Europe, Information From German Sources', Part 3, Appendix D.

Part 2

Operation Switchback

Chapter 3

The Days of Victory,
September 1944

In the first days of September 1944 the Allies experienced the sweet taste of victory when they broke free of the Normandy bridgehead. The advance of British and Canadian armour from the bridgeheads over the Seine at Vernon, Louviers, Elbouef and Rouen was remarkable in many ways. It was this break-out and subsequent surge through France and Belgium up to the Dutch frontier that stretched Allied supply lines and made freeing Antwerp a necessity.

The German armies that had relentlessly tried to hem the Allies into their Normandy bridgehead and then drive them back into the sea had suddenly, and inexplicably, collapsed. Allied armour roared past the bewildered enemy as resistance melted away. Villages and towns that had been oppressed under the Nazi boot for four long years suddenly found themselves staring wide-eyed at the sight of Allied tanks and trucks thundering through their streets now filled with the sounds of tank tracks on pavement, engines roaring, gears grinding, the fumes of engines at full tilt. For those people living a life under occupation it must have been a glorious sight. The people poured from their houses, throwing flowers and kisses at their liberators, showering them with whatever they had, food, fruit, wine, their pent up emotions let loose as they realised that freedom was theirs.

On 27 August, the Allies crossed the Seine at Melun and the River Yonne at Sens. That same day orders were issued for 21 Army Group's advance to the north. They were to wipe out any enemy concentrations in Pas de Calais and Flanders and then drive on to Antwerp. The orders for the Second British Army were:

1   To cross the Seine near Vernon with 30 Corps on the right and on the left in the area between Les Andelys and Louviers with 12 Corps. 11 Armoured Division was to lead the advance of 30 Corps to the Seine with 50 Division following while 43 Division waited in the

      reserve to force the crossing. 15 Division was to lead the advance of 12 Corps across the Seine with 53 Division following.

2   To advance north and capture the Arras – Amiens – St Pol triangle as quickly as possible regardless of the progress of the armies on either flank. Both Amiens and the Somme crossings had to be captured quickly and for this phase, 30 Corps regrouped with the Guards Armoured Division leading the advance on the right. On the left, 11 Armoured Division thundered onto the Somme crossings near Amiens. Following behind them was 50 Division while 43 Division was to secure the Seine bridgehead. 4 Armoured Brigade, and later 7 Armoured Brigade, led 12 Corps' drive to the area north west of Amiens with 53 Division protecting the Left flank.[1]

First Canadian Army's orders were:

1   To cross the Seine in the area between Pont de L'Arche and the sea then advance north towards St Omer and Bruges.

2   To capture Dieppe and then Le Havre.[2]

In addition, 2 Canadian Corps on the right were ordered to cross the River Seine near Rouen, along with 4 Canadian Armoured Division and 3 Canadian Division and attack any enemy positions there, capture the town then drive on north-north-east to the Somme in the area between Abbeville and the sea. At the same time, 2nd Canadian division was tasked with capturing Dieppe.

Also, on the left, 1 British Corps was to cross the Seine west of Rouen, while 51 Division, moving forward on the right, was to capture St Valery and then advance along the cost as quickly as possible. While this was taking place, 49 Division was tasked with seizing Le Havre. However, if they couldn't take the entire town their primary objective was to capture the port and then begin the necessary build-up for capturing the town and continuing on.

In the final days of August, the Allies realised that the Germans were in disarray, their resistance collapsing across the British Second Army's front. The Germans were withdrawing into the Channel ports in a last ditch attempt to deny the port facilities to the Allies, forcing a much longer supply line. Allied Headquarters ordered the Second British Army to capture Brussels and Antwerp and secure a bridgehead over the Albert Canal. The responsibility of clearing the coastal belt fell to the First Canadian Army.

With bridgeheads across the Seine established at Vernon and Louviers, the advance by 30 Corps began in earnest on 29 August 1942. Despite bad weather and some enemy opposition, 11 Armoured Division broke out and thundered all night through towns and villages and crossed the Somme at Amiens. Further east on their left the Guards Armoured Division was advancing along the Albert Road near Amiens while some elements of 50 Division were in the town. This was a night drive of some 80 miles.

As the British armour thundered forward like a juggernaut it bypassed pockets of German resistance that would be later mopped up by the infantry coming up behind them. The British tanks smashed aside any German armour or vehicles that dared oppose them directly and just kept going. On 30 August the advancing 12 Corps pushed more than 30 miles to Gournay, while 53 Division reached Lyon la Forêt. The following day 7 Armoured Division had roared through Poix while behind them 53 Division took care of the enemy positions overlooked by the armour.

Arras was bypassed on 1 September by the Guards Armoured Division which pressed on to Douai and Lens, while on their left flank 11 Armoured Division arrived at the Arras–St Pol road, went past enemy defenders at Airaines and crossed the Somme.

88 Corps had been aroused from its static role on 29 Aug when the Armed Forces Commander in the Netherlands gave orders to withdraw one division from the coast and prepare it for a move elsewhere. 347 Infantry Division (860 and 861 Gren Regiments) was selected. Proceedings were speeded up on the evening of 30 Aug after Field Marshal Model on the telephone had described the situation as burning and demanded the immediate despatch of the Division. Two days later 719 Infantry Division was withdrawn from coastal defence. Early on 2 September it was en route to the area South East of Brussels. Late on 3 September the Corps Commander suggested vainly to bring the Division to a halt at the Albert-Canal. On the morning of 4 September Army Group B gave orders to rush the bulk of the formation to Antwerp. At that time substantial elements of 347 Infantry Division were already returning from the northern outskirts of Brussels to Antwerp by rail. They were supposed to detrain at Antwerp and take part in its defence under 719 Infantry Division but the trains rolled on to Capelles (7 miles north of Antwerp). Army Group B had been anxious to defend the city. And by 0915hrs it had even demanded the use of every type of civilian vehicle to rush all available naval and air force fighters to the defence of Antwerp. But the British had moved very fast, the slow moving coastal divisions had been pulled out too late, and all chance of holding Antwerp had been lost.[3]

Bewildered German forces reeled under the onslaught of British and Canadian armour which seemed totally unstoppable. The Guards Armoured Division, with the Belgian Brigade under command, captured Tournai and crossed the Escaut River on 2 September. On the afternoon of 3 September the division arrived in Brussels and by the end of the day controlled all the main routes in and out of the city. Meanwhile, 11 Armoured Division had captured Lille and kept on going until by nightfall on 3 September they arrived in the area of Alost.

> With a sharp thrust to Antwerp, Second British Army on this day completely separated the German Fifteenth Army from the Fifth Panzer Army. 'This advance to Antwerp has closed the ring around Fifteenth Army. A thrust to Breda must be expected . . .' To all appearances the Fifteenth Army's situation was now hopeless. But the unexpected happened, the Woensdrecht isthmus and the Breda area remained unmolested and events evolved in a different way.[4]

For the British and Canadian tank crews and infantry passing through French and Belgian towns and villages, seeing the people and the overwhelming displays of gratitude this was the moment they had lived for, the moment they had signed up for. A brief moment when the brutality of the war they were fighting turned to glory. 'In that hour there was the feel and the knowledge of all the chariots, and all the cavalry that had ever charged through to victory.'[5]

In five days, the 11th Armoured Division, with the 8th Armoured Brigade under its command, had driven more than 250 miles from their bridgeheads over the Seine and now, on 3 September, had stopped at Alost, 15 miles north west of Brussels. Here, the division remained, exhausted, jubilant and only 10 miles from the port of Antwerp. At that moment this was the Allied spearhead, the juggernaut that could have kept going, and should have. The 50th Infantry Division, moving behind the 11th Armoured Division, took care of those enemy troops still able to mount whatever resistance they could but against the Allied tide it wasn't much. While the 50th mopped up the remnants of the enemy, the 7th Armoured Division on their left was advancing rapidly towards Ghent, while on their left the Guards Armoured Division had rolled into Brussels. Canadian and Polish armour in the west was pushing through into Flanders, capturing the same ground that the Allies had fought for in the long years of the First World War. Now, it seemed they were unstoppable.[6]

Perhaps what is the most amazing fact is that only ten days before 3 September the Allies had been hemmed in by the Germans, locked in a bitter struggle for every inch of ground against a determined enemy. But German resistance had been crushed by the combined might of air bombardment and Allied artillery fire, by the combined attacks of attrition from tanks and infantry. Rather than just withdrawing, the Germans had been destroyed and that had been the impetus that gave birth to the Allied juggernaut racing across France and Belgium in the early days of September 1944. Wherever last remnants of resistance could be found, Allied armour simply brushed it aside, the machine guns from the tanks taking their toll on the bewildered enemy. French and Belgian Resistance fighters rounded up prisoners from the wrecks of enemy transport that lined the roads as the Allied armoured juggernaut roared on.

This was no organised withdrawal by the enemy and subsequent pursuit of the enemy by the British and Canadians. Simply put, the British armour had broken free and now rolled forward limited only by its fuel supply. After having been involved in bitter house-to-house fighting, battling for every inch, foot and yard of ground in a tight bridgehead, the Allies were riding the crest of a wave that would take them as far as they could go. When they reached that place on the evening of 3 September, on the threshold of Antwerp, it must have seemed like the end had arrived. For surely there could be no more fighting? They were to find, however, that the end was far from near.

Thompson paints a vivid picture of what it was like in those first few days of September when the Allied advance seemed unstoppable. He tells us how, on 30 August 1944, the commander of 30th Corps, Lieutenant General Horrocks, ordered his troops to drive on all night by whatever means and to brush aside any resistance they met. So they did, with the 11th Armoured Division driving through a night of torrential rain and pitch darkness some 55 miles, crossing the Somme and passing less than a mile from German Seventh Army Headquarters. The German officers in that headquarters didn't know what hit them and were soon caught up in the advancing armoured column. They reached Amien and continued on. The roads ahead held no fear for the men of the 11th Armoured division. There were no booby traps or mines because these were the German communication roads and now they lay open to the Allied advance. Instead of finding well-established German defensive positions along the routes, at junctions, bridges, checkpoints and culverts, they found men of the Belgian Resistance, the Germans either dead or prisoners. Those Germans that were organised, in any way they could be, tried to mount whatever defensive posture they could but they were brushed aside in the same manner as one would swat a fly.

Yet, despite the fantastic break-out and dash across France and Belgium in those first days of September, the eyes of the Allied High Command, that is Field Marshal Montgomery, lay fixed on the east. Had Antwerp been the focus of command the possibilities become truly astonishing, as Thompson tells us:

Not only was the road to Bergen open, but through to the whole of North Holland. Utrecht, Amsterdam and Rotterdam could have been freed in the first ten days of September, and the Mass and the Rhine would have been crossed. The German Fifteenth army would have been lost, and the positions of all the garrisons from Le Havre to Walcheren would have been hopeless.[7]

Had the focus been on Antwerp, not only would the city itself and the its port facilities have been in Allied hands, but also all of North Holland and the road through to the German North Plain would have been free for the Allies to mount a drive to Germany and ultimately Berlin. Could the war have been won by the end of 1944?[8] That's something we will never know. However, we do know that it didn't end that year and that the operations to clear North Holland up to Walcheren and the Scheldt were a long, hard, bitter struggle for the Allies.

But the heart of this book is not about the 'what ifs' and the 'maybes', although they will be mentioned in order to let the reader consider their significance. This is about documenting the events, the struggles, and the highs and the lows that culminated in the German surrender on Walcheren.

For the Allies in the first days of September the struggle for the Scheldt was yet to come. Indeed, just before dawn on 4 September, the 3rd Royal Tank Regiment rumbled through the town of Malines on the road to Antwerp. Reaching the main bridge into the city, it quickly brushed aside the German defenders and rolled on into the city. As dawn came and the Allied tanks slowly moved along the streets of Antwerp the crowds began lining the main thoroughfares. By the afternoon the throngs of people were everywhere and the tank crews grinned and smiled as they slowly moved among the crowds. However, while the tanks crews bathed in the glory, the infantry units were on a mission that would bypass the crowds. Their goal was to get to the docks as quickly as possible and secure them. They had, at this stage, no idea what shape the port would be in but they assumed the worst. How could the Germans have failed to destroy the main infrastructure of the docks? It was inconceivable and so the Allied infantry units made all speed to salvage and secure what they could.

What the Allied troops discovered when they reached the docks was that the men of the Belgian Resistance organisation had, with great foresight the moment they'd heard of the break-out in Normandy, seized key areas with such speed that they shocked the Germans. By manipulating the swing bridges and dock gates they created a system of islands across the dock areas to ensure they could defend these vital points and deal with any counter-attacks that the enemy might mount during the hours of darkness.[9]

For the Allies however, securing the docks would prove to be a difficult and time-consuming process even with the help of the Resistance. During the night of 4 September, Allied infantry units secured the main sluices and moved through the warehouses, around the cranes, over the swing bridges, down cobbled pathways and streets, securing what they needed to and bypassing what wasn't important. These were troops from the 7th Manchester Regiment and the Rifle Brigade and as they moved through the docks the Belgian Resistance helped them secure the principal areas.

It wasn't easy going. For not only did the British not know the area of the docks but German snipers were very active making the task of clearing the docks much more difficult for the Allies. Even, so, by morning on 5 September, 'the Rifle Brigade and the Manchesters discovered to their infinite relief that the docks were intact, and that somehow, crawling about the nightmare of the night, they had managed to occupy all the key points'.[10]

Yet, in the northern edges of the city German defenders fired their machine guns at the Allied troops, while artillery fire from their 105mm guns began pounding the centre of Antwerp. Also, from the northern bank of the Albert Canal, German snipers harassed Allied vehicles and troop movements with deadly results. Of course, this should all have been quickly and ruthlessly attacked by Allied armour and artillery fire. However, 11th Armoured Division was at the end of the line and, now supporting 30th Corps, was aiming in an eastward direction for what would become Operation Market Garden. Still, the 11th was, on 5 September, ordered to establish bridgeheads over the Albert Canal and once that was done be ready to move forward. The Allies were only just beginning to realise that the battle for Antwerp had only just begun.[11]

The Germans were far from finished. Even though the Allies had control of the city of Antwerp and the dock area, on the northern bank of the Albert Canal and in the northern suburbs of the city the Germans had strengthened their positions and were now making a stand. 21st Army Group had been stretched beyond its limits. In order to sustain the advancing columns in the heady days of early September the resources were unable to keep up the pace. Indeed, Thompson tells us that more than 1,400 3-ton trucks were unserviceable. For the Seine crossings the Allies had brought up 7,500 tons of bridging from the Normandy bridgeheads, which was 'a foretaste of the immense tonnages which were needed for innumerable lesser waterways at increasing distance from Normandy, and which would soon be needed for the crossings of the Maas and Rhine. It was almost inconceivable that such supplies could come through any other channel but Antwerp.'[12]

While Montgomery concentrated his plans on Operation Market Garden, the crossing of the Rhine at Arnhem, it fell to the First Canadian Army to take on the task of clearing the Channel ports as well as the Scheldt Estuary. In the First Canadian Army sector, 4 Canadian Armoured Division had crossed the Somme and concentrated east of Abbeville, while 3 Canadian Division had reached the Boulogne to Calais area by 2 September.

Most of the Channel ports were useless to the Allies. Successive heavy bombing of enemy railheads and lateral communications had devastated many of the port facilities of Calais, Dieppe, Dunkirk, Le Havre and Boulogne. On 1 September 2nd Canadian Infantry Division liberated Dieppe and managed to get parts of the port back into operation but it wasn't enough for the immense amount of stores and materiel that would have to come through to support the advancing armies. From Dieppe, the Canadians moved north, bypassing the fortress of Dunkirk on 8 September. Two days later, Ostend and Nieuport had fallen and were in Canadian hands. Not prepared to rest on their laurels, the Canadians began pushing north, probing enemy defences in Zeebrugge.

While the Canadians were moving forward so too did the Polish Armoured Division, which had crossed the Somme and pushed onto the Ghent–Bruges Canal. Here they ran into heavy resistance, but with the help of 4 Canadian Armoured Division moving up on their left they managed to clear Bruges by 11 September and crossed the canal. These two divisions rolled up to the Leopold Canal where the Germans were making their main defensive stand. The fighting in this area is detailed elsewhere in this book.[13]

Throughout the first ten days of September 1944 the Allies had rolled across France and Belgium to the Dutch frontier, liberating Ghent, Brussels and most of Antwerp along with all the towns and villages along the way. With the exception of Le Havre, Boulogne, Calais and Dunkirk, the coast was cleared of German troops and armour. Dunkirk was to be sealed off while the other coastal towns were to be dealt with by the Allies.

The first of the German fortresses of the 'Atlantic Wall' to be attacked by the Allies was Le Havre. The German garrison in this town was made up of more than 12,000 troops. From a point on the Seine, approximately 6,000yd east of the port, the German defences ran in a semi-circle down to the coast of the English Channel about 10,000yd north of the port. On the eastern side that was dominated by high ground was a flooded valley, while along the northern perimeter was an extensive anti-tank ditch sited together with extensive minefields and barbed wire. Along the anti-tank ditch were a series of strongpoints built of reinforced concrete which contained several large-calibre machine guns and the 88mm anti-tank guns used so effectively by the Germans. 'In the town there were two forts, numerous pill-boxes and fortified buildings and anti-tank guns sited to cover all approaches. Of guns capable of being used in a ground role there were 108 of 88mm calibre or over.'[14]

In the four days preceding the attack on the German defences at Le Havre, the Naval Bombardment Squadron pounded the enemy defences relentlessly with their 15in naval guns. At the same time, more than 4,000 tons of bombs smashed into the enemy positions, dropped by aircraft from RAF Bomber Command. Another 4,600 tons of bombs plastered the German defences just in the 90 minutes before H-Hour, the start of the attack, took place.[15]

When the attack began on 10 September more than 350 artillery guns opened up on the German defences in support of the infantry and armoured columns, whose attack went in at 1245hrs. A brigade from 49 Division managed to smash through the minefields and breached the German positions in the north-east corner of their defences. On their right, 51 Division smashed through their defences at midnight. The following day the breakthrough was increased as German defences were overrun in the rear. By nightfall on 11 September, Allied infantry from both divisions, supported by tanks and mobile guns, broke into the town and reached the high ground that overlooked the harbour. Throughout the night the drive continued as the Allies pushed deeper and deeper into the town, fighting from house to house, with machine guns, mortars, artillery and tanks. By 1145hrs on 12 September the German commander surrendered. The Allies had taken some 12,000 prisoners including 500 found in the hospitals! This action, which took only 48 hours of fighting, meant that one of the strongest garrisoned fortresses of the German 'Atlantic Wall' now lay in Allied hands having been attacked from the landward side.

Next Boulogne was to be assaulted. Here the German garrison numbered around 9,000 troops. As with Le Havre, the defences for Boulogne also ran in a semi-circle. This time it was around high ground punctuated by features that had been organised as fortresses. The defensive positions had been made of earthwork and reinforced concrete for the gun emplacements, dug-outs and bunkers covered by wire and extensive minefields. The gun batteries in the emplacements housed guns up to 305mm acting as coastal guns pointing out to sea. Intelligence reports estimated that the Germans had more than ninety guns at Boulogne of more than 75mm in calibre

Bad weather forced the Allies to postpone the attack on Boulogne for two days. Finally, the weather lifted on 17 September and the RAF bombers dropped more than 300 tons of bombs on the hapless German defenders. At 1025hrs the assault began when two brigades of 3 Canadian Infantry Division attacked supported by approximately 340 artillery guns pounding the German positions. However, Allied progress was slow going as they fought their way past obstacles while facing determined artillery fire from the heavy gun batteries and the guns at Cap Gris Nez. Notwithstanding the slow progress, the Allies managed to crush all German resistance and liberated the town on 22 September.

The task of clearing Calais of the German defenders fell to 3 Canadian Infantry Division but operations to carry out this task had to be postponed because of the Boulogne operations. The Calais assault also included the capture of Cap Gris Nez and the gun battery at Sangatte. The defences were roughly similar to those found at Le Havre and Boulogne, although at Calais the Canadians ran into something different. The Germans had flooded the area east, south and south west of Calais which meant they could only attack from the western side of the town.

Once again, two brigades launched the assault on 25 September at 0815hrs, supported by heavy bombers pounding the German positions from the air. As the Allies gained more and more ground they reached and secured the high ground south west of Escalles. On 28 September the citadel fell to the Allies and they entered Calais, still facing determined resistance. In order to evacuate the civilians both sides agreed to a ceasefire that lasted until midday on 30 September when the Allies resumed the assault. By the evening, German resistance had collapsed and by the morning of 1 October, the last of the German units still fighting had been overrun and captured by the Allies. On 29 September Cap Griz Nez had been taken as well.

By this point the Allied supply line from Normandy north to the Dutch frontier was more than 350 miles long. For several days, vehicles from 1 Corps and 8 Corps had been used to support the drive north and nearly 9,900 tons of supplies had been airlifted for forward areas between 5 and 30 September to support the Allied drive north.[16] This airlift was separate to the Allied airlift for Operation Market Garden.

The Germans had done their best to wreck the port and dock installations at Le Havre. But both the British and US navies began the task of clearing the wreckage and getting the port up and running as soon as possible after the town had been captured and secured. For this task the British used thirty minesweepers. At this point, according to the Canadian historian, the smaller ports of Dieppe, Boulogne, Calais and Ostend, were soon functioning, albeit on a reduced scale, and these aided the Allies to some degree, but they desperately needed the massive port facilities at Antwerp to be opened.

Although heavy casualties were inflicted on all enemy formations engaged on 21 Army Group front, no specific formation was destroyed. Some 67,000 prisoners were taken during this period, mostly from the ports of LE HAVRE, CALAIS and BOULOGNE. The fortress of DUNKIRK, with its garrison of 15,000 men, mostly from 226 Infantry Division, was now isolated.[17]

Allied Losses from 25 August–30 September 1944

	Killed	Wounded	Missing	Total
Allied Contingents	147	422	50	619
British	4,944	12,923	6,245	24,112
Canadian	751	3,802	580	5,133
Total	5,842	17,147	6,875	29,864

Cumulative from D-Day

	Killed	Wounded	Missing	Total
Allied Contingents	437	1,445	151	2,033
British	17,272	57,220	12,885	87,377
Canadian	3,812	14,843	2,537	21,192
Total	21,521	73,508	15,573	110,602

Notes

1. Report No. 89, 'The Operations of 21 Army Group 6 June 1944 – 5 May 1945, HQ British Army of the Rhine', September 1945.
2. Ibid.
3. See 'Report No. 69, The Campaign In NorthWest Europe, Information From German Sources', Part 3.
4. Ibid.
5. See Thompson, *Eighty-Five Days*, p. 47.
6. Ibid. .
7. Ibid., p. 52.
8. Ibid.
9. Ibid., see Thompson's excellent description of these events.
10. Ibid., p. 53,
11. Ibid., p. 54.
12. Ibid.
13. See 'Report No. 89, The Operations of 21 Army Group 6 June 1944 – 5 May 1945, HQ British Army of the Rhine', September 1945.
14. Ibid.
15. Ibid.
16. Ibid.
17. Ibid.

Chapter 4

The Allies Draw Their Plans

With Operation Market Garden in tatters the urgency for the Scheldt to be cleared had now finally hit home with the Allied High Command and, in particular, with Montgomery. At Lieutenant General Henry Duncan Graham Crerar's headquarters there was no doubt about the urgency and there hadn't been any doubt for sometime. Operations had to be undertaken to clear the Scheldt and get the port facilities at Antwerp up and running. Yet, even though Montgomery's main focus was on Market Garden throughout September 1944 and even while the Canadians were dealing with the German garrisons in Boulogne, Calais, Dieppe and Dunkirk, the importance of opening the Scheldt was not entirely lost on him:

> The early opening of the port of Antwerp is daily becoming of increasing importance and this cannot, repeat cannot, take place until Walcheren has been captured and the mouth of the river opened for navigation. Before you can do this you will obviously have to remove all enemy from the mainland in that part where they are holding up north east of Bruges. Airborne army considers not possible airborne troops in the business. Grateful for your views as to when you think you can tackle this problem.[1]

The Allies originally believed that using airborne troops was the best solution to the Walcheren problem. They would be landed in South Beveland and Walcheren Island and then fight their way through, clearing the enemy as they went. However, the Allied Airborne Army believed that the use of airborne troops was untenable and would only mean greater risk because the waterlogged and confined areas to be attacked where the enemy was dug in would make it extremely difficult for the Allies to deal with. A light airborne force would not do the trick and the reasons why were were recorded by Lieutenant General Lewis H. Bereton, Commander of the Allied Airborne Army, in his diary and cited in the Canadian report on the clearing of the

Scheldt: 'I refused Operation Infatuate because of intense flak on Walcheren, difficult terrain that would prevent glider landings, excessive losses likely because of drowning, non-availability of U.S. troops, and the fact that the operation is an improper employment of airborne forces.'[2]

However, Montgomery was unconvinced. In a letter to General Crerar in which Montgomery asked Crerar to give immediate thought to the operations required for clearing the Scheldt while the Canadians were still fighting in the Channel ports, he intimated that paratroops would be part of the operation. This helped the Canadians in their assessment of the operation's feasibility.

My Dear Harry,

Since last meeting you, we have had a great victory with SHAEF and the main weight of maintenance is now to be diverted to the northward thrust against the Ruhr.

I am delighted that you have captured Havre, and please give my congratulations to 1 Corps and the Divisions concerned.

The things that are now very important are:

1   capture of Boulogne and Dunkirk and Calais
2   the setting in motion of operations designed to enable
     us to use the port of Antwerp

Of these two things, (b) is probably the most important. We have captured a port that resembles Liverpool in size, but we cannot use it; if we could use it, all our maintenance troubles would disappear. I am very anxious that (a) and (b) should both go on simultaneously if you can possibly arrange it, as time is of the utmost importance. I wonder whether you could possibly use 1 Corps HQ to control the operations from Boulogne to Dunkirk, and the other corps HQ to control the operations for the opening of Antwerp. Perhaps you would let me know what you think about this.

For the operations concerned with Antwerp, you will need a great deal of air support. I have ordered that bombing to destroy the forts on Walcheren Island is to begin at once. On the day concerned we can lay on for you the whole weight of the heavy bomber effort from England, both Bomber Command and Eighth Air Force. I would like you to take over the city of Antwerp itself from Dempsey as soon as possible; you will want that place and certain ground east of it, so that you can develop operations to push the enemy northwards from the city. You may also possibly want to develop operations westwards along the neck of the peninsula towards Walcheren.

Dempsey is launching Operation Market Garden on Sunday 17th September. This is the operation designed to secure the crossings over the Meuse and the Rhine in the Arnhem area, and three Airborne Divisions are being used.

I have arranged that Airborne Forces (paratroops) will be available for you to assist in the capture of Walcheren Island. The really important thing is speed in setting in motion what we have to do. I hope very much that you will be able to tackle both your tasks simultaneously, i.e. the Pas de Calais ports and the Antwerp business.

Yours ever

B. L. Montgomery[3]

At SHAEF Montgomery's argument for the use of airborne troops fell on deaf ears. Those who knew the ins and outs of using airborne forces loudly proclaimed that they could not and should not be used. The final nail in the coffin was recorded in Lieutenant General Bereton's diary:

Paris, 21 September 1944 (d-plus-107).

Called to a conference at SHAEF to discuss general Montgomery's urgent request for an airborne operation on Walcheren Island. With the backing of ACM Leigh-Mallory, I Convinced General Eisenhower that the airborne operation was not sound. General Eisenhower sent a message to Field Marshal Montgomery informing him that airborne troops would not be employed against Walcheren. He stressed also that this decision was in no way due to a possible high rate or loss being suffered by airborne troops, but was due entirely to terrain characteristics which made the operation intrinsically unsuited as an airborne task.[4]

On 11 September General Crerar's planning staff began studying the feasibility of operations on South and North Beveland and Walcheren Island. The studies proceeded on the assumption that airborne troops would be thrown into the mix of troops landing by sea and attacking up the South Beveland isthmus. It was clear that the operation would have to be combined and that the closest relationship between the services maintained if the enemy was to be cleared of the whole watery and intricate region of the West Scheldt. Despite these studies, the Allies knew the task would not be easy. Replying to Montgomery's letter, General Crerar provided a first look, before his staff had time to make a further detailed study, on how extricating the Germans from the Scheldt Estuary was going to require 'the heaviest of implements':

The capture of Walcheren and Beveland islands looks like very tough propositions to me – at this stage – and will require a lot of 'doing'. I certainly will want to secure the mainland end of the peninsula leading from South Beveland before launching a final assault, but my studies have not yet proceeded sufficiently to indicate how I would propose to conduct that operation as a whole. In any event, I feel that maximum heavy bomber effort on these islands should be carried out whenever Bomber Command is not required by me for specific support of attacks on Boulogne, Dunkirk and Calais.[5]

Lieutenant General Simonds, commanding 2 Canadian Corps, had the responsibility of carrying out these operations to clear the Scheldt. His planning staff, and those at Army Headquarters, on closer study, confirmed General Crerar's impression. In a directive issued by Montgomery on 14 September there was encouraging news in the form of strong support for the use of heavy bombardment from the air:

> First Canadian Army
> • Complete the capture first of Boulogne, and then of Calais.
> • Dunkirk will be left to be dealt with later; for the present it will be merely masked.
> • The whole energies of the Army will be directed towards operations designed to enable full use to be made of the port of Antwerp.
> • Airborne troops are available to co-operate. Air operations against the island of Walcheren have already commenced and these include:
> > • the isolation of the island by taking out the road and rail bridges
> > • attacks on coast defence guns
> > • attacks on other artillery, including flak[6]

To the Allies it was evident that bombardment from the air would be needed to destroy the heavy, complex defences built by the Germans, which included large coastal guns built in concrete emplacements, as well as the more topographical barriers such as water barriers, dykes and polders.

The north shore of the West Scheldt, that is the South Beveland and Walcheren Island shoreline, was comparatively inaccessible and would make achieving military objectives difficult. The Canadian historian outlined the topographical area as it faced the Allies in September/October 1944:

> The islands of Walcheren and North Beveland and the peninsula of South Beveland can only be approached on the landward side across a narrow

isthmus of salt flats and polders joining South Beveland with the mainland and supporting the causeway, which carries the main road and railway line into Brabant. Some 23 miles farther east, another causeway links the peninsula with Walcheren. On the way, road and rail cross the South Beveland Canal over a double bridge. There are other canals on the peninsula but the South Beveland Canal is the most formidable as a military obstacle. It gives access to barges moving up from the West Scheldt to thread the northern channels of the archipelago and in normal times takes more traffic probably than any other canal in Europe, a burden of about 28 million tons passing through in a year. It is about four and a half miles long, 21 feet deep and between 130 and 160 feet wide. Farther west, the peninsula itself at its widest part is eleven miles from shore to shore, although there are other secondary roads, the main highway is the only one that runs from one end of South Beveland to the other, and in view of the difficulties of deployment over the sodden country on either hand, it afforded good defensible advantages to the enemy. This was particularly true at the narrowest part of the isthmus, where although there are also two subsidiary roads on the south, the Germans, when forced back upon it, would be holding a front of only 2000 yards.[7]

Further examination by Allied planners showed that an amphibious attack was a strong possibility depending on the right conditions. At the time of the operation, a dyke that lay behind a shore of mud, salt marsh and some grass that could provide a foothold for tracked and wheeled vehicles, if conditions were right, protected the whole of the coast of South Beveland. Allied intelligence reports indicated that the seaward slope of the dyke was moderate enabling infantry to negotiate it with reasonable speed and would allow tracked vehicles, if landed at high tide, to cross the dykes at most points and move inland. On the south shore there were small tidal harbours, such as Hoedekenskerke, which would enable tracked and wheeled vehicles to drive up the ramps and move inland to the South Beveland road.[8] 'Given the necessary craft and crews, high tide and suitable timing, a landing was not, therefore, out of the question so far as topography might affect the issue.'[9]

However, the heart of the Allied strategy for clearing the Scheldt lay in Walcheren Island, the outermost island and the heart of the German fortified defences for the estuary. No Allied ship could pass through the approaches to Antwerp without passing the coast of Walcheren and being blasted to bits by the heavy guns that ringed the coast of the island. A treacherous gap of mud, silt, ooze, runnels and water separated South Beveland and Walcheren. This channel, known as the Slooe Channel, was forbidding and virtually impossible to cross. The only way across was via a causeway between South Beveland and the island that carried a road and railway line.

> The island is about nine miles from north to south and roughly the same distance across at its widest part from east to west. The same landscape of polders and intricate system of drainage prevails as elsewhere throughout the region, though with rather more rough pasture and with the attendant hindrances to movement across country, especially after rain. For the level of saturation underground is never deep, and towards the end of September a very slippery surface laced with ditches would slacken and hinder the passage even of tracked vehicles off the roads, and the pace of infantry would be slow.[10]

At the time, there were two main towns on the island. Flushing, sitting at the south end of the Walcheren Canal, was a travel destination and well known to English holidaymakers before the war. The second was the capital of the island, Middelburg, which was also the island's main market town. For the most part, Walcheren Island lies below high water level and it is only the dykes and dunes that keep it from being lost to the sea.

In order to make a seaward approach on the north-west or south-west shores the Allies realised that it would have to be made through various local channels, or gaps. Along the north-west shore were 8 miles of sandy beach 'backed by dunes and in part protected by groynes'.[11] At Westkapelle the western tip of the island was solidly buttressed by a dyke, so to the Allies the best foothold seemed to be the broad beach in front of the dunes on the south-western shore which stretched almost as far as Flushing. However, this foothold was only suitable for lightly armed infantry, it was not suitable for heavy armoured vehicles. 'For the rest, the dykes march with the sea, except when the flats and salt marshes are left bare beneath them by the ebbing tide, and for one small beach, not thought suitable for landing, on the north-east.'[12]

The Allies realised that in most places along the shoreline of Walcheren they could only land infantry. The dunes were too steep for vehicles to move up the loose soft sand.

> Here and there men could get up a more gentler slope and squeeze through the rows of stakes set along the bases of the dykes to support them. Apart from the occasional small harbour, the only possible landing places for mechanical transport were through two sandy exits from the beach on to a brick road leading from the village of Domburg, on the North-west coast, or over the eastern dykes by a similar road into Flushing.[13]

From there a broad main road ran to Middelburg and then on to South Beveland via the causeway. However, for an attacking army it would be difficult to use the road as it was highly likely the Germans would have created heavy defences along it and would probably blow the bridge at Middelburg to ensure that no invading force could follow this route to South Beveland or come that way from South Beveland onto Walcheren.

North Beveland was the final outermost island in the group of islands of the East Scheldt and as such its topography was much the same as Walcheren's. This made a seaborne landing onto this island much more difficult. To clear the enemy from North Beveland a landward attack was needed, as shall be discussed later in this book.

However, before Walcheren and the Bevelands could be considered it was the German defences dug in on the southern shore of the Scheldt Estuary that demanded the Allies immediate attention. For if the Germans were not cleared from this area then mounting an amphibious invasion of Walcheren and South Beveland would not be possible. As with Walcheren, the terrain favoured the defender. This area of Holland was contained by water, with dykes and canals crisscrossing the region.

There were two negotiable waterways that were also obstacles for the Allies. These were the Leopold and Terneuzen Canals. The first was to prove to be the main obstacle in the Allied operations to clear the south shore of the West Scheldt, while the second was to be invaluable in helping the Allies break the German grip from the rear.

> Within the confines of this area along the shore, enclosed on the east by the Braakman Inlet and for 25 miles on the south and west by the Leopold Canal the Germans could expect to stand at bay and hold us off from the main onslaught against Walcheren. For beyond these water barriers the ground, which the enemy defended, gave him many advantages.[14]

Lying almost at sea level and honeycombed with polders fringed on the coast by dykes and dunes, the entire area was liable to saturation or flooding. Trees were few and far between except along the edges of an embankment or a canal or in some occasional wooded depression. 'Ditches took the place of hedges, and a sparse population had scattered its farmhouses wherever the soil was firm and dry, or strung its cottages along the roads or on the brink of the polders. It was not a country for armour, and amphibians were the only other sort of vehicle likely to flourish there.'[15] In terms of built-up areas that might offer good defensive places for the Germans were villages such as Eede, Oostburg, Sluis and Cadzand, Knocke and the port of Breskens, as the Allies would soon discover.

At first glance it would appear as if the battle to clear the Scheldt Estuary in order to use the port facilities at Antwerp entirely favoured the defenders. Indeed, the terrain was so poor that it would seem as if the Allied attackers would have no advantage whatsoever. However, it was not entirely one-sided. Once the Allies sealed off the isthmus into South Beveland, the Germans on Walcheren and on South and North Beveland would be cut off by land. Only by sea could they maintain some form of contact with their own military. They would also be susceptible to the hazards of tide and flood, as were the local population.

Deliberate inundation was a two edged weapon, a fact not to be missed by General Simonds in the calculation of his requirements for reducing Walcheren, that first and final obtrusion in the neck of the Scheldt. Were it not for the dunes and dykes which surround the island as rim to a saucer rising up with arduous ingenuity by countless generations of Dutchmen in their own unending war against the sea, its cultivated fields and thriving communities, like those of the entire group, would be reduced to the banks of mud from which they were reclaimed. All that would be left above water at high tide would be some of the roads, irrelevant on their dykes, the remnants of the sea defences and the dunes on the perimeter, tree-tops, the roofs of farm buildings, the port of Flushing and the town of Middelburg, itself an uncertain and dwindling island. Such a calamity, faced through the centuries of their tireless engineering, now overhung the helpless Dutch.[16]

Flooding would be a main weapon in the Allied armoury to defeat the Germans and there were several ways that this could be done. The Canadian historian cites the method used by the Germans in Normandy and Flanders to prevent the drainage system working. By stopping the pumps from working, the flow from ditch to canal and to the sea stops, the ditches begin to fill, the polders become saturated and flooding eventually takes place. The Allies also knew that this method could be used by the Germans in order to make it difficult for their troops to advance, especially across the isthmus. Of course, one other method was to breach the dykes that would then let in the sea and bring with it the destructive power of the tides. Allied intelligence believed that if the breaching took place at high tide there would be a deluge of some 8–10ft which would rush through the gaps in the form of a tidal wave and begin the reclamation of the land by the sea. Allied planners estimated it would take about three days for Walcheren to be covered.[17]

The planners also realised that the western parts of the island, where the dykes were strong, would see the worst results but it was also thought that destroying the dykes in this area would prove to be too difficult. The Allies also believed that if the dykes were breached in other areas the devastation would not be as sudden or as dramatic as in the west. However, the loss and misery to the local population would remain high. Allied intelligence believed there was a moral case to be had for breaching the dykes and causing such unprecedented misery to the local population: 'Apart from the physical difficulties involved are the moral questions. At this stage of the war, and for purposes so fleeting, it is unlikely that even exponents of total war would bring down on their nearest neighbours a calamity equal to an earthquake or volcanic eruption. It is possible but improbable.'[18]

The appreciation for breaching the dykes and causing the flooding of the interior of Walcheren was made on 16 September, the day before Montgomery proposed to drop his airborne troops over the rivers into northern Germany and bring about a swift victory and an end to the war. Of course, this was not to be. The war was to go on for another two long, bitter seasons into the spring of 1945 against an enemy determined to fight to the last, as can be seen by the use of the V weapons on Antwerp in the autumn and winter of 1944/45. It was clear, as far as the Germans were concerned, that Antwerp was the issue around which everything revolved. 'So it fell out that to hobble and distress the in place and resistant garrison and thus to ensure the success or our hazardous enterprise and diminish the number of our casualties which promised to be heavy, the Canadian command came to consider the drastic and terrible device of letting in the sea.'[19]

Yet, as far as the land operations were concerned, the Allies most immediate task was to clear the southern shore of the Scheldt, which ultimately meant clearing the Germans from the area of the Leopold Canal and the Breskens Pocket. It was a task that would prove to be monumental in its undertaking.

Notes

1. 'GOC C-in-C Operations 21 Army Group', fol. 77, 12 September 1944, cited in 'Report No. 188'.
2. Lieutenant General Lewis H. Brereton, *The Brereton Diaries*, pp. 340, 341, cited in 'Report No. 188'.
3. 'GOC C-in-C Operations 21 Army Group', fol. 79, 13 September 1944, cited in 'Report No. 188'.
4. Brereton, *The Brereton Diaries*, p. 353, cited in 'Report No. 188'.
5. 'GOC C-in-C Operations 21 Army Group', fol. 82, 13 September 1944, cited in 'Report No. 188'.
6. 'GOC C-in-C Operations 21 Army Group', fols 86, 87, 14 September 1944, cited in 'Report No. 299, The Westkapelle Assault on Walcheren'.
7. AEF/21 Army Gp/C/F, Docket III, fol. 3, p. 12, cited in 'Report No. 299'.

8. Ibid.

9. Ibid.

10. Ibid., fol. 55.

11. Ibid.

12. Ibid.

13. Ibid.

14. The Braakman Inlet was better known during the actual course of the battles as the Savojaards Plaat, which is the name of the shoal rather than the opening itself. AEF/21 Army Gp/C/F, Docket III, fol. 3, p. 12, cited in 'Report No. 299'.

15. AEF/First Canadian Army, Intelligence Summary No. 66, 3 September 1944, Appendix D, cited in 'Report No. 188'.

16. See 'Report No. 299'.

17. AEF/First Canadian Army, Intelligence Report, No. 2, Vol. 2, fols 31 and 76, cited in 'Report No. 299'.

18. Ibid.

19. See 'Report No. 299'.

Chapter 5

Plan of Attack

Lieutenant General Simonds, commanding Canadian 2 Corps, was the man entrusted with the Allied operations to clear the Scheldt. On 19 September the Allied Plans Section at Army Headquarters issued an appreciation that would help Simonds to evolve his plan. This appreciation, primarily for the clearing of South Beveland and Walcheren Island, was based on all the available information and the assumption that the Allies had cleared the south shore from Antwerp to the sea of enemy positions. A situation that had not yet occurred and that Operation Switchback was to achieve. While preparations for Operation Switchback were underway, planning for clearing Walcheren Island and South Beveland began in earnest with the appreciation from Allied planners.

Taking into account considerations of topography, intelligence reports, the availability and condition of equipment, how the Germans might react and any other alternatives open to the Allies, the planners compared these considerations, looking at the advantages and disadvantages of each one then provided a set of recommendations under which the assault could most favourably be launched.[1]

As far as equipment was concerned the appreciation showed that progress had been made in providing the necessary specialty craft, vehicles and naval support for the operation and by 24 September, 5 Assault Engineers of 79 Armoured Division had been reinforced to a full complement of 5 squadrons, comprising 40 Terrapin amphibious vehicles and 100 tracked vehicles, assembling in the area north of Antwerp in readiness.

The availability of Weasel amphibious vehicles was more doubtful. Only sixty were within relatively easy reach and could float but none could move under their own power. That made them useless for the operation. However, another 100 completely amphibious Weasels were available in the UK and were due to be shipped to France on 20 September. The timing was very fine indeed.

The Royal Navy was able to provide seventy assault landing craft (LCA) and twenty tank landing craft (LCT) with some being carried by tank transporters over rough roads from Ostend to the estuary by inland waterway.[2]

Allied engineers then realised that work would need to be done to clear demolished bridges and damaged lock gates in order to make the canals usable. There was no certainty that the Bailey bridges used by the Allies would be high enough to allow the landing craft to pass safely underneath them.

Another problem faced by the Allies was that the crews for the landing craft did not have the appropriate training for carrying out large-scale amphibious operations. The logistics for getting the men afloat would not be easy either. However, once the landing craft were on their way to assault South Beveland and Walcheren they would have assistance from the monitors HMS *Roberts* and HMS *Erebus*, which were to use their four 15in guns to pound German coastal batteries and other installations.

The Planning Section knew that the Germans had a heavily defended garrison on both South Beveland and Walcheren Island. They also knew, from past experiences in Normandy, that the Germans would hold out for as long as they could. The planners believed a heavy bombardment by the Allies on the German positions might convince the enemy to withdraw. They argued that:

> If he is faced with the possibility of these forces being cut off by the thrust of Second British Army, and if his defences of these islands are subjected to heavy bombardment by naval and ground artillery together with heavy air attack, he may decide to leave only a small retaining force. Therefore any plan for the capture of these islands by us should embrace plans for the quick exploitation of light enemy resistance.[3]

However, there was no chance of this taking place as the Germans believed the risk of losing the entire garrison on Walcheren Island was an acceptable one 'as the strategic issues at stake were of sufficient magnitude to render the sacrifice a cheap one'.[4] The appreciation by the planners at Army Headquarters never really believed that heavy bombardment with high explosives from artillery and the air would not be needed:

> Each of the courses to be considered is based on constant efforts to neutralize the enemy's battery positions and to destroy his defences on the islands of WALCHEREN and South BEVELAND by naval and ground artillery fire and by heavy and medium bombing together with attacks by RP and fighter bombers. The ground artillery, apart from the divisional artillery of the force working along South Beveland from the East should be placed as soon as possible in suitable areas along the South side of the West Schelde so that this artillery can continually carry on the neutralisation of the enemy's batteries as well as being able to support the advance of the troops from the East.[5]

A number of different alternatives were considered by the Allied planners that included an assault by land along the South Beveland peninsula right up to the South Beveland Canal, and if airborne forces were available to send in a parachute brigade to capture the small harbour at Hoedekenskerke through which waterborne troops could strike inland.

In addition, if airborne forces were available, troops could parachute onto the German side of the causeway into Walcheren. They could then secure a bridgehead that would free the causeway that linked South Beveland to Walcheren for the land forces on South Beveland to cross over. But if no airborne troops were available the next best alternative was to mount amphibious landings on the German right flank from the south shore of the estuary to support the landward Allied assault into South Beveland.

Once Beveland had been captured and cleared of the enemy, the Allies could then attack the German positions along the causeway, enabling them to establish a bridgehead on the Walcheren side. German defences at Flushing and Middelburg would then be overwhelmed by further attacks across the island from the bridgehead.[6]

These alternatives put forward by the Allied planners were based upon the assumption that Walcheren Island would be too difficult to assault before the landward approach via South Beveland had been completely secured. The planners also believed that they should 'discard at the outset the possibility of mounting a successful combined op to capture WALCHEREN island by assaulting the only possible suitable beaches, which are on the North West and South West coasts because this could only be done after considerable time spent on combined training and preparations'.[7]

For General Simonds, however, an attack on the causeway without a diversion or assault on the Germans elsewhere would be a costly failure. The causeway was heavily fortified and the Allies knew this. They had no doubt about the risks involved in attacking the German positions on the Walcheren side of the causeway where they were heavily dug in. Much of the coastline of Walcheren Island was quite treacherous and unsuitable for an amphibious assault. Yet despite this, Allied planners believed that diversions and extreme attacks on the Germans had to be tried, even given the risks and the short amount of time available to mount such operations. 'It was concluded that only by tormenting and distracting the Germans and by attacking them in such a way that they believed was impractical would it be possible to persuade them that their position was untenable.'[8] The comments by General Simonds on the appreciation submitted to him by Allied planners at Army Headquarters illustrate the originality and incisiveness that he brought to bear on the very serious problems he faced in clearing the enemy in the Scheldt Estuary. On 21 September, he wrote a memorandum to General Crerar where he introduced his ideas: 'As I understand it, the object of the operation is NOT to capture the islands of WALCHEREN and South BEVELAND but to destroy, neutralize or capture enemy defences which deny us free passage through the West Scheldt to the port of ANTWERP.'[9]

There was a fine distinction between capturing the islands and destroying the enemy defences. The first concern that Simonds outlined in his comments was the assumption that the Allies would quickly be able to hold the south shore opposite Flushing, where they could bring up all available artillery guns and begin pounding the German coastal gun batteries on Walcheren from across the Scheldt until they were neutralised and not a threat to any amphibious assault on Flushing.

Simonds believed that gaining the area of the south shore would involve a bitter struggle for the Allies to capture and secure the low-lying terrain of dykes and canals between Antwerp and the sea:

> The Appreciation begins with the assumption that we hold the whole of the south bank of the Scheldt. At the present time the enemy is strongly posted along the line of the LEOPOLD CANAL from about HAVEN to EEYST. With the exception of a few dyked roads, the areas between HAVEN and OOSTKERKE and HEYST are inundated. The gap between these inundations is the only approach to enemy positions NORTH of the LEOPOLD CANAL and most of this gap is covered by the dual courses of the LEOPOLD and LYS CANALS – a most difficult obstacle. It is within the enemy's power to increase the inundations or indeed, except for the dune area along the NW coast, to 'sink' the whole of the area between LEOPOLD CANAL and the SCHELDT. The clearing of this area may be a major operation and barring the fact that it will deny to the enemy the employment of his guns around KNOCKE, it may be so saturated that it would be useless to us for gun positions from which the WALCHEREN defences may be commanded.[10]

Fully aware of the skill of the Germans in exploiting the terrain where the battles would be fought, Simonds realised that the Germans did not need to flood the area in front of their defences as saturation would achieve the same result. Water-logged fields, soggy land, mud and ooze would force the Allies to use only the roads and the dykes, thus bringing the Allied troops into the concentrated fire of the German defenders.

> In most military appreciations the ground is the one constant on which firm conclusions can be based. This is not the case in the particular problem under consideration. A German document in our possession

makes it clear that the conditions most advantageous to the defence and most disadvantageous to us are those of 'ground saturation'. This denies to us the use of the ground for movement to exactly the same extent as if it was completely flooded but allows the enemy the use of his roads, avoids the flooding of buildings, stores and many works, which must be of importance to him. Attacking across a 'saturated' area, movement is possible only on top of dyked roads. We sacrifice every advantage, which we normally possess in the offensive. The defensive firepower can all be concentrated on narrow approaches. Mines and obstacles are most effective. With room to deploy on a 'dry belt' behind a saturated area, the enemy can concentrate their fire while keeping their dispositions well concealed and well dispersed. The land approach via SOUTH BEVELAND appears attractive but it may well turn out to be an approach down a single stretch of road some five miles in length, bordered by impassable ground on either side. It would be equivalent to an assault landing on a 'one craft front' on a coast where it was only possible to beach one craft at a single pre-known point on which the whole firepower of the defences could be concentrated. I consider that the project of an assault across water cannot be ruled out if Walcheren Island must be taken. It may be the only way of taking it. Though it would be a last resort and a most uninviting task, I consider it would be quite wrong to make no preparations for it, and to be faced at some later time with the necessity of having to improvise at very short notice. I am strongly of the opinion that the necessary military and naval forces should now be earmarked, married up and trained against the contingency that they might be required.[11]

Simonds also realised that the state of the ground would also affect airborne troops. 'Intelligence sources state that thoroughly saturated ground is impassable to infantry and therefore is equivalent to flooding from the point of view of landing airborne infantry upon it.'[12] The General was convinced that the strength of the German defences on Walcheren required the Allies to use variety and ingenuity if they were to overcome the advantages of terrain enjoyed by the Germans. One solution he came up with was, according to the Canadian historian, an original idea and a rather drastic remedy that would ultimately lead to the clearing of the Scheldt. Simonds believed that the Allies should use the following techniques for the capture of Walcheren Island:

• Bombing operations to break the dykes and completely flood all parts of the island below high water-level.
• Those parts of the island remaining above the water should then be

systematically attacked by heavy air bombardment day and night to destroy defences and wear out the garrison by attrition. RDF stations should have an early priority as 'point' targets.

• Whenever possible, heavy bombers proceeding to or from targets in Western Germany by day or night should be routed over WALCHEREN so that the garrison can never tell whether the approach of large numbers of aircraft indicates attack or not. This combined with heavy bombing attacks will drive the enemy to cover an approach of large aircraft formations and will help to 'cover' an eventual airborne landing.

• When it is considered that the morale of the German garrison has sufficiently deteriorated, water-borne patrols may be sent to determine the situation.

• If found to be ripe, airborne, followed by water borne, troops should be landed immediately following a bomber raid (when defenders have been driven to ground) and mop up and take the surrender.[13]

From that point, Simonds then set forth the conditions in which he wished to discuss the broader plan of operations:

• 2 Canadian Infantry Division to push North to cut off South Beveland and exploit the land approach along South Beveland as far as possible.

• 4 Canadian Armoured Division to continue its operations to clear the north of the Leopold Canal up to the West Scheldt until 3 Canadian Infantry Division was available to relieve it. 'This is a highly unsuitable task for an armoured division but I have nothing else available within the present constitution and tasks of 2nd Canadian Corps.'

• As soon as 3 Canadian Infantry Division can be released from Boulogne – Calais area, this division less one infantry brigade will relieve 4 Canadian Armoured Division and complete the clearing of the area North of the Leopold Canal if not completed by that time.

• One infantry brigade of 3 Canadian Infantry to be earmarked with necessary Naval counterpart to train at Ostend for seaborne operations against Walcheren.

• Airborne forces earmarked for this operation, to study and train for landings on those parts of Walcheren Island that cannot be sunk by flooding.

• Bombing –
  • To break dykes and flood WALCHEREN ISLAND.
  • Destroy defences and break morale of defenders of 'unsinkable' portions of the island, be instituted forthwith.[14]

On 23 September, these views were presented to General Crerar at a conference at his headquarters. Here Simonds was able to go into greater detail for the benefit of the representatives of the other services and headquarters that would make the decisions regarding the Allied air attack.

However, while all these plans and preparations were being made, the south shore of the West Scheldt still needed to be cleared. Operation Switchback had not yet run its course and that, at this point in time, was the Allies' most immediate concern.

Notes

1. Appendix 17, Operation Infatuate – An Appreciation, cited in 'Report No. 188', Part IV, p. 24.
2. Ibid., stated by the Allied Naval Commander Expeditionary Force.
3. Ibid., cited in 'Report No. 188', Part IV, p. 25.
4. Ibid.
5. Ibid., p. 26.
6. Ibid.
7. Ibid.
8. Ibid., p. 27.
9. AEF/First Canadian Army/C/E, Docket II, No. 28, fol. 50, cited in 'Report No. 188', Part IV.
10. Ibid., p. 28.
11. Ibid., fols 49, 50, p. 29.
12. Ibid., fol. 49.
13. Ibid.
14. Ibid., fols 48, 49, p. 30.

Chapter 6

Final Preparations

Throughout September 1944 General Crerar had been working despite his steadily declining health. Yet he would not leave until the basic plans and preliminary plans were in place for the next phases of the operation to clear the Scheldt Estuary of the Germans. As each day went by his condition threatened to hinder his ability to carry on in command. Finally, on 26 September, after being thoroughly examined by doctors at the Canadian General Hospital in St Omer, who advised him to return to the UK for further treatment and tests, Crerar flew to Headquarters 21 Army Group to chat with Montgomery about the situation. Field Marshal Montgomery agreed with the doctors and that he should return to the UK for further treatment. At this meeting, Crerar put forward the name of the replacement he wanted to take over his command while he was away. That replacement was Lieutenant General Simonds and Montgomery agreed with this decision. That same afternoon, at First Canadian Army Headquarters in Ghent, the handover to General Simonds was completed and he became the Acting Army Commander while Crerar was away. Other appointments saw Major General C. Foulkes taking over the command of 2 Canadian Corps from General Simonds, while Brigadier R.H. Keefler was appointed to command 2 Canadian Infantry Division. General Crerar flew back to the UK on 27 September 1944.

General Simonds lost no time in resuming the argument for breaching the dyke around Walcheren as part of his plan to the capture the island with the least possible loss of life. On 29 September he called a special meeting to look into the issue with senior officers of 84 Group and with Group Captain P.B. Lucas of the Allied Expeditionary Air Forces, and Air Commodore Dickens of Bomber Command. Captain A.F. Pugsley attended to represent the desired air support by the navy.[1]

At this meeting Simonds announced there would be no airborne troops involved in the operations to clear the Scheldt Estuary. Other methods would have to be found that would provide the best chance of success. One key method was flooding the inland area behind the dykes on Walcheren Island. At the time,

Allied intelligence showed that a large proportion of the island was under sea level and if the dykes were breached the subsequent flooding would compel the Germans to concentrate their forces in a smaller area, making them much more vulnerable to air, sea and land attack. Simonds believed that points where the dykes were breached could be used as entry points for amphibious vehicles to land troops, vehicles and materiel on the other side of the German positions. Indeed, from his study of intelligence reports and aerial photographs and the opinions of the engineers, Simonds believed that much of the island could be flooded to the point that the ground would become soggy and impassable: conditions that would give the Allies the advantage they were looking for. 'If the dyke that ringed the Walcheren coast was to be breached "the land on the inside was low enough to be inundated, a conclusion borne out by the testimony of Dutch civilians who had said that if the dyke was broken the island would sink."'[2] He used other air photographs of bomb-patterns caused in previous operations by the RAF to show that as in the case of the attack on the Ems–Dortmund Canal, similar tasks had been carried out with a degree of accuracy commensurate with that required for the proposed target of Walcheren.[3]

According to the report from the Canadian historian, the dyke around Walcheren was approximately 20ft high. On the seaward side it was faced with stone some 3ft above the height of the highest tide while the top of the dyke was approximately 25ft across. The top was either covered by turf or more often than not carried a double-tracked road. The outer slope was 30 degrees and the inner slope no more than 45 degrees. At the time, the base of the dyke was approximately 150ft, the core of which was made of sand bound by a layer of clay at least 3ft thick.[4]

There were three points that Simonds suggested where the dykes could be breached prior to the spring tides of 3 or 4 October 1944. These three areas were 1,000yd to the north of the coastal town of Westkapelle. From the meeting on 29 September it was decided that: 'Bomber Command would make a deliberate attempt to breach the dykes as soon as a) authority was obtained from the Supreme Commander and notified to them through normal channels and b) weather and technical conditions permitting.'[5] The wait for the decision would not be long.

The experts accepted the practicality of the plan as well as the cost on behalf of the troops who would have to assault the German positions by land and water in the face of concentrated, withering enemy fire, if the breach was not made. In this case, the saving of life had a stronger case than the loss of land and livestock and the subsequent dire hardship that would befall the Dutch local inhabitants. 'Too much depended on silencing the German guns for these unhappy alternatives to be avoided, and Walcheren's rich acres were condemned to the ravages of the sea.'[6]

Finally, on 1 October, a signal came through from Montgomery: 'Op Infatuate: The Supreme Commander has approved the project to flood the island of Walcheren.'[7] And: 'The wholesale destruction of property is, in my view, always justified if it is calculated to save casualties.'[8]

Anticipating the approval to breach the dyke, Headquarters 21 Army Group had already begun warning the local inhabitants of the coming calamity. This information was made known to Headquarters the First Canadian Army from a message sent to SHAEF on 27 September 1944: 'TOPSECRET: Ref operation Infatuate. Request immediate preparation and drop leaflets Scheldt Estuary Islands warning civil population imminent heavy prolonged air bombardment. Leaflets should stress danger flooding and urge immediate evacuation of islands or if this is not possible of military objectives and low-lying ground.'[9]

Within a week of that signal the first bombing attack on the dyke took place. On 3 October, heavy bombers attacked the chosen breaching point near Westkapelle.

The target was a small section of sea-wall approximately 330 feet x 200 feet in area. A total of 237 4,000 pound bombs and 1742 1,000 pound bombs were used in the attack, as well as a smaller number of 500 pounders. The seawall was successfully breached, four gun emplacements were drowned, and seven other batteries were surrounded by flood waters as the sea spread inland during the next three or four days. The seawall was again successfully breached near Flushing on October 7th and again near Veere on October 11th. A final attack on the wall at Westkapelle on October 17th deepened the breach in that area and completed as far as possible the flooding of the island.[10]

That same week, General Simonds issued a directive to his corps commanders, Generals Foulkes and Crocker, that recognised the increasing urgency for the Allies to open up the port facilities at Antwerp and the pressing need to clear the Scheldt of the enemy as quickly as possible.

I appreciate that the greater the success of the offensive of the First US and Second British Armies, the greater will become the demand for the use of the port of Antwerp and concurrently with this, First Canadian Army may be required to extend its right Northwards and Eastwards to cover the outer flank of Second Brit Army and isolate, and ultimately destroy, the German forces cut off in HOLLAND. It is important that the large forces required for offensive operations to clear the Scheldt Estuary should be released for operations further Northwards as early as possible – unless engaged offensively they constitute an uneconomic and bad detachment. In spite of the immediate priorities given to First US and Second British Armies, the importance of quickly clearing the Scheldt Estuary is increased, NOT diminished.[11]

In his directive, Simonds added that the First Canadian Army would:

• Clear the Western flank of the Second British Army by a thrust North Eastwards from TURNHOUT on HERTOOENBOSCH
• Develop operations to clear the SCHELDT Estuary and open the port of ANTWERP
• Use the Czech Armoured Brigade to contain Dunkirk[12]

His instructions for 1 British Corps were to:

• Push North Eastwards on Hertogenbosch
• Clear the area North of Antwerp using 2 Canadian Infantry Division then advance to the eastern end of the South Beveland isthmus and close it
• From there develop successive operations towards BREDA and ROOSENDAAL in order to cover 2 Canadian Infantry Division's eastern flank and rear as they were directed westwards onto South Beveland.[13]

The orders from Simonds to 2 Canadian Corps were equally specific. They were to:

• Attack, capture or destroy all enemy troops and units remaining in Belgium and Holland on the southern shore of the West Scheldt (Operation Switchback)
• Once Operation Switchback had concluded, develop operations with 2 Canadian Infantry Division to clear out South Beveland of the enemy, and
• Capture the Island of Walcheren (Operation Infatuate).[14]

On 2 October, the same day that General Simonds issued his directive to his corps commanders, General Foulkes produced an outline plan for his commanders. The clear objective of Foulkes' plan was to attack and destroy the enemy north of the Leopold Canal right up to the south shore of the Scheldt Estuary. This would silence the German guns that covered the approaches to the Scheldt, as well as provide suitable gun emplacements for pounding German positions on Walcheren in support of the Allied amphibious assault on the island.

The plan called for the Allies to force a bridgehead and clear the area between the Braakman Inlet and the Belgian border during the first phase of the operation. In the second phase, the Allies would concentrate their efforts in the area around Knocke-sur-Mer and all the roads leading into it. While this was taking place, the tasks of 4 Canadian Division were to:

• Hold the line of the Leopold Canal and secure a base that would cover the concentration of assaulting troops that would carry out the crossing of the Canal.
• Carry out feints and diversions in order to pin the Germans down during the actual assault.
• Ensure that all the assaulting troops had the necessary information.
• Prepare and improve roads, approaches or tracks required by the assaulting troops.[15]

The 3 Canadian Infantry Division, supported by 5 Assault Battalion Royal Engineers, along with a squadron of amphibious tanks, would carry out the attack and were tasked to:

• Break into the area across the Leopold Canal and across the Braakman Inlet or Savojaards Plaat.
• Ensure that the enemy escape routes through the ports of Breskens and Hoodfplaat were cut off.
• In the area between the Braakman Inlet (Savojaards Plaat) and the Dutch border ensure all the enemy had been cleared.
• At Sluis and Retrenchment secure a crossing as a preliminary Phase II.[16]

Rocket-firing Typhoon fighters, fighter-bombers and medium bombers were to be on call whenever they were required.

With everything ready, Operation Switchback began.

Notes

1. 'G' Plans, H.Q . First Canadian Army, September 1944, Appendix 28, Operation Infatuate.
2. Personal Diary, Major W.E.C. Harrison, 8 November 44, cited in 'Report No. 188'.
3. Information given by Lieutenant General Simonds to Lieutenant Colonel W.E.C. Harrison, 10 September 1947.
4. First Canadian Army, September 1944, Appendices 'Y–Z', 'AA–PP', fol. 97, cited in 'Report No. 188'.
5. 'G' Plans, H.Q. First Canadian Army, September 1944, Appendix 28, Operation Infatuate.

6. Ibid.

7. AEF/21 Army Gp/C/H, Docket II, tele message, 1 October,1150hrs.

8. This quote is from Air Marshal Sir Arthur Harris, *Bomber Offensive*, new edn Pen & Sword, Barnsley, 2005, p. 237.

9. See 'Report No. 188'.

10. First Canadian Army/S/F, fol. 19, Bomber Command Attacks, cited in 'Report No. 188'.

11. Ibid.

12. Ibid., pp. 1, 2.

13. Ibid., p. 2.

14. Ibid.

15. Ibid.

16. Ibid.

Chapter 7

Break-Out

In describing the Allied operations to clear the southern shore of the Scheldt and South Beveland the sources used are based on a series of reports written by Canadian and British military historians shortly after the war. Other sources also include publications such as Gerald Rawling's excellent book *Cinderella Operation*.

The First Canadian Army had been tasked to clear the south shores of the Scheldt Estuary as well as North and South Beveland and the island fortress of Walcheren. They were also committed to relieving the left flank of the Second British Army so that General Dempsey could bring his forces to bear in the north west for the main Allied offensive against the Ruhr. This would help Allied forces to advance along the lower reaches of the Scheldt in order to seal off the Beveland isthmus prior to the Allied invasion of South Beveland.

However, before any of this could take place the area known as the Breskens Pocket had to be cleared of the enemy. This was a chunk of the Netherlands heavily defended by the Germans that commanded the southern bank of the West Scheldt Estuary and, before any attempt at attacking Walcheren and South Beveland could be contemplated, the Pocket had to be cleared. The area was bordered by two major canals running from the North Sea at Zeebrugge then inland for 10 miles on a parallel course before the northern canal, the Leopold Canal, circled around past the village of Eede, up to the Braakman Inlet, a 5-mile long, 1-mile wide body of water connected to the Scheldt Estuary. At Eede, the other canal, the Canal de la Derivation de la Lys, ran south away from the Leopold Canal past the town of Eeklo and beyond. The Germans fortified a defensive line that largely ran the course of the Leopold Canal, from Zeebrugge to Terneuzen, a seaside town that lay on the other side of the Braakman Inlet.[1]

In mid-September, General Simonds issued instructions to the commanders of his armoured divisions to move north from Antwerp in a rough line that followed the Ghent–Terneuzen Canal. The area running up to Breskens on the left was given to 4th Armoured Division, while in the right area, north-west of Antwerp, it was the task of 1st Polish Armoured Division to clear out the German defenders.

The first Allied unit to run into the strong defensive German positions of the Breskens Pocket was the 4th Canadian Armoured Division. The Canadians managed to establish a bridgehead over the Ghent Canal in order for them to approach this German defensive line. Once they did they found themselves facing a much larger and more heavily defended line that followed the Leopold Canal and the Derivation Canal.

Major General Foster, not realising the depth and strength of the German defences, decided on a night attack for crossing both canals. This was to take place in the Moerkerke area and would kick off at 2200hrs. Once across, 4 Canadian Armoured Division was to clear the north bank of the Leopold Canal and then spread out, advancing as quickly as possible some 12 miles to Fort Frederik Hendrik 'on the coastal side of the Pocket'.[2]

Unfortunately, the initial attack was not a success. The Canadian Algonquin Regiment attacked using four rifle companies supported by artillery, mortar and machine-gun fire. To scale the steep banks of the canals they used grappling hooks and special ladders. Both canals were crossed by the four rifle companies and once on the far bank of the second canal the Canadians began digging in. During the night the Germans counter-attacked, which the Algonquins were able to repel. However, the following morning the Germans attacked again with a ferocity that left the Canadians reeling. They hammered the forward Algonquin position with heavy artillery and shellfire, forcing the engineers building the bridges across the two canals to withdraw. The enemy shellfire also destroyed many of the assault boats the Algonquins had used to cross the canals. The bridgehead itself, however, bore the brunt of the German counter-offensive. It was plastered and pounded with everything the Germans could throw at it and the Algonquins clung on, suffering heavy casualties. On 14 September they were ordered to withdraw, which they did, leaving behind many dead and dying. One company alone suffered nearly 75 per cent casualties. As Rawling states, this was the Canadians' 'baptism of fire' and first taste of what faced them in the Breskens Pocket.[3]

The goal for the 1st Polish Division in the east was to reach the port of Terneuzen, situated on the south bank of the Scheldt and the other side of the Braakman Inlet. Having pushed out of the Ghent area, the Polish headed north east and by the 15 September managed to take the small village of St Paul. The following day, the Polish 10th Dragoon Regiment, dealing with what German defences there were, established a bridgehead across the Hulst Canal having crossed the Dutch frontier to get to it. This canal connects to the Ghent–Terneuzen Canal and runs in an east–west direction. The problem for the Poles was that the country they were in was not suitable for armour so the going was slow.

On the morning of 17 September, the Germans counter-attacked, battering the Poles so badly that the bridgehead was completely wiped out. In this attack, the Poles suffered heavily. But they were undaunted and the following day they attacked the Germans again. This time it was further west along the Hulst Canal at Kijkuit where the Polish 3rd Infantry Brigade mounted their assault. Crossing the canal easily, their engineers managed to construct a bridge enabling the armour to cross as well. From there, the Poles rapidly expanded their bridgehead up to the small town of Axel, which they occupied, 5 miles from Terneuzen. They were now some 20 miles east of the terrible fighting and heavy German defences established in the Breskens Pocket. On 20 September, as the Canadian battled it out in the Pocket, the Poles tore through what enemy defences there were and in several places reached the coastline, capturing several boats used by the Germans for moving men and equipment across to South Beveland. Terneuzen was quickly captured and occupied that same day. This action meant that the Poles had managed to clear the area from Terneuzen right through to Antwerp of all German defences.

Early in October 1944, General Simonds wrote that:

The First British Corps was: 'making rapid progress north-eastward from its bridgehead over the Antwerp–Turnhout Canal. The 1st Polish Armoured Division had elements as far as Poppel. During the next few days it became apparent that the enemy was fighting a delaying action, while withdrawing on his left flank under pressure from the Poles on the Tilburg and giving way more gradually before the 2nd Canadian Infantry Division on his right north of Antwerp.'[4]

The battle of the Leopold Canal will be examined a little later in this book but, for now, it is worth looking at the operations north of Antwerp. The plan for these operations was ultimately to reach the isthmus of South Beveland. So the Second Canadian Infantry Division, rolled out of Antwerp, mopping up any last elements of German resistance in that area and headed north. On the left flank 4 Canadian Infantry Brigade, under the command of Brigadier F.N. Cabeldu, early on 2 October entered Merxem and pushed on. In the centre of the advance, the northern bank of the canal at Sternhoven and Lochtenberg was taken and held by 6 Canadian Infantry Brigade, commanded by Brigadier J.G. Gauvreau, while on the right, at Brecht, was Brigadier W.J. Megill's 5 Canadian Infantry Brigade.

German resistance at first was spasmodic. They still held out north of Antwerp, almost in the suburbs of the city just north of the Albert Canal. This waterway linked Antwerp to Liège, some 80 miles away.[5] The Germans that were in the area were part of four combat-hardened and tired divisions. A reinforced German 711 Division and a depleted 346 Infantry division were positioned in the area of St Leonard and Brecht. Allied intelligence estimated this enemy formation to be about the size of three infantry battalions. Elements of the 70 Infantry Division had been reported in the front line west of Antwerp and were estimated to be nearly up to full strength. However, from prisoners captured days before, the Allies discovered that morale was low.[6] The Canadian historian who wrote about the Canadian operations in clearing the Scheldt Estuary states that east of Antwerp, at Baarle-Nassau, the Allies captured several prisoners from the 719 Infantry Division that had been virtually wiped out.

> These formations, together with various satellite battle groups, were clearly in the process of being reorganized and strengthened as fast as the German command could produce the necessary personnel. After a disheartening series of retreats, prisoners had a pessimistic view of the future. Contrasting the previous headlong flight of the German Fifteenth Army with the present effort to defend Walcheren, they gloomily quoted an epigram attributed to one of their battalion commanders: 'You can't turn a hare into a porcupine.'[7] But as time would soon show, this unlikely metamorphosis was entirely possible, and it was to take us some weeks in the field to scotch the animal.[8]

As the Germans withdrew, the Allies followed. On 3 October the Camp de Brasschaet was captured by 6 Canadian Infantry Brigade, without loss, in a swift action that took the Germans completely by surprise. The next day, Allied troops occupied the important junction of Capellen, while Eckeren and St Mariaburg fell to 4 Canadian Infantry Brigade which then advanced up the main road, passing through St Mariaburg up to the canal before attacking enemy positions in Putte.[9] On 5 October, the Canadians entered Holland when they crossed this canal in front of Putte. It was here, on the Dutch/Belgian border, that the Essex Scottish faced a determined enemy and after some severe fighting finally managed to enter the town and capture it.[10] Once cleared of the enemy, the Canadians moved on from Putte. On 6 October, 3 miles to the west, Berendrecht was taken while elements of the brigade pushed further northwards up the road through thickly wooded country where German defenders continuously fired on the advancing Canadians. This was more harassing fire as their strength and numbers were not enough to halt the Allied advance or to stop them taking Osendrecht and Hondseind by nightfall. To the south, the town of Santvliet fell to the Canadians who liberated more than a hundred German and Polish political prisoners. This is an example of some of the discoveries the Allies would make as they pushed deeper and deeper into Nazi-occupied territory.[11]

Operation Switchback was now well under way. However, the Germans, realising what the Allies were trying to do, began strengthening their resistance. Von Rundstedt was ordered by General Jodl to hold the line that ran from Antwerp–Tilburg–Hertogenbosch to the very last man, with the 'obvious intention of denying the Allies access to Woensdrecht and by that convenient corridor to the Bevelands and the fortress of Walcheren'.[12]

The primary objective for Operation Switchback was to isolate the enemy on South Beveland. Allied concentration at this stage was to ensure continued advancement north towards Woensdrecht, Korteven and the coast. To achieve this plan, the Canadian historian wrote that the idea was to:

> strike simultaneous blows north and north-east, one in the hope of being able to sever the connection between the highway from the peninsula and the road to Bergen Op Zoom, and the other to improve the position on our flank, which was now becoming dangerously extended. We could hardly expect that the enemy would regard such a severance lightly, since the tactical and strategic consequences would be decisive. The phase of the pursuit was over. The enemy had regained both the willingness and the ability to stand and fight.[13]

For this next phase of the operation some changes were made that saw 2 Canadian Infantry Division revert to the command of 2 Canadian Corps on 7 October. Further changes included 7th British Armoured Division and 51 (H) Division coming under the command of Lieutenant General Crocker. His sector had been extended by 25 miles and now took in 12 British Corps in the east.[14] The right boundary for the First Canadian Army now ran east of the road between Eindhoven, Veghel and Uden then north east towards the Maas River. These new changes meant that the entire Allied front for the Scheldt operations was 50 miles long.[15] The road between Oostmalle, St Leonard and Brecht was the boundary between 1st British Corps and 2 Canadian Corps giving Wuestwezel and Achterbroek to the Canadians, while Esschen and Dinteloord went to the British.

To achieve its objectives, 2 Canadian Infantry Division had a two-pronged plan. The first was to drive northwards in order to strengthen the extended Allied flank. The second was for 5 Canadian Infantry Brigade to mount an attack on the town of Korteven by passing through 4 Canadian Infantry Brigade, then deployed in the Ossendrecht and Santvliet area, to carry out the assault while elements of 6 Canadian Infantry Brigade were used for shoring up the right flank. In each case, 4 Canadian Infantry Brigade seized and secured the start lines for the attack. The first start line was through the woods between Calfven and the Groote Mer, while the second hugged the tree line that bordered the Witte Hoevenscheheide.[16] However, preparations for enabling the battle group to move forward were not ready on time and an entire day was lost.[17] On 7 October, despite the lack of preparations, 5 Canadian Infantry Brigade mounted the assault northwards on their own.

This northern assault was made with two battalions of 5 Canadian Infantry Brigade. On the left were the Calgary Highlanders while Le Regiment de Maisonneuve (R de Mais) took up the right positions. The Germans were not ready to let the Canadians move forward without a fight and while the Highlanders managed to get through to Hoogerheide, the R de Mais were stopped 1,500yd north east of their own start line. Their objective had been Hujbergen but the vicious fighting left them 1,000yd south east of the Highlanders.[18]

With the Highlanders occupying Hoogerheide they halted their advance and waited for the Royal Highland Regiment of Canada (RHC) to move through their positions and continue the assault on Korteven. By remaining in Hoogerheide the Highlanders were now approximately a mile away from the main prize, Woensdrecht.[19]

At 1030hrs the next morning, the RHC rolled out of Hoogerheide to attack enemy positions at Korteven. By now the Germans were reinforcing the line bringing up new units to meet the Allied advance. Bitter fighting broke out all along the line and the Canadians fought hard for every step forward. However, the RHC bore the brunt of the new German reinforcements and were thrown back to their start line by heavy mortar, machine-gun and artillery fire. The German 88mm anti-tank gun put in a sterling performance as the gun crews hammered away at Allied armour. However, the Canadian historian tells us that the Calgary Highlanders remained in Hoogerheide fully engaged in 'mopping up' enemy positions. On the right flank, the R de Mais managed to push forward and by 1730hrs they had entered the outskirts of Huijbergen.[20]

By nightfall the Allies received some startling news. Local intelligence from Dutch civilians indicated that a large enemy force of between 2,000 and 3,000 troops, with guns and tanks, was concentrating in the wooded area around Bergen Op Zoom. Upon hearing this, the Allies immediately ordered aerial reconnaissance flights to verify if this information was true or not. By 2030hrs they knew that it was.[21]

Armed with this knowledge, 5 Canadian Infantry Brigade began quickly dispersing its positions to try to foil the counter-attack they knew would be coming. The battalions were ordered onto the defensive. The situation by the time darkness fell on 8 October was that the Calgary Highlanders were on the left, RHC held the centre in Hoogerheide with R de Mais strung out along the right side of the line towards the outskirts of Huijbergen.[22] And so they waited. Later that night the German counter-attack came with a ferocity the Canadians were not expecting. Using infantry, armour and paratroops, the Germans hammered the Canadian lines around Hoogerheide.[23] The following day even more counter-attacks came, each with their own level of ferocity and viciousness. Some of the Canadian troops were forced to make local withdrawals.[24]

It was clear that further consolidation, regrouping, and above all, reinforcement would be necessary before we could hope to get much farther along the vital road to Bergen Op Zoom. Our inability to exploit fast enough once Antwerp had fallen into our hands and the absence of our armour on the Leopold Canal was to cost us dearly both in casualties and in time.[25]

To the east, on the attenuated right flank, the Canadians mounted an armoured attack by 6th Brigade.[26] This thrust combined elements of Les Fusiliers Mount Royal (Fus M.R.), a squadron of tanks from 10 Canadian Armoured Regiment, plus a squadron from 8 Canadian Reconnaissance Regiment along with supporting arms. The plan for this thrust was to capture and hold the country towards Achterbroek and Wuestwezel. Initially, the thrust failed to get going because the start line was still not secure. When another squadron of tanks arrived to shore up the initial force, the plan was for the assault to begin the next morning at first light. The armour was to drive at full speed straight through to Achterbroek, capture it then continue on up to Wuestwezel. From there they were to sweep down to the south west to Klein Gooreind in order to link up with Fus M.R. 'The object of the excursion was to create confusion amongst the enemy along the whole of the brigade's sector and give him the impression that he was surrounded by tanks.'[27]

However, on the morning of the assault, 8 October, heavy thick fog clung to the muddy ground. With such poor visibility armour was all but useless. As the morning wore on conditions worsened as the fog thickened. While the armour didn't move forward, the troops of Fus M.R. fought their way up to Punt Heuvel, which they captured at 1400hrs. It was a slow process of moving over the sodden ground trying to peer through the fog while attacking the enemy with machine-gun fire, grenades and mortars. By noon, as the fog slowly lifted, the Fusiliers were joined by tanks and the entire force began a long slow slog towards Dorp. Hour by hour the enemy resistance was growing as casualties in men and materiel on both sides began to mount. By 1830hrs the Fusiliers had managed to capture the town of Dorp after some difficult fighting. But all around them the Germans were reinforcing. Brigadier Gauvreau had been warned by the Divisional Commander that the Germans were reinforcing and threatening the battalion's flank.

As the day came to a close and dusk arrived the Canadians clung on to Dorp, doing their best to hold the slim link they had with Essex Scot, the same road they had used to attack the German positions in and around the town of Dorp.

> The divisional flank thus remained without the hoped for buttress in the large triangle between the Groote Meer, the Camp de Brasschaet and Brecht. Some assistance in guarding this long, lean flank, while 2 Canadian Infantry Division renewed its effort to put a stopper in the Beveland bottle, was provided on 9 Oct by 29 Canadian Armoured Reconnaissance Regiment, with a company of Algonquin Regiment under its command, an instalment of the larger reinforcement from 4 Canadian Armoured Division, which became an increasingly urgent necessity as the days dragged on.[28]

Elsewhere, 1 British Corps were still trying to protect the flank of 2 Canadian Infantry Division which was attacking enemy positions on and around the South Beveland isthmus as well as trying to clear any remaining enemy south of the Maas River.[29] The front was so extended that all they could do was wait for reinforcements. No advance or assault could take place without them. These included 4 Canadian Armoured Division, that once they were released from the operations at the Leopold Canal, would be able to provide close protection for 2 Canadian Infantry Division. But in the meantime, they had to sit tight, wait and beat off any counter-attacks by the Germans.

Notes

1. The detail on this can be found in Rawling, *Cinderella Operation*, p. 27.

2. Ibid., p. 33.

3. Ibid., p. 34.

4. First Canadian Army/C/G, Report by Lieutenant General Simonds, 22 November 1944, Forwarded by Lieutenant General Crerar as Despatch to Minister of National Defence, cited in 'Report No. 188'.

5. See Rawling, *Cinderella Operation*, p. 34.

6. 2nd Canadian Corps/L/F/, Docket I, Intelligence Summary No. 63, 5 October 1944, Appendix 'B', cited in 'Report No. 188', Part IV.

7. Allied Expeditionary Force/2, Canadian Infantry Division/L/F, Interrogation Report on Prisoners of War, 4 October 1944, cited in 'Report No. 188'.

8. 'Report No. 188', Part IV.

9. H.Q. 6 Canadian Infantry Brigade, 3, 4 October 1944. On 4 October, the Division being

directed to continue the advance through Merxem to Bergen Op Zoom, as well as to maintain a protective screen covering the approaches to Antwerp westwards from Brecht, 2nd Canadian Infantry Division/C/I, Docket III (d), Operations Instruction No. 2, 4 October 1944.

10. See Rawling, *Cinderella Operation*, p. 35.

11. H.Q. 4 Canadian Infantry Brigade, 4–6 October 1944, cited in 'Report No. 188'.

12. See Rawling, *Cinderella Operation*, p. 37.

13. See Canadian Military Headquarters, Historical Section, cited in 'Report No. 188', Part IV.

14. GOC C-in-C, First Canadian Army, October 1944, letter from Simonds to Crocker and Foulkes, 12 October 1944, cited in 'Report No. 188'.

15. 1st British Corps Operational Instruction No. 16, 8 October 1944, cited in The Operations of 21 Army Group 6 June 1944 – 5 May 1945, HQ British Army of the Rhine, September 1944.

16. H.Q. 2 Canadian Infantry Division, October 1944, Appendix 19, Operational Instruction No. 3, 6 October 1944, cited in 'Report No. 188'.

17. H.Q. 6 Canadian Infantry Brigade, 7 October 1944, cited in 'Report No. 188'.

18. W.D., H.Q. 5 Canadian Infantry Brigade, 7 October 44.

19. See Rawling, *Cinderella Operation*, p. 38.

20. H.Q First Canadian Army, October 1944, Main Operations Log, 8 October 1944, Serial 61.

21. Ibid., Serial 69.

22. See 'Report No. 188', Part IV.

23. First Canadian Army/L/F, Docket I, Vol. I, 1–14 October 44; Intelligence Summary No. 100, 8 October 44; H.Q. 2 Canadian Infantry Division, October 1944, Appendix 2, Intelligence Summary Nos 79, 80, cited in 'Report No. 188'.

24. H.Q. 2 Canadian Corps, October 1944, Appendix 3, Operations Log, 9 October 1944, Serials 3, 11, cited in 'Report No. 188'.

25. See 'Report No. 188', Part IV.

26. See Rawling, *Cinderella Operation*, p. 38.

27. H.Q. 6 Canadian Infantry Brigade, 7 October 1944; 2 Canadian Infantry Division/C/I, Docket III(d), 2 Canadian Infantry Division Operational Instruction No. 4, 8 October 1944, cited in 'Report No. 188'.

28. Ibid. See also 'Report No. 188', Part IV.

29. 1 Brit Corps/C/I, Docket III(d), Operations Instruction No. 16, 8 October 1944, The Operations of 21 Army Group.

Chapter 8

The Battle for the Leopold Canal

For the Allies, the main ingredient for mounting the assault across the Leopold Canal was, in addition to gaining a foothold on the further bank, to break through the defiles and deploy before the enemy realised that it was here that the Allies really intended to strike rather than further to the east or west.

While operations were under way for breaking out north from Antwerp towards Bergen Op Zoom, taking Woensdrecht and cutting off the Germans on South Beveland one other major thing had to be done. That was clearing the south bank of the Scheldt Estuary or, to put it bluntly, breaking the Breskens Pocket. The Germans called it Scheldt Fortress South.[1]

The operation to break the Pocket and clear it of German defences would be done over some of the most difficult terrain the Allies had yet encountered, for, apart from the formidable obstacles of the Leopold and Derivation Canals, the landscape was mostly made up of flat, flood waters with only a few spots of dry land. The country itself was so flat that there was literally nowhere for reconnaissance parties to hide or shelter. Only aerial photographs would give the Allies an idea of where the enemy was.

The plan was to establish a bridgehead on the opposite bank of the Leopold Canal. The canal was 90ft wide. To do this two battalions of 7 Canadian Infantry Brigade, commanded by Brigadier J.G. Spragge, were to mount an assault with the Regina Rifles on the left directed on Middelburg and 1 Canadian Scottish Regiment on the right making for Aardenburg, with the Royal Winnipeg Rifles to follow up and occupy Heille.[2] Shock and surprise were to be the order of the day. The suddenness of the assault was designed to take the Germans by surprise, while the shock element would come from a wide use of flamethrowing converted Bren gun carriers known as Wasps.

Thereafter, Allied artillery would begin pounding the German positions. Once the Allies had taken possession of the German burnt-out posts on the far bank, they would have the immediate support of 12 and 23 Canadian Field Regiments and 107 Medical Regiment Royal Artillery and all available 4.2in mortars. When the operation was fully under way the number of cannon firing across the whole of the Allied front would be 144 25-pounders, 128 medium guns and 55 heavy and super-heavy artillery guns; a total of 327 guns of all calibres.

The place chosen for the assault was the point where the Leopold and Derivation Canals diverged, with the Derivation running south east away from the Leopold. The Dutch frontier, marked by houses on the outskirts of the southern side of the village of Eede, was little more than a mile away from the canal. The only vegetation that stood above the flat landscape were the poplar trees that lined the canal and the dykes. The church spire of Eede could be clearly seen in the distance. In the words of R.W. Thompson, the only thing stopping people from seeing the North Pole 'was the curvature of the earth and poor visibility as there was nothing in the way'.[3]

On the reverse side of the steep banks on the opposite side of the canal to the Allies, the Germans were dug in. This meant that attacking these slit trenches with standard high explosives and small arms fire would be difficult because the enemy were dug in just short of the crest of the canal. It was decided that flamethrowers would be the best way to dislodge the enemy by projecting the burning fuel into their defensive positions. Trials were undertaken converting several Bren carriers to Wasps. The trials showed the range and effectiveness of the flamethrowers and provided evidence that a good proportion of the ignited fuel could be splashed into the enemy trenches if the flame was aimed at the edge of the dyke just below the crown.[4]

In addition to the units mentioned above, 4 Canadian Division was to use the surprise and shock tactics by attacking German positions behind the canal, while also simultaneously mounting two diversion raids, one south of Watervliet and the other east of Moerkerke, as the main assault went it. Where they could, the Allies tried regularly to probe the German defences. They discovered that through barbed wire fortifications, mines, water, concrete strongpoints and well-dug slit trenches the Germans were immune to serious conventional attack, which only helped to increase their confident, aggressive defensive behaviour. However, the Germans had been kept so busy by Allied probing thrusts that they had failed to notice the arrival of another Allied formation and only became aware of 3 Canadian Infantry Division when they were under attack by them.[5]

For the operation the Allies assembled twenty-seven Wasp tracked vehicles, eleven of which were positioned behind the near bank at intervals of 60yd. Their job was to support 1 Canadian Scottish Regiment while other machines were able to support the left flank where the Regina Rifles were ready to go. These vehicles had been brought up to their positions under the cover of darkness on the night of 5 October.[6]

The orders for the assault across the Leopold Canal were clear. '7 Canadian Infantry Brigade will destroy or capture enemy in the area of Moershoofd –

Arednburg – Oostburg – Schoondijke. Assault and seize a crossing of Leopold Canal. Enlarge bridgehead. Mop up to west.'[7]

D-Day for the assault was 6 October 1944. It was a bitterly cold morning without rain. That would come soon enough. All the troops received an issue of rum and a promise that this issue would become a daily stipend. The men would soon find that in the days to come it would be badly needed, yet it would have no more effect on them than water did.[8]

Throughout the night the Germans had been subjected to a heavy artillery bombardment, yet they remained firmly dug into their positions. Finally, at 0525hrs, the Wasps let loose their terrible inferno, their flames shooting across the water, licking the tops of the canal and running down the banks into the enemy positions. Under this inferno the troops of the 7th Brigade scrambled up the steep slope of the canal, threw their assault boats into the water, jumped in and rowed furiously across the canal. For this, ferrymen were provided by members of the North Shore Regiment under the command of 7th Canadian Infantry Brigade. Stunned by the ferocity of the flames they were subjected to, the Germans did not return fire for more than 10 minutes giving enough time for both companies of 1 Canadian Scottish Regiment to cross the canal and 'establish Kapok bridges without opposition'.[9] One enemy strongpoint was immediately set on fire and 30yd from the canal several houses were burnt from the flames fired by the Wasps.

Both D and B Companies reached their positions on the right near Oosthoek, while the Wasps poured their liquid fire on the enemy, burning them out of their defences or reducing them to a state of terror. However, the Germans soon began to recover from the Allied onslaught and began returning heavy, accurate artillery, mortar and machine-gun fire. But it was not enough and soon A and C Companies were across the canal with the entire battalion successfully across in under an hour.[10]

The Canadians found themselves with two separate and very tenuous holds on the enemy side of the Leopold Canal. In some areas the bridgeheads were no deeper than the canal bank and the Canadians faced a ferocious onslaught of machine-gun and rifle fire from the Germans. Shells hammered into the bank of the canal just above their heads, while mortar bombs landed on their side of the banks, or in the water. The two separate bridgeheads were at Moershoofd and Oosthoek. A maze of dykes around the towns and villages, designed to keep the water out, held the well-entrenched defenders. Thompson tells us that a bitter battle broke out between the villages of Eede and Moershoofd as the Allies tried to link up both bridgeheads to form a more secure one. Some difficulty was experienced throughout the battle in finding vantage points from which artillery officers could observe and direct the fire of the guns. Overhead, Typhoon fighter-bombers rolled into their dives and peppered the enemy positions with rocket and cannon fire. In some areas this helped, such as in the sector between St Kruis and Aardenburg but the German resistance remained strong, almost untouchable. The intense fire from the Germans held the Canadians to the northern bank of the Leopold Canal, unable to break out or even try to link up with the other bridgehead. They were pinned down. One company of troops of the Canadian Scottish tried desperately to break out, but the Germans quickly captured them.[11]

But on the left side of the Allied side of the canal the assault had not gone well. After the flames from the Wasps stopped firing the right-hand company of the Regina Rifles hesitated in launching their boats and in that slight delay the Germans were able to creep back to their positions where they rained down a vicious curtain of machine-gun fire on the Canadians. The left company of the Regina Rifles got across safely without encountering the same resistance as the right company had. This left company was the Army Headquarters Defence Company of the Royal Montreal Regiment.[12]

However, once the right-hand company of the Reginas had launched their boats the enemy fire was so intense that A Company was forced back to their start line unable to launch at all. However, B Company, commanded by Captain R. Schwob, managed to get across the canal but suffered severe casualties in the process. By 1300hrs only a handful of men from B Company were left standing so they were attached to another Regina company, also heavily depleted. All three of the remaining Regina Rifles companies were eventually ferried across the canal on the left flank, where troops were already holding a narrow bridgehead with steadily increasing casualties. Against this small bridgehead on the left the Germans mounted counter-attack after counter-attack, pouring mortar, machine-gun and small arms fire onto the entire position.[13] Under this inferno of shells any chance of expanding the bridgehead, let alone uniting the two bridgeheads, was out of the question. The German defenders were dug into positions on a narrow island at a point where the Leopold and Derivation Canals converged, just west of Strooiburg.

Despite the hellish conditions suffered by the Allies as they clung to their two bridgeheads, Canadian morale did not waver and the standards of leadership, especially junior leadership, remained high. An example of this is that of Rifleman S.J. Letendre of the Regina Rifles who, when his section commander was killed, took over command, reorganised the section and 'set an example of initiative and fighting spirit that made an important contribution to preserving the position'.[14]

By the time darkness fell on 6 October the Allies still held two tenuous bridgeheads on the far side of the Leopold Canal. On the right side the bridgehead had been pushed a little further from the bank when 1 Canadian

Scottish Regiment had taken Moershoofd and Vuilpan. Behind them, the engineers of 16th Field Company, under enemy fire, had managed to build a footbridge (Kapok) across the canal and later that same day managed to construct another one on the left near the Reginas.[15] However, according to the Canadian historian, the bridgehead on the left held by the Regina Rifles 'consisted only of a line of soldiers that stretched from Graaf Jan to the main road'.[16] Both battalions made repeated efforts to expand their bridgeheads but in each case they were pushed back by strong, concentrated enemy fire.

At 2330hrs that evening, Brigadier Spragge, commanding the Royal Winnipeg Rifles, ordered his four rifle companies to cross the canal in order to link up the two bridgeheads the following day, 7 October.

It was not to be. Both Allied positions on the far bank, especially where what was left of the Regina Rifles were dug in, proved to be too precarious for the link-up to take place that day.

> The Royal Winnipeg Rifles were only able to fight their way about 1000 yards westwards along the side of the canal before the enemy's unrelenting fire brought them to a halt. Not the least of their tribulations in that windswept, soggy and coverless landscape, never more than 200 yards from the bank, was the slow evacuation of their wounded across the flooded fields.[17]

Meanwhile, 1 Canadian Scottish Regiment was kept busy beating off the unrelenting German counter-attacks that threatened their positions. They suffered a further sixty casualties during these counter-attacks. Eventually, the Canadian Scots were reinforced by a dismounted squadron from 7 Canadian Reconnaissance Regiment. The Regina Rifles, clinging to the bank on the left flank, were in no better shape as, in addition to the counter-attacks, they suffered the relentless pounding from German high-powered, large-calibre artillery guns firing from coastal positions.

It would take several days of fighting before the two bridgeheads could be unified, strengthened and extended. 'The enemy showed no signs of slackening, and it was another four days before it was possible to build the required bridges near Strooiburg.'[18]

Throughout 8 October there was little the Allies could do to improve their situation. The intense fighting had taken its toll on the Royal Winnipeg Rifles (RWR) who were now reduced to three companies. They tried to get through to the depleted Regina Rifles but failed to do so.

> In many places the Allies had been unable to move much further forward than the edge of the canal bank, where there was some possibility of

digging slit trenches to an adequate depth. Elsewhere, they could only be scooped out to a shallow foot or so before water was reached and any hole in which a man might take refuge rapidly filled and had to be baled out many times a day. This meant that any coordinated action, even at platoon level, was impossible. In front, the ground as far as the villages of Graaf Jan and Eede was flooded. Routes had to be tested by patrols. Parties of the enemy were frequently encountered and violent skirmishes ensued.[19]

For the Canadians advancing and attacking the enemy was an extremely slow process. It was not a question of standing up and running across dry land to find cover in hills, behind rocks or in the ruins of bombed or shelled buildings. This was men advancing, often up to their necks in water carrying their guns and ammunition above their heads, through a mass of dykes, channels, flood water and polders. To the Canadians, it seemed as if the Germans had thought of everything and had every approach covered by heavy machine guns or mines. Indeed, Rawling tells us that the Germans had taken to 'booby-trapping their own dead'. Compassion disappeared after the Canadians suffered a few casualties in trying to rescue the enemy dead. They became hardened to any suffering of their enemy.[20]

Early on 9 October, the RWR tried again to link up the two bridgeheads and attacked the German positions between them. At 0500hrs they launched the assault that finally cleared and destroyed the German defenders enabling them to link up with the depleted Regina Rifles. The two bridgeheads were now a single consolidated item and the immediate requirement was to push north and especially west, to capture the main road to Aardenburg, 'which would have to be well within Allied lines in order to enable the sappers to construct their bridges and join the end of the highway together over the two canals'.[21]

On 9 October the rain came. Not just any rain, but a non-stop torrential downpour of cold, miserable, rain. For the Allies to expand their bridgehead the plan was for the brigade on the left flank of the bridgehead to be compressed and deepened in order to assault and capture the village of Eede and the main Aardenburg road.

In the small hours of 12 October, 1st Canadian Scottish Regiment attacked enemy positions dug in along the road and quickly cleared them out so much so that by early morning they held both sides of the road. They spent the rest of the day consolidating and securing their positions on hard ground and early the following morning began their assault towards Eede. Towards the end of the day the Canadians had reached the outskirts of the town, while behind them engineers from 8th and 9th Field Squadrons 'brought their efforts to a climax in completing the two Bailey bridges carrying the road from Maldegem to Aardenburg by 2000hrs on the same day, and with Royal Winnipeg Rifles in the outskirts of Graaf Jan, Allied prospects seemed likely to improve'.[22] And so they did.

> With the Leopold Canal now secure, and the bridges over it secure, the Allies began moving armour and men across it. On 14 October tanks from 28 Canadian Armoured Regiment, now across the canal in support of 1st Canadian Scottish, attacked enemy positions in Eede forcing the Germans to surrender. 'Nevertheless, the pressure against the Allies continued to be unyielding until the first signs of relief came on 16 October as the result of the successful penetrations into German strongholds from the east.'[23]

In the assault to establish a bridgehead across the Leopold Canal and expand out from there, Allied casualty rates had been high. The 7th Brigade alone suffered 533 casualties with 111 dead, the rest wounded and unable to fight. The Regina Rifles had incurred the highest number of casualties in terms of percentage rate, with 51 men killed and 229 wounded.

It is fitting that for the Battle of Leopold Canal the final words should go to the Canadian historian who detailed the operations for this assault:

> The German defenders paid a heavy price for their attempts to keep the Allies at bay and throw them back across the water. If freedom of movement had been denied to the Allies by the flooding, the German approaches were also limited to two routes on which the Canadian hard-pressed infantry brought down the fire of their supporting artillery. Under this barrage the enemy could only close by stealth and infiltration and bitter fighting with grenades and small arms and hand-to-hand took its toll of 64 Infantry Division. The bravery of the men of 7 Canadian Infantry Brigade had the effect of forcing the German commander to commit the reserve battalions of his three infantry regiments – a substantial contribution to the German ultimate overthrow.[24]

Notes

1. See Rawling, *Cinderella Operation*, p. 41.
2. Ibid.
3. See Thompson, *Eighty-Five Days*, p. 91.
4. See 'Report No. 188'.
5. According to the Canadian historian who wrote 'Report No. 188', Part IV, troops of this

division had maintained radio silence since they'd left Calais, thus adding to the shock and surprise tactics of the Allies.

6. Ibid.

7. See Thompson, *Eighty-Five Days*, p. 91.

8. See Rawling, *Cinderella Operation*, p. 41.

9. 'Report No. 188', Part IV.

10. See Rawling, *Cinderella Operation*, p. 42.

11. See Thompson, *Eighty-Five Days*, p. 92.

12. See Rawling, *Cinderella Operation*, p. 42, who states that the Royal Montreal Regiment had been temporarily subsumed into the Reginas in order to gain 'battle experience'.

13. 'Report No. 188', Part IV.

14. See Rawling, *Cinderella Operation*, p. 43.

15. Ibid.

16. See 'Report No. 188', Part IV.

17. Ibid.

18. Ibid.

19. Ibid.

20. See Rawling, *Cinderella Operation*, p. 44.

21. See 'Report No. 188', Part IV.

22. Ibid.

23. Ibid.

24. See 'Report No. 188', Part IV.

Chapter 9

Across the Braakman Inlet

While the attack on the German Defences at the Leopold Canal was under way and 7th Brigade was hanging onto the tenous bridgehead for dear life, the Allies planned another assault to put pressure on the Germans from a different direction. This attack would be by amphibious vehicles across the mouth of the Braakman Inlet. Once across they were to land near Hoofdplaat with the ultimate goal of seizing the harbour town of Breskens.[1]

The German defences were concentrated along the line of the Leopold Canal. The German commander, Major General Eberding, had discounted the possibility that the Allies would attack his positions from across the inlet in the north east. Yet, it was here that the Allies noticed a definite thinning out of the dense coastal fortifications. At Breskens the heavier defensive constructions came to an end, and the beach beyond showed only a few prepared positions. This lead the Allies to believe that the Germans assumed the mud flats beyond Breskens were a natural effective obstacle against any attempted assault and so had not prepared defences there. This was a mistake.

From aerial photographs and details supplied to them by a Dutch engineer, the Allies knew what the shoreline from the inlet along the southern shore of the West Scheldt was like and they realised that as long as they had suitable vehicles available the mud flats would not be impassable.[2] Major General Eberding had positioned his three infantry battalions along the length of the Leopold Canal and as such barely had enough trained men to meet another threat from another direction. Under his personal command, Eberding kept his reserve, a variety of troops from various battle groups, including marines and artillery troops turned infantry, in the centre of the Breskens Pocket. Allied patrols in the Leopold–Isabella Canal area gave Eberding the impression that another Allied attack would come across the canal on his flank. As such, he moved a company of infantry into the area to meet this suspected assault, based on the aggressive patrolling from 4 Canadian Armoured Division. 'Afterwards, as a prisoner, he confessed that he had not considered that the Allies had the equipment to mount a water-borne operation.'[3]

For the assault across the mouth of the inlet, the Allies would bypass the German defences and be able to attack them from the rear. The troops that would carry out this attack were mainly from 9 Canadian Infantry Brigade commanded by Brigadier J.M. Rockingham, supported by 5th Assault Regiment Royal Engineers, part of British 79th Armoured Division. For the assault the Canadians had driven their Buffalo tracked amphibious vehicles some long 40 miles to the docks north of Ghent. Known officially as LVTs (Landing Vehicle Tracked), the Buffaloes were American and variously armed with machine guns and/or cannon. At the front of the vehicle was a large ramp that enabled small vehicles such as Jeeps, equipment and men to be offloaded quickly. The Canadians also used another amphibious vehicle, the Terrapin, a six-wheeled British vehicle similar to the American DUKW.[4]

On 6 October training on these two amphibious vehicles began in earnest on the Ghent–Terneuzen Canal. The assault force was divided into four groups. In terms of vehicle allotments, the two forward infantry battalions had six Mk II Buffaloes for carrying troops along with around forty Mk IVs for transporting materials, small vehicles and equipment. Tactical and Main Brigade Headquarters had similar arrangements. The small vehicles carried by the MK IVs were mostly Bren gun carriers and a few Jeeps, while for those Buffaloes that carried troops only the full complement was ninety men including officers.

The four groups of the assault force were: the Assault Group made up of troops from the North Nova Scotia Highlanders, Highland Light Infantry of Canada and Tactical Brigade Headquarters; the Follow-up Group, carrying troops of the Stormont, Dundas and Glengarry Highlanders (SD&GH), one platoon of D Company, Cameron Highlanders of Ottawa (CH of O) (MG) and their 4.2in mortars, C Company CH of O (MG) and Main Brigade Headquarters; the Build-up Group, included several Jeeps and one company of 23 Canadian Field Ambulance along with carriers and anti-tank guns. The fourth group was the Residue Group. Both the equipment and the specialised assistance required were supplied by 5 Assault Regiment Royal Engineers of 1 Assault Brigade (79 Armoured Division) that would carry 9 Canadian Infantry Brigade to the beaches. More engineers from 18 Canadian Field Company, Royal Canadian Engineers, were tasked to prepare exits from the beaches and maintain them as well as marking the routes, making smoke and fixing beacons.[5]

From the docks near Ghent the distance up the canal to Terneuzen was 20 miles. Once landed, the plan was for the flotilla to create a bridgehead to include the Thomaes Polder and Biervliet and then seize the entire area lying between Ijzendijke, Schoondijke and the sea, including Breskens.[6]

The plan for the assault was that the North Nova Scotia Highlanders would land on Green Beach on the right a few miles east of Hoofdplaat, while on the left, the Highland Light Infantry of Canada (HLI of C) were to land on Amber Beach in the Paulina Polder. They would then relieve the North Nova Scotia Highlanders by taking over the bridgehead while the Highlanders were to capture Biervliet and push on to Breskens. Once the SD&G Highlanders had landed they were to attack and take the town and harbour of Hoofdplaat then push on south to create a firm base near Sasput.

The assault group was to have artillery support from 4 Canadian Armoured Division. This included a light observation aircraft, heavy anti-aircraft guns, a heavy battery of 155mm guns and searchlight to light up the beaches.[7]

The Allies knew they had to make the roads leading to the bridgeheads extremely dangerous for the German defenders to use. They devised an artillery firing plan that would begin 50 minutes before the Buffaloes and Terrapins landed and stop once this had been achieved. The Canadian historian tells us that for each regiment, 12 rounds per artillery gun were allotted for a total of 288 rounds.[8]

Once the troops had landed and established the bridgehead, the artillery barrage was to stop but remain on constant readiness. Allied planners believed that this barrage would not arouse German suspicions because they had been pounding various enemy positions in this area for some time. It should seem to be nothing new for the watching Germans.

However, from South Beveland and from Flushing, the Germans had excellent vantage points from which they could see the Allied landings and would then be able to direct artillery fire onto the beachheads. The dark of night would obscure their vision but during daylight something had to be done to ensure the Germans could not see the beaches. A smoke screen would be laid to cover the landings.

> In order to ensure the smoke did not obscure the landing craft the screen would have to be laid in the estuary itself in a north-westerly direction from outside Terneuzen harbour, a requirement complicated by the presence of sand bars, a difference of 16 feet in the tides and variations of the wind. As the Chemical Warfare Officer of 2nd Canadian Corps was already engaged with 7 Canadian Infantry Brigade, this complicated experiment in obscurity was to be carried out under the direction of Major J.T. Hugill at Headquarters First Canadian Army.[9]

By late afternoon on 7 October 1944 all was ready. At 1730hrs the flotilla of nearly 100 Buffaloes and 40 Terrapins faded into the darkness, their tail lights dimly glowing as they sailed slowly up the canal towards Terneuzen.[10] The Buffaloes were difficult to handle at such low speeds as they wallowed in the water, their engines roaring and clattering, echoing across the silent, sodden landscape. The flotilla sounded so much like approaching aircraft that some watchful German gunners in Flushing fired their flak guns spasmodically into an empty, black night sky. The troops sat helplessly in their vehicles wishing the artillery guns were firing to cover the sound.[11]

When they reached Terneuzen, to their dismay, the Allies found the locks were so badly damaged that they had to get the Buffaloes and Terrapins out of the canal, drive across land past the locks and then into the sea. Because of the mud on the canal banks, and the difficulty manoeuvring at slow speed, the Buffaloes had to be hauled out of the canal, one by one. Originally, the engineers built ramps for the vehicles but these soon became unusable so each Buffalo climbed out of the water partly under its own power and partly from the power of a bulldozer hauling it onto dry land. Using this method, the vehicles all managed to get out of the canal by 0300hrs, well past the planned midnight time of departure. Once out of the water, lined up and ready to depart across the inlet, it was then discovered that fifteen vehicles couldn't start so the operation was postponed for 24 hours.

However, this delay brought dangers to the waiting force and meant that the troops on the bridgehead across the Leopold Canal would continue to bear the brunt of the enemy's defensive fire. It also meant that now there was a danger that the Germans might discover the waiting assault force on the flat countryside around Terneuzen.

Vehicles and men were dispersed among the neighboring farms and orchards, nets were draped over the ramps, marking lights were removed and a cordon was put round to restrict the movement of civilians. The waiting men suffered some additional strain, and those of 7 Canadian Infantry Brigade had another day of dealing with a still confident and untroubled enemy. Allied safety measures proved to be effective and the Germans were unaware of the assault force until the blow fell and took them completely by surprise.[12]

The delay was not entirely bad news for the Allies as it gave them time to add to their knowledge of the coastline the assault force would be landing on. Two Dutch pilots were engaged to provide local information on the shoals and banks, the local waterways and the beaches of the coastline. Their job was to guide the assault force into the beaches in two motorboats.[13] However, the two local men were nowhere to be seen when the time came to launch the assault. Fortunately for the Allies, Lieutenant Commander R.D. Frankes, the Dutch Naval Liaison Officer to Canadian Army Headquarters, was on hand and volunteered his services. During the 24-hour delay Frankes spent the day pouring over charts, assessing the tides and making a careful reconnaissance of the coastline by peering over the dykes in various locations.[14]

The force was divided into two flotillas, each with forty-eight Buffalo and Terrapin landing craft. The flotilla carrying the North Nova Scotia Highlanders was to sail for the northerly beach marked out by a breakwater, while the one carrying the HLI of C was to make for the small harbour on the bulge of the Paulina Polder, west of the first flotilla. Lieutenant Commander Frankes provided some detail of the landings in his report:

By 0030 hours we were lying off the sea ramp in our little motorboat showing two dim red lights astern. Well on time the first LVT waddled down the ramp and splashed into the water. We led slowly out of the canal entrance as more and more took to the water and formed up astern. It was nearly an ideal night, calm and quiet with a half moon behind light cloud, but a bit of haze that restricted visibility to a mile at the most. We were quite invisible from the north shore of the Scheldt, where all was quiet.

We soon reached the main part of the river and turned west along the coast, keeping about half a mile off until we reached Nieuw Neuzenpolder. We went slowly, and as far as could be seen, all our LVTs were formed up and following. I then set course due west across the entrance to Savojaards Plaat (Braakman Inlet). Just as we cleared the land, our artillery barrage started up, plastering the far beaches and other targets. The noise effectively blanketed our sounds and was generally most heartening.

Our landfall on the far side was satisfactory and we set course up the channel between the coast and the large sand bank, at a distance of about half a mile from the shore. There was supposed to be a prepared position on the northeast corner of the island and momentarily I expected enemy fire, but we continued unmolested, with the artillery barrage still thundering away and occasionally putting down star shells, which I personally found of little use.

Our touch down was planned to be on either side of a groyne that proved to be a good landmark and we were able to identify it and then lie off flicking our lamps to guide the LVTs in. They deployed and thundered in past us, looking, and sounding, most impressive. Landing was successful and I could see, through my binoculars, the infantry disembark on dry land and form up and move off. The artillery barrage had by now, of course, ceased and there was silence except for the roar of the engines and an occasional rifle shot.[15]

An infantry landing craft (LCI) approaching the shore to take off wounded from Walcheren, Holland, November 1944. (Wikimedia Commons, IWM, Public Domain)

A German 75mm anti-tank gun emplaced in a bandstand at Nieuland, near Middelburg in Holland, November 1944. The Germans installed this gun in the bandstand at Nieuland to cover the crossroads in the town. (Wikimedia Commons, IWM, Public Domain)

'Buffalo' amphibious vehicles taking troops of the Canadian First Army across the Scheldt in Holland, September 1944. (Wikimedia Commons, IWM, Public Domain)

Allied bomb damage to railway sidings at Middelburg station in Holland, November 1944. The railway lines were blown over adjoining buildings. (Wikimedia Commons, IWM, Public Domain)

British assault troops landed on Walcheren at dawn on 1 November 1944 and most of Flushing was included in the first bridgehead. The landings were supported by fire from British warships. The object of the assault was to silence the enemy guns menacing the Scheldt passage to the port of Antwerp. This image shows British assault troops operating in Flushing. (Wikimedia Commons, IWM, Public Domain)

British landings on Walcheren. British assault troops are seen advancing through the streets of Flushing where there was sharp fighting. (Wikimedia Commons, IWM, Public Domain)

A wrecked landing craft on the beach, Walcheren. The occupation of Walcheren Island progressed quickly. With Flushing in the hands of the British, troops fanned out to the west close to the Marine Commandos coming down from the Weskapelle beachhead (where this picture was taken). (Wikimedia Commons, IWM, Public Domain)

The final phase of the battle to free the approaches to the Belgian port of Antwerp began when Royal Marine Commandos landed at dawn at Westkapelle, the western most point of Walcheren. Here LCG survivors are being picked up by an LCI(S) acting as a hospital ship. Smoke from battle ashore is in the background. (Wikimedia Commons, IWM, Public Domain)

German coastal guns and blockhouses on Walcheren Island which the British forces quickly put out of action. (Wikimedia Commons, IWM, Public Domain)

German prisoners on Walcheren in a prisoner of war cage. (Wikimedia Commons, IWM, Public Domain)

An aerial photograph taken shortly after the daylight attack on the sea wall at Westkapelle, Walcheren (the Netherlands), showing a breach in the wall at the most westerly tip of the island. The Allies decided that the dykes had to be breached before the Allied assault in order to flood the inland areas and restrict movement by the German defenders. On 3 October 1944, 252 Avro Lancasters and 7 De Havilland Mosquitoes of RAF Bomber Command attacked the sea wall and dykes at Westkapelle, Flushing and Veere. (Wikimedia Commons, IWM, Public Domain)

Oil being unloaded from the SS *Fort Cataraqui* in the port of Antwerp. This was the first ship to berth at the port following the opening of the Scheldt Estuary, 30 November 1944. (Wikimedia Commons, IWM, Public Domain)

An RAF Humber light reconnaissance car in Middelburg, Holland, November 1944. (Wikimedia Commons, IWM, Public Domain)

British assault troops landed on Walcheren at dawn on 1 November 1944 and most of Flushing was included in the first bridgehead. The landings were supported by fire from British warships. The object of the assault was to silence the enemy guns menacing the Scheldt passage to the port of Antwerp. The area of the Walcheren coast seen here was affected. (Wikimedia Commons, IWM, Public Domain)

The wounded being taken to a British medical officer following the British landings on Walcheren. (Wikimedia Commons, IWM, Public Domain)

Troops advancing along the waterfront near Flushing with shells bursting ahead. (Wikimedia Commons, IWM, Public Domain)

Royal Marine Commandos going down the ramp of a LCT in an Alligator amphibious personnel carrier, while some more men in a Weasel amphibious carrier are about to follow. The LCT has just beached on the island of Walcheren at Westkapelle during the final phase of the battle to free the Belgian port of Antwerp. Note the badly damaged buildings and sea defences in the background. (Wikimedia Commons, IWM, Public Domain)

A column of Alligator amphibious vehicles passing Terrapin amphibious vehicles near Terneuzen, 13 October 1944. (Wikimedia Commons, Canadian Archives, Public Domain)

The Buffaloes of both flotillas were quickly ashore and encountered virtually no opposition. A couple of miles east of Hoofdplaat on Green Beach, the North Nova Scotia Highlanders came ashore while at the mouth of the Braakman, at Amber Beach, the HLI of C landed also unmolested by enemy artillery fire. On landing, the North Nova Scotia Highlanders and HLI of C quickly reorganised under the cover of darkness. However, as dawn approached the Germans suddenly realised the extent of what the Allies had done. The HLI of C ran into small arms fire as they landed and on the extreme left some companies had difficulty overcoming enemy positions on the junction of the dykes between Elizabeth and Paulina polders. However, by 0730hrs, both battalions made contact and the bridgehead was formally established and by 0900hrs it had been pushed out to a depth of 1,500yd. 'By this time the Germans had woken up to the danger and began calling down fire from artillery, more especially from the big guns at Flushing, that made movement for allied vehicles a tricky and precarious situation.'[16]

With the bridgehead established and the two main battalions moving inland, the reserve battalion, the SD&G Highlanders, clattered ashore in their Buffaloes at 0930hrs. Even though the Germans were now firing their big guns from Flushing on Walcheren Island towards the Allies, a smoke screen in the inlent prevented them from accurately hitting their targets and the bridgehead continued to be reinforced without the Allies suffering casualties. The Brigade Commander, Brigadier J.M. Rockingham, ordered the SD&G Highlanders along with the machine guns and heavy mortars of the CH of O to move to Green Beach, which they did at 1030hrs.[17]

Noon that day saw the Allies moving along the coast towards Hoofdplaat while German artillery fire became more accurate and more intense as the day progressed. Major General Eberding, fully aware of the danger of the 9th Brigade's landing at the north end of the Pocket, threw his 64th Division into the battle, to ensure that every yard was fiercely defended. Enemy gun batteries at Flushing, Breskens and Cadzand regularly harassed the Allies as they moved forwards. The elusive enemy mortars also kept up a regular barrage on the attackers. Each time the Allies attacked a mortar position the crew quickly moved back several yards to a new position and then opened fire again.[18]

The following day, 10 October, Hoofdplaat was taken by the SD&G Highlanders, who had to contend with severe enemy shelling and several counter-attacks. The success of the landings, the establishment of the bridgehead and the break-out depended in many ways on the skill of the British 79 Armoured Division in handling the Buffaloes, as well as a platoon from 18 Canadian Field Company which ensured the traffic of Buffaloes moving to and from the bridgehead and across the inlet kept going.

The constructions and maintenance of loading ramps for the amphibians and work on the roads were both heavy and hazardous as much of it had to be carried out under continuous shellfire. The tide gave much trouble for the inflow of water set the timber afloat and caused the ramps to distintegrate. Considerable ingenuity was needed to keep the exits open.[19]

The Divisional Commander, Major General Spry, realised that with 7th Canadian Infantry Brigade stuck on the far bank of the Leopold Canal unable to expand its bridgehead and move out the best place to send in reinforcements to alleviate the situation was across the Braakman Inlet to the bridgehead held by 9th Canadian Infantry Brigade. Spry now decided to move his reserve brigade, the 8th Canadian Infantry Brigade, to that bridgehead where the going was much better.[20] On the morning of 11 October, the North Shore (New Brunswick) Regiment, the 8th's leading battalion in this case, was ashore and the following day the entire brigade was safely ensconced in the bridgehead and relieved the 9th Brigade on the left. The Allies had effectively turned the axis at right angles with the main thrust of the assault on the Breskens Pocket coming from the east, rather than the south.

That same morning troops from 7th Canadian Reconnaissance Regiment landed at the bridgehead while HLI of C attacked Biervliet, which they captured by dusk. Throughout the night heavy enemy counter-attacks took place but these failed to dislodge the Canadians from the town. At the same time, the Nova Scotia Highlanders had moved across the polder and in the evening linked up with the HLI of C in Biervliet. As the first battalions from the 8th Canadian Infantry Brigade arrived, the North Shore Regiment (New Brunswick) took up positions between the Nova Scotia Highlanders and the HLI of C on this left flank. The following day, 12 October, the entire brigade was ashore and had taken over the responsibility for the left sector.[21]

On 13 October the North Shore Regiment arrived in Biervliet and made contact with elements of the Queen's Own Regiment of Canada, which had relieved HLI of C and now held the town. In the rear, the Regiment de Chaud took up positions behind the two forward battalions. Once again, the Allies decided to change their tactics with 9th Canadian Infantry Brigade set to push towards Schoondjike in the west, while 8th Canadian Infantry Brigade would join up with 4th Canadian Armoured Division in the south probing the enemy defences in the Isabella Polder. From there the 9th was to continue its advance west through the towns of Ijzendijke and Oostburg.[22]

Meanwhile, on 12 October, the bridgehead was still being expanded by the 9th Canadian Infantry Brigade and the SD&G Highlanders, holding Hoofdplaat, now moved south attacking German positions, killing and capturing several of the enemy.[23] That same day, the North Nova Scotia Highlanders who had been advancing west ran into heavy fighting on the Driewegen Road, which later caused Brigadier Rockingham to state that this was the most intense and bitterest fighting that his troops had been involved in. The infantry had little protection against the constant German artillery fire. Yet, while the Germans were putting up a ruthless, bitter resistance they were now under attack from three brigades from 3 Canadian Infantry Division coming at them from different directions.

> He was now beset by all three brigades of 3 Canadian Infantry Division and the growing encroachments on his eastern flank during 13 October, and his continuously heavy losses both there and in the centre were beginning to erode his self-confidence and sap his powers. It was still too early to claim that the defending Germans were hard pressed but that the strain was beginning to tell there could be no doubt.[24]

On 14 October the 10th Canadian Infantry Brigade finally managed get across the Leopold Canal. Up until this point the German defences had been repulsing Canadian attempts for the 10th to advance towards the Isabella Polder to the head of the inlet. Along that part of the front, Allied patrols had probed and attacked key points in the German-held territory but had been pushed back by strong resistance from old fortifications on the Dutch/Belgian border. However, the Argyl & Southern Highlanders of Canada had been steadily advancing and on 14 October their patrols crossed the canal near the main road leading to Watervliet where they discovered the Germans had withdrawn. They immediately moved into the town and occupied it. Meanwhile, the Algonquin Regiment advanced slowly from the Isabella Polder through a maze of traps, mines and concrete strongpoints, waiting for the inevitable machine-gun fire from the enemy with each step they took. But none came. The Germans were nowhere to be seen. That evening, the Algonquins linked up with the Queen's Own Rifles of Canada who had moved southwards and captured the Angelina Polder.[25]

These actions now put pressure on the German 64th Division's eastern flank. A slice of the Pocket had effectively been cut off and now the Allies had an overland supply route that ran through the Isabella Polder from the bridgehead at the Leopold Canal. At this point, the ferry service of Buffaloes and Terrapins leaving Terneuzen and crossing the Braakman Inlet could now be discontinued.[26]

On 15 October, advancing out some 2,000yd from Hoofdplaat, the SD&G Highlanders attacked and captured Hoogeweg and Roodenhoek, while the North Nova Scotia Highlanders arrived on their left flank. In 8th Brigade's sector in the south, the Queen's Own Regiment of Canada captured Ijzendijke on 16 October.[27]

The Canadian historian recorded an interview with Major General Eberding who stated that when 7th Canadian Infantry Brigade advanced towards Erskens, while 8th Canadian Infantry Brigade cleared the area south around Isabella Polder, it was his most alarming moment of the battle for the Breskens Pocket.

> It was this stage that he was forced to commit most of his reserve divisions against 7 Canadian Infantry Brigade in the Leopold bridgehead and against 9 Canadian Infantry Brigade in order to keep it at arm's length from Breskens. The strength he could deploy in front of 8 Canadian Infantry Brigade was not great and he feared that if the Allies were to strike due west from the northern limit of the flooded area, they would penetrate right to the heart of his system with little cost to themselves.[28]

The Allies did not strike due west. The Canadian historian states that it was Major General Spry's intention instead to capture Breskens and its port facilities in order to deny the Germans their supply routes from Walcheren. For Eberding this was yet another headache, as he knew he could not reinforce Breskens because his troops were tied up elsewhere.

Yet, despite Eberding's manning problems his troops ensured that the Allies would have to fight hard for every inch, every foot, every yard they advanced. The Germans had fallen back to a new defensive line that ran from Breskens on their left, through Schoondijke and Oostburg to Sluis. From there, it followed the Sluis Canal down to the Leopold Canal.

On 16 October 1944, the Allies discovered that the Germans had withdrawn from Eede and so they promptly marched into the village. Almost immediately the Germans counter-attacked, pouring mortar and machine-gun fire into the village. Pinned down, the Allies brought up a troop of anti-aircraft guns that began firing on the German positions killing several enemy soldiers, destroying their equipment and neutralising their positions. This allowed the Allies to penetrate and attack the enemy defences over the flooded country to the north as far as St Kruis. The road they used was, in some places, flooded up to a level of almost 3ft and the men slipped and sloshed through the dirty, muddy, foul water. In the east the Allies captured Kantijne and in the west they took Demdoorn, while the Regina Rifles advancing on the left flank attacked and occupied Middelburgsche and Doopers Dijks.[29]

After twelve long days of fierce and ruthless fighting 7th Canadian Infantry Brigade was finally relieved on 18 October. The 157th Infantry Brigade marched in to take over the 7th's positions and command officially passed over to it at 2230hrs. For the 157th its task was to expand the Leopold bridgehead and patrol the Lembeck to Watervliet crossing as far as Moekereke.

The top priority for the Allies at this stage of the battle was to unite the Leopold bridgehead with the battalions pushing the Germans from the east. As the German defensive line shrank against the advancing Allies the possibility of this unification came ever closer. Indeed, the 8th was continuing its advance from Ijzendijke heading for Oostburg on the German's left flank while the 9th had taken Nommer Een on the coast and was ready to continue its advance.[30] As the Allies continued their assault so the Germans withdrew, particularly to the north west.

The expectation for the unification of the bridghehead at the Leopold Canal with those advancing brigades was that it would be 7th Canadian Reconnaissance Regiment that would make first contact. The joining up took place on 19 October at both St Kruis and at Moershoofd.

With the bridgehead now unified, 157th Infantry Brigade was able to advance and they quickly captured Aaardenburg and Middlebourg without any resistance. The Germans had simply melted away from their defensive positions in these villages. They had withdrawn into the rings of concentric dykes around Zuidzande and Cadzand – much more favourable ground for defence.

> This hard core of the German defences left the Allies with some ugly work to do, for the line through Breskens, Schoondijke, Oostburg and Sluis, then from Sluis to the Leopold Canal was a strong one, studded with fortified towns and thick-set with those barriers of earth and water normal to this part of the continent.[31]

The towns along the German defensive line had not been left untouched. Regular attacks by rocket-firing Typhoons plastered the German positions and gun batteries with 60lb rockets and 20mm cannon fire in and around the towns causing mayhem and devastation. Spitfire fighter-bombers regularly dive-bombed the same positions keeping the pressure on the defenders. These attacks by the RAF were set to increase in ferocity as the Allies, day by day, grew closer to breaking the Breskens Pocket and clearing it of the enemy. Up to this point the Germans had lost more than 3,000 troops as prisoners of war. Their casualty rates were even higher.[32]

The next big town for the Allies to capture and hold was Breskens. This was the key. The Allies wanted to capture the town and the harbour, which would deny the Germans the ability to bring in supplies and reinforcements from Walcheren Island. On 21 October the Allies attacked German defences in and around Breskens. The assault was mounted by the SD&G Highlanders who drove through enemy defences, including a 30ft-wide anti-tank ditch that contained more than 12ft of water. The German guns at Flushing laid down a heavy barrage of artillery fire, but this was nothing compared to the strikes the enemy received from the air. Heavy bombers pounded the guns at Flushing, while medium bombers hammered the enemy gun batteries and emplacements at Cadzand. Lying north west of Breskens was an old strongly built fortification called Fort Frederick Hendrik which was strafed heavily by fighter-bombers supporting the attack on Breskens.

That day, more than 232 sorties were flown by fighter-bombers and rocket-firing Typhoons. Instead of defending the port of Breskens, the Germans had decided to concentrate on the eastern approaches to the town. However, with the air support on that day, the Allied infantry had little trouble clearing it. 'In fact, the enemy had neglected even to blow his prepared demolitions, a failure accounted for on the claim that our artillery had prevented the German sappers from fulfilling their tasks.'[33] Occupation of the town by the SD&G Highlanders was completed by next morning. Forward patrols and reconnaissance parties from the Highlanders began probing the defences at the fort. With Breskens in Allied hands, the Germans were now cut off from all hope of escape or reinforcement. It was only a matter of days, depending on their stamina and how much ammunition they had left, before they would have to capitulate. Yet they fought on.[34]

The Allies now needed to break the next link in the German defensive chain, the town of Schoondijke and this action was handed to 7th Canadian Infantry Brigade to complete. Since taking Biervliet the 7th had reorganised and enjoyed a few days' rest. The attack on Schoondijke took place in the afternoon of 22 October and by next morning it was securely in Allied hands. The concrete gun emplacements the Germans had built here all faced out to sea making them useless against an attack from the land.[35]

The next target for the Allies was the German positions at Fort Frederick Hendrik and 23 October was set for the assault on the fort. That day two companies of the North Nova Scotia Highlanders attacked the German positions and managed to penetrate the outer defensive perimeter. They were thrown back by heavy mortar, machine-gun and anti-tank-gun fire and as a result they had to be withdrawn. The Allies then began planning an attack using air support from medium bombers and this was set for 25 October. Yet early that day the Allies heard through the Dutch that the German defenders in the fort wanted to surrender. The assault was stopped and the troops of the North Nova Scotia Highlanders entered the fort, rounded up the German garrison and marched them all out as prisoners of war. With the fort now in Allied hands and the Highlanders having consolidated their positions there, they then pushed the line forward another mile with their patrols.[36] 'The capture of the fort marked the disengagement of 9 Canadian Infantry Brigade, and its withdrawal into Divisional reserve, well to the rear around Biervliet.'[37]

Astonishingly, Allied intelligence reports stated that news of the 9th's withdrawal was announced on the BBC. The Germans, hearing the report were baffled and Major General Eberding, commanding the German 64th Infantry Division, began to worry about the whereabouts of the 9th. Interviewed as a prisoner of war after the surrender, Eberding stated that he had set his entire front on alert because he was unsure as to where the 9th would be committed next.[38]

Hearing this unexpected piece of news, General Eberding then changed his tactics and reinforced Oostburg because he felt that was the point where the Allies would most likely commit the 9th.

The German plans were thrown awry when 7th Canadian Infantry Brigade struck out of Breskens with such speed and ferocity it took the defenders completely by surprise.[39] On 24 October, both the Germans and Allies agreed that Groede would be an open town as it was full of civilians and wounded from both sides. With Fort Frederick Hendrik now in Allied hands, the Canadians were moving fast along the coast, attacking pockets of resistance and capturing and killing as many Germans as they could. Their main goal was to take Cadzand, where intelligence reports indicated the enemy's Divisional Headquarters were located. 'We attempted an outflanking movement by pushing past the place as far as the entrance to the Uitwaterings Canal. 1st Canadian Scottish Regiment came close to accomplishing this feat, until the enemy, taking alarm, threw in a strong counter-attack which overran our leading company.'[40]

But by 29 October, the Canadians discovered that the Germans had abandoned Cadzand.[41] The Allies quickly moved in and liberated the town. In the south 8th Canadian Infantry Brigade, which had come from the sector between Sluis and the Leopold Canal, advanced rapidly on Oostburg. The most logical approach to the town was from the north east and the Germans had heavily fortified this area. Hunkered down in their concrete gun emplacements, behind barbed wire and anti-tank ditches, the Germans waited, their machine-gun crews ready, their anti-tank guns and mortar crews prepared. But the Allies did not come the way the Germans expected, instead they mounted a flanking manoeuvre and attacked the town from the south, taking the Germans by surprise. Oostburg fell to the Allies on the evening of 25–6 October. The fighting here was intense but the Germans soon capitulated, knowing their defences were untenable due to their complete isolation.

On 28 October, the Allies noticed a sudden slowdown in the German resistance which they believed signified a general withdrawal. Indeed, the following day the Regiment de Chaud easily captured Zuidsande as they advanced on it from the south east.

> The amputation of these places and the incision made by 7 Canadian Infantry Brigade along the coast left the enemy's system with little more to sustain it. His plans disrupted and his vitality diminished, he was retiring for a last stand beyond Retrenchment and the Uitwaterings or Lesser Derivation Canal. General Spry's intention was to follow him across, to break through with 9 Canadian Infantry Brigade and finish him off.[42]

However, in the dunes north west of Cadzand the Germans were still manning their coastal guns by 30 October. These gun emplacements were fortified with concrete, bunkers, trenches, tunnels and pillboxes that, one by one, had to be cleared of the enemy. According to the Canadian historian, this job occupied the 7th Canadian Infantry Division for several days.

> The emplacements and bunkers had first to be isolated, and then their occupants slowly extricated a process for which crocodiles would have been most useful had we been able to get them over the loose, sandy soil. As it was, this tedious bit of ferreting prevented 7 Canadian Infantry Brigade from wholly joining in the pursuit and destruction of the enemy's main body.[43]

For the 8th it was a different story. They were driving hard against limited, if not, negligible resistance. The town of Retrenchment was reached and captured by the Queen's Own Rifles of Canada on 30 October. The Rifles pushed through the town and advanced towards the line of the canal of the same name, while to the south the Regiment de Chaud reached the bank of the canal north east of Sluis.

The Allies were advancing now on almost all fronts, pushing the Germans into a corner. For example, the 9th followed up the advance to the canal when they broke out of their positions between Cadzand and Zuidsande. Passing through the positions of the Queen's Own Rifles of Canada on the night of 30 October, the SD&G Highlanders and HLI of C crossed the canal at Retrenchment. Working as fast as they could, while enemy shellfire fell around them, the Engineers finished constructing a bridge on 31 October. Almost as soon as it was completed the Allies began roaring across it. Regiment de Chaud moved across quickly, as did the 9th which roared on for Knocke where the Germans, and their Divisional Headquarters, were making a last stand.

On 1 November the North Nova Scotia Highlanders advanced on a pillbox on the Het Zoute golf course where they found Major General Eberding and quickly took him prisoner. While this was taking place and the 9th was encircling Knocke, the 8th Canadian Infantry Brigade guarding the flank enabled 7 Canadian Reconnaissance Regiment to take over from the 52nd Reconnaissance Regiment the line from the Leopold Canal to Zeebrugge. Acting as infantry under the command of the 8th, the 3rd Canadian Anti-Tank Regiment moved up to fill the gap in the Allied line near Sluis.

The capture of Eberding was the end of the German resistance bar those Germans who had either not heard of his capture or were fanatical enough to hold out until death.

In the south the 8th Canadian Infantry Brigade conducted operations to clear large numbers of enemy troops from the canal area. On 1 November the North Shore Regiment, attacking from the north east, captured Sluis. 'Opposition proved light, and the battalion pushed on westward towards the Belgian border to take St Anna Ter Muiden, the last Dutch village, without much difficulty. The line of the Sluis Canal was cleared by 3 Canadian Anti-Tank Regiment, which then went on to capture OosTankerke.'[44]

Still resistance from fanatical Germans continued in the coastal strongpoints near Cadzand until they were either killed or captured by the 7th Canadian Infantry Brigade on 2 November. The Belgian coastal resorts of Knocke and Hoyst were liberated the same day after some heavy fighting by 9th Canadian Infantry Brigade. In the south, the Queen's Own Rifles of Canada captured the Belgian town of Westcappelle. That same day, the 8th Canadian Infantry Brigade Headquarters was able to report that the fighting was finally over. The Breskens Pocket had been broken and no longer existed. That evening, the ceasefire order was issued.

Thus at 0950 hours on 3 Nov Operation 'SWITCHBACK' was declared complete and Belgium, the first occupied country to be free of the Nazi oppressor, prepared, through its fine city of Ghent, to offer the tribute of a warm, civic hospitality to the tired troops of 3 Canadian Infantry Division who, after a period of almost unbroken fighting since June, were now withdrawn for a week's rest.[45]

Notes

1. See Rawling, *Cinderella Operation*, p. 45.
2. 9 Canadian Infantry Brigade/C/D, Docket 1, fol. 1, Account of Landings, see 'Operations of 21 Army Group'.

3. Interview with Major General Eberding, cited in 'Report No. 188', Part IV.

4. See Rawling, *Cinderella Operation*, p. 47.

5. Battle Narrative, Historical Officer, H.Q. 3 Canadian Infantry Division, cited in 'Report No. 188'.

6. H.Q. 9 Canadian Infantry Brigade, October 1944, Appendix 6, No. 3, 6 October 1944, as cited in Report No. 188. For Order of Battle see Appendix A.

7. 'Report No. 188', H.Q. 4 Canadian Armoured Division, October 1944, Appendix 1, Operation Order No. 1, Switchback, 7 October 1944.

8. 'Report No. 188', Part IV. Out of this allotment the medium guns would fire eight rounds per gun and the heavier artillery guns one round every 2 minutes with the anti-aircraft guns firing two rounds a minute.

9. First Canadian Army Report on the Smoke Screening for Operation Switchback, cited in 'Report No. 188', Part IV.

10. See Rawling, *Cinderella Operation*, p. 47.

11. See 'Report No. 188', 9 Canadian Infantry Brigade, Headquarters, October 1944, Battle Narrative, Historical Officer, H.Q. 3 Canadian Infantry Division.

12. See 'Report No. 188', Battle Narrative, Historical Officer, H.Q. 3 Canadian Infantry Division; Interview with Major General Eberding, cited in 'Report No. 188', Part IV.

13. The Canadian historian states that these motor launches were the type used by the Royal Canadian Army Service Corps (RCASC) for bridging.

14. 'Report No. 188', Narrative of the Amphibious Operation.

15. Ibid.

16. Battle Narrative, Historical Officer, Headquarters 3 Canadian Infantry Division, cited in 'Report No. 188', Part IV.

17. 'Report No. 188', 9 Canadian Infantry Brigade, October 1944.

18. See Rawling, *Cinderella Operation*, p. 49.

19. Battle Narrative, Historical Officer, Headquarters 3 Canadian Infantry Division, 'Report No. 188', Part IV.

20. See Rawling, *Cinderella Operation*, p. 49.

21. 'Report No. 188', Battlefield Narrative, Historical Officer, H.Q. 3 Cdn Inf Div.

22. Headquarters 8 Canadian Infantry Brigade, 14 October 1944; Headquarters 3rd Canadian Infantry Division, October 1944, Appendix 12, Operational Instruction No. 2, cited in 'Report No. 188', Part IV.

23. See Appendix 12, Report No. 188.

24. See 'Report No. 188', Part IV.

25. See Rawling, *Cinderella Operation*, p. 50.

26. Ibid.

27. 'Report No. 188', Queen's Own Regiment of Canada, 17 October 1944.

28. See 'Report No. 188', Part IV.

29. See 'Report No. 188', Headquarters 7 Canadian Infantry Brigade, 17, 18 October 1944.

30. Interview with Major General Eberding, cited in 'Report No. 188', Part IV.

31. See 'Report No. 188', Part IV.

32. 'Report No. 188', Battle Narrative, Historical Officer, Headquarters 3 Canadian Infantry Division.

33. 'Report No. 188', Interview with Major General Eberding.

34. 'Report No. 188', Battle Narrative, Historical Officer, H.Q. 3 Canadian Infantry Division.

35. Ibid.

36. 'Report No. 188', H.Q. 9 Canadian Infantry Brigade, 23–5 October 1944.

37. Ibid., 25 October 1944.

38. 'Report No. 188', Interview with Major General Eberding.

39. Ibid.

40. 'Report No. 188', Part IV.

41. 'Report No. 188', Battle Narrative, Historical Officer, H.Q. 3 Canadian Infantry Division.

42. Ibid.

43. Ibid.

44. Headquarters 8th Canadian Infantry Brigade, 31 October 1944, cited in 'Report No. 188', Part IV.

45. 'Report No. 188', Battle Narrative, Historical Officer, H.Q. 3 Canadian Infantry Division.

Chapter 10

The Battle for Woensdrecht

While the battle for the Leopold Canal and the operations against the Breskens Pocket raged, the Allies were pushing further and further north from Antwerp towards the isthmus of South Beveland.

For the Allies, 9 October was an important day. According to Thompson, it was the day that marked the true start of the opening battles for clearing the Scheldt Estuary and opening up approaches to the port of Antwerp.[1] With Lieutenant General G.G. Simonds' command of the Canadian First Army having bedded in after Lieutenant General Crerar had gone on sick leave, changes in the structure of the Allied command were now put into practice. These changes, by Simonds, would help him to realise his ideas for clearing the Scheldt. Simonds has been variously described as an ambitious and ruthless general. At the age of 41 he was the most experienced general the Canadians had and one of the most experienced of all the Allies.[2]

Some of the changes instituted by Simonds included Major General Foulkes taking over the position vacated by Simonds for temporarily commanding Canadian 2nd Corps. Foulkes' old command of 2nd Canadian Infantry Division was then eventually handed to Brigadier R.H. Keefler.

Adding to the changes and the confusion that arose from them was the Royal Navy's statement, by Commander T Force, that they believed the Canadian First Army would run out of ammunition before the end of October. This statement provoked Montgomery to issue an order to open the approaches to Antwerp without delay.[3]

Operations to open the Scheldt would enable General Dempsey to concentrate his efforts on clearing the south west of Holland up to the Maas Line. By doing this, Dempsey's 2nd Army would relieve the British 1st Corps, thus shoring up the western battlefield.[4] Other changes saw the 4th Canadian Armoured Division move out from its positions in the Leopold Canal area to take up positions between the Canadian 2nd Division and the British 49th Division. The US 104th Infantry Division was moved up to strengthen British 1st Corps. These changes meant that the Allies were strong enough to attack the Germans across south-west Holland, putting pressure on the German defences while also poised to assault the Bevelands and 'seal off the Scheldt'.[5]

These changes however, would take two weeks or more to bed in. In the meantime, the hold the Germans had on the Breskens Pocket had to be broken and the crucial town of Woensdrecht had to be cleared and held. It was the only way the Allies could break the German iron grip on South and North Beveland and, ultimately, Walcheren.

Before looking at the Canadian historian's account of the assault on Woensdrecht it is worth considering other moves that took place which also made 9 October a watershed for the Allies.

On this day, Brigadier Megill, commanding 5th Canadian Infantry Brigade decided it was time that the brigade had a go at taking the South Beveland isthmus. However, the battalion commanders believed that their resources were insufficient for mounting an attack to the north west while also mounting a defensive manoeuvre to the north east to stop the Germans from penetrating the Allied line.[6] The Brigade then withdrew back to the line around Hoogerheide while waiting for the Royal Hamilton Light Infantry (RHLI) to arrive and hold their positions. From there, the full might of 5th Canadian Infantry Brigade would assault the isthmus while 4th Canadian Infantry Brigade attacked German positions on the left flank.[7]

The Allies had a brief moment where they felt that they could seal off the Bevelands and Walcheren Island. This was a moment when the Allies, as Gerald Rawling puts it in his book, *Cinderella Operation*, had the chance to 'cut off the neck of the chicken'. This occurred when 4th Brigade, using the Royal Regiment of Canada (RRC), managed to slip and slide through the mud and slime to arrive at a position just west of Woensdrecht. Indeed, they had reached a point where they were within 'rifle shot' of the embankment that crossed the isthmus into South Beveland at the narrowest point.[8]

The only thing stopping the Allies from securing the isthmus and entering South Beveland, was, of course, the enemy. With six battalions of paratroopers the Germans were deeply dug in. Before them lay open fields that gave them a wide arc of fire for their mortars, snipers and machine guns.

Terrible weather also played a part in halting the Allied advance. Up to this point it had been primarily damp and cold, with oozing mud underfoot. Now, from 9 October it rained for four days in a row. But not just rain, a downpour that soaked the Allied attackers who crept and crawled forward towards the enemy through the mud and the rainwater.[9]

Advancing for the Canadians often meant wading through murky, chest-deep water in some dyke or lying prone in the wet mud, rain hammering their backs as they inched forward trying to avoid trip wires, mines and booby traps. All the while enemy machine-gun shells whizzed over their heads. In that moment of time, when they slowly moved forward, their world was one of soaking, sodden misery. To them it must have seemed as if the lowering, heavy grey skies and the pouring, driving rain would never stop. This day was the beginning of a nightmare for the Allies that would last for a little more than a month.

For the Essex Scottish and the R de Mais their ordeal began at dawn on the following day. As the grey gloom of early morning light slowly grew, the rain pounding the sodden earth, they crept forward through soaked woodlands towards their objectives; the enemy positions around the Groot de Meer lake. This was not one lake but several lakes linked by woodland. Ordinarily the definition between water and land would be pronounced but on this day, water mingled and flooded the land, the earth turning to slime and oozing mud, squelching as the Canadians moved slowly forward. Conscious of concealed mines and trip wires, they paid scant attention to the regular thump-thump of artillery fire and instead concentrated on the whine of machine-gun and rifle bullets hurtling past them, ploughing into the mud and saturated trees. In addition to this was the regular sound of exploding mines, each detonation denoting a casualty. The blood of the men that fell simply mingled with the oozing, waterlogged earth until it became indistinguishable.

By now, the Canadians were some 3,000yd west of Woensdrecht. The 5th Infantry Brigade held positions on either side of the main road that led into the town. They covered the road with small arms fire and were up against an entrenched enemy using their 88mm anti-aircraft guns as effective anti-tank guns. With these guns, their machine guns, rifle fire and other anti-tanks weapons the Germans had woven a lattice of defensive fire. Tanks of the 8th Reconnaissance Regiment repeatedly attacked these positions but each time the German anti-tank fire was too much and they were pushed back. In the dykes and drains alongside the main road lay the men of the Canadian 5th Infantry Brigade, covered in mud and soaked to the skin. Mercilessly, the rain pounded their positions while the enemy was there to pick them off if they moved or stood out in any way. They knew there was no way for them to go around Woensdrecht, they were going to have to attack it head on and take it. But if the tanks couldn't do it, how could they?

Guarding the north-west corner of the isthmus leading to South Beveland, Woensdrecht stands on a shallow mound that lies on the edges of the polders. During those days of continuous downpours, with visibility down to a few yards, the Canadians would not have seen that 1,000yd beyond the town was the embankment that carried the railway line from Walcheren along the causeway right along South Beveland across the isthmus curving north to Bergen Op Zoom. Thompson tells us that at the point where the railway embankment comes out of the isthmus and curves away, immediately behind it is the Verdronken land van Zuid Beveland, or 'Drowned Land'.[10] Even though this land had been reclaimed by the Dutch, to the Canadians on 10 October, as they crawled forward in the brown, tepid, squelching earth, it must have seemed as if the water had claimed the land for its own.

As far as the German defences were concerned for Woensdrecht they were more than 1,000yd in depth 'to the final barrier of the railway embankment'. Four battalions of German paratroopers, well-armed and deeply entrenched, held these positions while two more battalions shored up the left flank, fighting a slow measured withdrawal to the main positions that kept the Allies from clearing the woods.[11]

At 1400hrs on 11 October, troops from the RHLI, stumbling and slipping through the saturated ground, fought their way forward and took up and held positions north of Nederheide at the main crossroads under intense and accurate enemy fire.[12] That same day the RRC attacked enemy positions west of Woensdrecht towards the main junction of dyke and railway.[13] But the attack completely failed and they were forced to return to their start line. Elsewhere, the South Saskatchewan Regiment tried to attack enemy positions south east of Hoogerheide but were unable to reach their objectives, stopped by a hail of enemy machine guns and mortar shells.[14]

The days of continuous downpours for the Canadians became a muddy hell. It was a hell where earth and water merged into a shapeless oozing slime, where the Germans laid down lethal, controlled, concentrated and accurate defensive fire from their positions on the embankment picking off the Canadians in the open polders. 'The enemy, buttressed against all the fire power the Canadians could bring to bear, thankful for the filthy murk of the sky that saved them from air attack, were men of the highest caliber Germany could still muster, and dedicated to death.'[15]

Yet the Canadians fought on. What drove them? They were hungry, beyond sleep, covered from head to foot in mud, soaked to the skin, their faces seemingly like those of the walking dead. From somewhere deep within them, these men gathered the will, the strength to push on. For them, what mattered was that they were part of something bigger, perhaps no more than a platoon, a section, a regiment but all moving with the same intent, the same purpose.

For six days they fought and paid for every yard they took. But by the third day, Thompson tells us that not one yard of ground had been taken. That day, 13 October, would be a turning point for the Allies.

The day before the Germans mounted several fierce and heavy counter-attacks on both the right and left of the Allied positions. In the area around Hoogerheide, held by the South Saskatchewan Regiment, the attacks were particularly heavy.[16] However, come the 13th the 5th Canadian Infantry Brigade was ready to take the fight to the enemy. The Canadian historian tells us that the attack was against the tenuous German lines of communications along the isthmus.

At first light, 0615hrs, elements of the Royal Highlanders of Canada (RHC) were thrown into the battle, their objective – to capture and hold the railway embankment west and north west of the town 'at the angle of the junction with the main dyke'.[17] The Germans reacted quickly. With anti-aircraft, mortar and machine guns they laid down such a heavy weight of fire that the Canadians were forced back to their start line. In late afternoon, the Allies tried again this time supported by tanks and flamethrowers. The fighting was ruthless and brutal, the Allied soldiers and tanks struggling over the sodden ground, fighting foot by foot, hammered by continuous rain while the Germans, deeply dug in, poured accurate fire on the attackers. In this case, some objectives were met, but the embankment remained in enemy hands. Casualties were appalling. Thompson tells us that in the ranks of the Black Watch of Canada every rifle company commander was killed. Yet, despite this, they would not withdraw but kept moving forward with a sense of purpose that defied logic and must have, to the Germans, seemed strange and frightening. For several hours the two depleted companies clung onto the ground they'd gained while exposed to a violent and continuous storm of fire.[18]

Under this storm of lead endured by the RHC and with their company commanders either dead or wounded, the regiment was ordered to withdraw at 0100hrs on 14 October. Reluctantly, the commanding officer of RHC, Lieutenant Colonel R.B. Ritchie, agreed and soon the withdrawal began.

> One company had been virtually wiped out and losses generally left the exhausted battalion completely unfit to take any further part in the fighting until it had been rested and reinforced. In this grim episode among the polders, such costly failure was charged not only to the nature of the ground, the eligibility of the objective itself as a target for the enemy's artillery, and the fighting quality of the defenders, but also to the lack of experience and even of elementary training among the more recent arrivals in the battalion itself.[19]

Yet, despite these setbacks, the Germans were being relentlessly pounded by Allied artillery fire. So much so that cracks were beginning to form in their defences.

On 16 October Allied fortunes changed for the better. Two days earlier, after the failure to reach the embankment, the Allies began restructuring. The 5th Infantry Brigade took over command of the left sector then held by the RRC. Command of the right sector went to 4 Canadian Infantry Brigade who took over from South Saskatchewan Regiment. The Calgary Highlanders took over from the RRC while Essex Scot relieved the RHLI, which was pulled back for an assault on Woensdrecht.[20]

In the early hours of 16 October the assault on the town took place. Troops from the RHLI attacked German positions at 0330hrs behind a dense curtain of artillery fire. The barrage contained all the divisional artillery supported by a heavy anti-aircraft regiment and three medium regiments of artillery.[21] This time they managed to gain a foothold in the village. During this action the Canadians took sixty prisoners, some from the German 6th Parachute Regiment. At last the Canadians had something to hold onto other than the sodden earth, mud and water. The straggling village lay on a hill and, even better, was dry land. In addition, the Canadians had the buildings and roads of Woensdrecht and nothing was going to push them off this patch of ground.[22] Together with a squadron of tanks from 10 Canadian Armoured Regiment the RHLI managed to consolidate their position by 0700hrs. During the assault, the Canadians had bypassed pockets of resistance and these continued to give them trouble until they were cleared.

The first of the German counter-attacks took place at 1000hrs when they threw in infantry supported by self-propelled guns with a ferocity that can only be described as fanatical.[23] The Canadian historian states that the Germans over-ran the right company of the RHLI north east of the village but they were unable to get closer so the counter-attack failed. In order to reinforce the depleted RHLI, a company of Essex Scot moved forward, supported by more tanks. For their part the Germans continued counter-attacking, pounding the Canadians with artillery fire and mortar fire throughout the day and into the night. As the shells exploded around them, the Canadians, cowering in the buildings and rubble hung onto their position, beating off the counter-attacks as they came.

The Canadian historian who wrote the report on Allied operations for clearing the Scheldt believed that one of the main reasons for the inability of the Allies to deal more effectively with the Germans than they did was because of the lack of trained reinforcements for the infantry battalions in the line. He states:

> We did not have enough bodies on the ground completely to control the Woensdrecht Feature and it was possible for the enemy to infiltrate. The enemy appeared to suffer very heavy casualties from our artillery fire which was used unsparingly, but he continued to reinforce his positions. We were prevented from probing forward as the average company strength was forty-five and the casualties amongst our officers and NCOs and older men were very heavy. The bulk of the men in the battalion at the present had not had very much infantry training, but had been re-mustered from other branches of the services.[24]

The following morning, RHLI Commander Lieutenant Colonel W.D. Whitaker reported to Brigadier Cabeldu who wrote the following on their situation at Woensdrecht:

> Feels his battalion very weak in men and lacking in training for the type of fighting necessary in that area. The hun is battling most bitterly and seems to have no shortage of weapons. It is close, hand-to-hand fighting – the enemy is not giving up here the way he has in the past. Lt-Col Whitaker reports our fire to have been most effective having inflicted heavy casualties on the enemy. He further reports what seems to have been the turning point in the battle during the enemy's counter attack two days ago was a heavy medium SOS task called for and put down within less than 100 yards of our own troops. The fire caught the enemy troops right out in the open whereas our own men were deep down in their slit trenches having been warned beforehand. Our troops cheered; the slaughter was terrific.[25]

These were the conditions under which the Canadians and Germans fought for the last strip of territory linking Walcheren Island, and the German garrison dug in there, with the mainland. The Allies now held the railway line on the left and partly held the village of Woensdrecht, putting them 'within an average of only about 1500 yards from that tenuous, contested thread'.[26]

In Report Number 188, the Canadian historian continues the theme of poorly trained reinforcements arriving at the front during the operations for clearing the south bank of the Scheldt Estuary. Within the 4 rifle companies of the Canadian Black Watch there were more than 174 men with only a month's training, amounting to 45 per cent of the total strength of all 4 companies, as can be seen in the Black Watch War Diary:

> The morale of the Battalion at rest is good. However, it must be said that 'Battle Morale' is definitely not good due to the fact that inadequately trained men are, of necessity, being sent into action ignorant of any idea of their own strength, and after their first mortaring, overwhelmingly convinced of the enemy's. This feeling is no doubt increased by their ignorance of fieldcraft in its most elementary form.[27]

Despite their lack of well-trained reinforcements, the Allies continued to put pressure on the German defenders. The Canadian 4th Armoured Division began moving on 17 October along the western flank of the British 49th towards Bergen Op Zoom. By the 22nd the tanks were across the Dutch frontier at Esschen and drove forward to Spillebeek, some 8 miles north east of Woensdrecht, completely outflanking the enemy positions.

By 24 October the Allies had finally opened the road from Antwerp to Bergen Op Zoom which completely cut the German escape route, forcing the enemy to move 'through the neck, and beyond the neck, on the canal, the dykes and in scores of defensive positions as good as the one they had yielded'.[28]

The Canadian 2nd Division moved onto the edge of the neck of the South Beveland isthmus, facing east, ready for what would be their final and heaviest battle for clearing the Scheldt.

Notes

1 See Thompson, *Eighty-Five Days*, p. 96.

2. Ibid.

3. Ibid.

4. Ibid., p. 97.

5. Ibid.

6. 'Report No. 188', H.Q. 5th Canadian Infantry Brigade, 9 October 1944.

7. 'Report No. 188', First Canadian Arm/C/H, Docket V, October 1944, Liaison Officer's Report, 1215hrs, 10 October 1944.

8. See Rawling, *Cinderella Operation*, p. 39.

9. Ibid.

10. See Thompson, *Eighty-Five Days*, p. 100.

11. Ibid.

12. 'Report No. 188', H.Q. Royal Hamilton Light Infantry, 11 October 1944.

13. 2 Cdn Corps Ops Log, 11 October 1944, Serial 31.

14. 'Report No. 188', H.Q. South Saskatchewan Regiment, 11 October 1944.

15. See Thompson, *Eighty-Five Days*, p. 101.

16. 'Report No. 188', 2 Canadian Corps Operations Log, 12 October 1944, Serial 1.

17. Ibid.

18. 'Report No. 188', H.Q. 5th Canadian Infantry Brigade, 13 October 1944.

19. 'Report No. 188', 5th Canadian Infantry Brigade/C/D, Docket IV, fol. 2, the Action at Woensdrecht 8–14 Oct 44, Account by Lieutenant W.J. Shea, IO, RHC, 15 October 1944.

20. Report No. 188', H.Q. 4 Canadian Infantry Brigade, 14–16 October 1944.

21. See Rawling, *Cinderella Operation*, p. 40.

22. Ibid.

23. Thompson, *Eighty-Five Days*, p. 101.

24. Ibid.

25. 'Report No. 188', H.Q. 4th Canadian Infantry Brigade, 18 October 1944.

26. 'Report No. 188', Part IV.

27. Ibid.

28. See Thompson, *Eighty-Five Days*, p. 102.

Chapter 11

The Assault on South Beveland

In the last days of October 1944 German resistance in the Breskens Pocket on the south shore of the Scheldt was beginning to crumble. The Allies, fighting fiercely for every yard, had pushed the Germans back into a shrinking defensive circle within the Pocket. The village of Woensdrecht, the key jumping off point for advancing into the isthmus, was in Allied hands. However, the German defences on the isthmus and the peninsula of South Beveland still remained, as did the fortress of Walcheren Island. Despite the fact that the southern shore of the Scheldt was virtually cleared of German defenders by the end of October, for the Allies to use the port facilities at Antwerp the northern shore of the Scheldt also needed to be cleared. It now remained for the Allies to advance into the isthmus, cross the Beveland Canal, clear South Beveland, take the causeway linking the peninsula with Walcheren Island and then clear Walcheren itself. The operations were far from over.

On either side of the isthmus that leads into the peninsula of South Beveland is the Scheldt Estuary. The East Scheldt borders the northern shore of South Beveland and the isthmus. At the end of this estuary is the large port of Bergen Op Zoom. The West Scheldt borders the southern shore of South Beveland and the isthmus and it is this leg of the Scheldt Estuary that has the approaches to Antwerp. Cutting the isthmus and South Beveland in half is the Beveland Canal, a barrier that would cause the Allies much grief.

In this flat, waterlogged landscape, replete with mud and silt, the going was more than difficult, it was almost impossible. The isthmus at the narrow point is little more than a mile wide. On the shore line of the East Scheldt ran a dyke with a railway line and a cratered, heavily mined road. From this main road ran secondary roads in strange patterns in and around the polders. Then after that, there was only grey turgid water and sticky, slimy mud. In advancing the only place the Canadians could go was along the banks of the dykes or the railway embankment, either crawling slowly forward, wading or, as Thompson tells us, sometimes swimming. What drove these men is difficult to say. The acceptance of their plight had been made long before the assault on South

Beveland. To say that they suffered discomfort is to do their situation an injustice. For many men had been up to their waists in cold water for more than two weeks, with nothing on their horizons but more water, more mud and rain that sometimes turned to constant drizzle. It is difficult for us today, in the twenty-first century, to understand what it would be like to be in water for two weeks, with nothing around you in either direction but water and mud, soaked to the skin. Nor can we imagine that in addition to these terrible conditions there was the constant threat of death as well. 'And death becomes personal, a daily and nightly lottery in which each man of the forward battalions held a ticket. Every day in every platoon someone "bought it", as they said.'[1]

The Canadians and the British troops, fighting the gruelling foot by foot advance, had by this time gone past the point of no return. They moved like robots, silent, staring, ghost-like figures that came out of the grey unforgiving landscape and even unnerved the German troops facing them. Thompson tells us that they were spurred on by the need to advance and, after the bitter fighting at Woensdrecht, 'the Canadians of the 4th Canadian Infantry Brigade had become a tight-knit organisation, sharing the hardships and suffering together, stoical in the belief that they were fighting this war alone'.[2]

The operations of 4th Canadian Armoured Division pushing towards the Maas River, clearing out the area in front of the isthmus and to the north east, as well as driving the Germans out of the region between Woensdrecht and Bergen Op Zoom, gave the Allies the chance to assault westwards along the isthmus without the worry of close-range enemy artillery. The advance into South Beveland was to begin on 23 October. The isthmus attack was code-named Vitality 1, while the amphibious assault was code-named Operation Vitality 2.[3]

According to the Cabinet Office report, the 'Clearing of the Scheldt Estuary', the ground of the isthmus is described as being an 'unsuitable piece of country in which to fight a battle'.[4] Most of it is reclaimed land held in place by dykes. At the time of the attacks there was only one main road, with a series of minor roads running south along the dykes that made movement extremely difficult. East of the Beveland Canal large areas were flooded and where flooding hadn't taken place the ground was saturated with water. Reports from captured prisoners indicated that the German strength on South Beveland was considerable at around 3,000 troops, including recently arrived reinforcements.[5]

Realising that the Germans could use the Beveland Canal as a strong defensive line, General Simonds ordered an amphibious assault to be mounted from Terneuzen, across the estuary, to land on the South Beveland peninsula between Hansweert and Borsselen.[6] The launch was timed to coincide with the assault of 2nd Canadian Infantry Division's leading brigade advancing from the east along the isthmus. However, Simonds decided that if things did not go according to plan, he would have 52 (Lowland) Division in reserve for the amphibious crossing and so ordered that that division was not to be used in the mopping up process in the Breskens Pocket.[7]

The primary task of moving along the isthmus in a westerly direction and securing a bridgehead over the Beveland Canal fell to 4th Canadian Infantry Brigade. While this operation was underway, 5th Canadian Infantry Brigade would mount the amphibious assault across the Scheldt.[8] The two forces would then link up at Gravenpolder.[9]

On 23 October 6th Canadian Infantry Brigade, directed from Heistraat, east from Woensdrecht, advanced to the high ground south of Korteven while on the left, 5th Canadian Infantry Brigade pushed north to cut off the isthmus between the sea and the railway.[10] Both brigades ran into fierce, ruthless German resistance that nearly stalled the advance. On the right flank, the Allies were hit by heavy enemy machine-gun and mortar fire and had to find whatever cover they could in that waterlogged landscape. They were forced to consolidate between Hooghuis and Zandvoort. In the centre of the advance, the Fusiliers Mont Royal had taken positions just east of the main road a little south of the Doolstraat.[11] In the afternoon, the attack went in on the left which placed Allied troops on either side of the railway line running along the isthmus before they were halted by withering enemy fire, mines and booby traps. Running into intense, accurate and lethal fire from the Germans, the Calgary Highlanders dug into the embankment where they stayed for the night, sheltering from the enemy's fire.[12] While they had limited success in achieving their objectives they consolidated their positions, tightening the Allied grip on the area, enabling 4th Canadian Infantry Brigade to begin their advance in the early morning of 24 October at 0430hrs.[13]

Allied operations on 24 October were much more successful. The road to the north of the railway was cleared and the enemy, aware of the danger of being cut off by 4th Canadian Armoured Division striking in from the east, hurriedly retired to the north of Korteven, with 5th Canadian Infantry Brigade in pursuit.[14] The north shoulder was now free, 4th Canadian Infantry Brigade drove into the neck of the isthmus and 6th Canadian Infantry Brigade, released in front of Korteven, prepared to follow through into South Beveland.

The RRC led the offensive westward and two columns of mounted infantry, with supporting armour, were ordered to bypass whatever opposition they could and push on with all speed to seize whatever crossings they could over the Beveland Canal. Behind them came the RHLI to deal with the defenders the RRC had left behind.[15] This offensive began at 0430hrs on 24 October after a half-hour artillery barrage by seven Allied field and medium gun regiments. After 90 minutes of fierce, vicious resistance from the Germans, the Canadians managed to overrun their first line of defence at the narrowest part of the isthmus. The units reported that mines, booby traps and mud made the secondary road on the south side of the isthmus impassable. Brigadier Cabeldu then ordered Essex Scot to drive north along the railway embankment.

During the advance along the isthmus the Canadians avoided using the main road, and captured the most difficult German positions in night attacks, usually after lengthy marches. The soggy, marshland around the dykes was not good tank country as 10th Canadian Armoured Regiment discovered. Variations on how the tanks would be deployed had to be invented on the spot in order to get around the difficult terrain. In most cases, a single squadron of tanks would support the infantry with one squadron or troop of tanks to one infantry battalion.

However, an incident took place on 24 October that illustrated the need for further refining the way in which armour was to be used in the campaign. On that day, an infantry company supported by a squadron of tanks and armoured cars from 8 Canadian Recce Regiment advanced along the railway line. The tanks and the armoured cars rolled on in front of the infantry, steadily advancing. Suddenly, the Germans opened up on the Allied armour, pouring shells from a 75mm anti-aircraft gun onto the advancing column. As the shells hammered down and exploded, one tank received a direct hit and blew up, while two more were hit in quick succession, catching fire. As the deadly, accurate enemy fire pounded the Allies, three armoured cars were hit. Casualties were heavy and one-sided. A decision was quickly made to pull the armour back behind the infantry to keep the casualties from rocketing. 'It was decided that this type of formation was inadvisable.'[16]

From that point onwards the tanks and armoured cars remained behind the infantry and were only brought up when amour was required. Generally, the tanks were placed on the flanks of the attacking force, which resulted in fewer casualties and greater advantage for the tanks. One effective use for tanks was for them to deploy into hull-down positions in holes in the dykes that had been previously blown open by the infantry using grenades. 'Further support was given by indirect shoots, using bursts of delayed action high explosives and directed by a FOO.'[17] With these changes being quickly incorporated, the small groups of tanks were able to provide support to the infantry when it was needed during the advance along the isthmus.

With the infantry now on foot, the going along the embankment, with nothing but the flat featureless, wet and exposed landscape as far as the eye could see, was extremely difficult. There was nowhere for the Allies to dig into under the withering enemy fire. All they could do was cling to the sides of the embankment or slip into the water. However, the Germans had plenty of cover and had dug their defensive positions into the dykes and the many junctions where the dykes intersected, while the advancing Allies had very little cover and were always under enemy fire. Advancing was yard by yard, foot by foot with shells pinging and exploding all around. Any real progress was made at night.

In the early hours of 25 October Essex Scot reported that attacks on German positions at the main crossroads north east of Rilland, which itself was cleared by the RHLI, had been successful. The RRC then leap-frogged Essex Scot and, encountering a large German minefield, managed to push the line 1,000yd beyond the Eerste Weg by 1600hrs. To the south, the large part of the Frederica Polder had been enveloped and captured by the RHLI.[18]

The following day, 26 October, Essex Scot was moved out of the positions currently held by the RHLI to march north west, while RHLI was ordered to advance behind the enemy who were dug in around the Krabbendijke and Roelshoek area and were menacing the RRC. This flanking manoeuvre could have succeeded, and nearly did, until around noon when Essex Scot were stopped in their tracks by deeply entrenched German defensive machine-gun and mortar positions along the dykes at the end of the isthmus, just before the canal. The extensive use of mines and booby traps gave the retreating Germans time and delayed the Allied advances along the roads, forcing them to bypass the roads and move into the saturated fields, wading through the water and mud. Allied troops were rapidly becoming exhausted. 'It was therefore with some relief that orders were received for the brigade to hold its positions in readiness for the advance to be carried on by 6 Canadian Infantry Brigade.'[19]

The next day, 27 October, when 6th Canadian Infantry Brigade reached the Beveland Canal their hearts fell. The Germans had destroyed most of the road and rail bridges crossing the canal.[20] Those that hadn't been destroyed had been heavily mined by the Germans. For the Allies to get across new bridges would have to be built, while in the meantime assault boats would have to be used to get across. In the early hours of 28 October, assault boats were quickly dropped into the water and troops from 6th Brigade clambered in, rowing the 300ft across to the other side as silently as possible. The South Saskatchewan Regiment established a bridgehead on the opposite side of the canal, south of Vlake, while the Fusiliers Mont Royal also got across and established their bridgehead at a point west of Kruinengen; but while setting up a third, the German gunners woke up and began pounding the third position forcing the Allies back.[21] The other two bridgeheads remained, secure, strong and viable.

At the same time, Allied engineers quickly got to work on constructing a series of makeshift crossings over the canal and by noon the following day the engineers had done their magic, and a Class 9 Bridge they'd built near Vlake was opened. Allied men and vehicles began to pour across the canal into South Beveland.

With Allied armour and men now swarming into South Beveland over the

Beveland Canal German resistance soon began to crumble. In the early hours of 26 October, the amphibious assault from Terneuzen across the Scheldt took place and with the Allies landing on South Beveland they outflanked the Germans. Once again, the defenders began to withdraw and on the night of 27 October, they abandoned their positions along the Beveland Canal, 500 evacuating across the Zandkreek into North Beveland while more than 3,000 German troops withdrew back into the fortress of Walcheren Island.[22]

Bergen Op Zoom had been captured by 4th Canadian Armoured Division on the same day while the push beyond the canal was joined by 5th Canadian Infantry Brigade, which had moved west to link up with other units involved in the same advance. Even though there were few defenders actually on the ground, for the Allies the going was still difficult as they picked their way around heavily mined dykes, booby-trapped roads and the constant enemy artillery fire from Walcheren.

North Beveland was quickly captured and occupied by the Allies without any resistance. Their backs to the sea, the 500 Germans had nowhere to go. In the face of the Allied forces they were outnumbered, bewildered, shocked and gave themselves up as prisoners of war. To all intents and purposes the Bevelands were now clear of enemy defenders.

While the Canadians were advancing along the isthmus as part of Operation Vitality 1, plans were quickly being made for the amphibious assault across the West Scheldt from Terneuzen. This was Operation Vitality 2. The task for this amphibious crossing fell to the British Army Scots 156th Infantry Brigade of 52nd Lowland Division.

The brigade, along with its landing craft, specialised troops, various vehicles to be carried, concentrated in the area around Terneuzen on the night of 23 October. According to Thompson, the whole plan and tasking for Vitality 2 had been given to the brigade less than 24 hours beforehand.[23] The plan was for the amphibious assault to take place on 24 October and for the Allies to land on two beaches, establish a bridgehead and push out, linking both bridgeheads into one. From there, they would then push out and link up with the Canadians at Gravenpolder.

While the Brigade Headquarters worked feverishly to plan the assault, the men of the brigade, the ones doing the landing, familiarised themselves with their amphibious vehicles – Buffaloes, Weasels, Terrapins, Aligators and Duplex Drive Tanks.[24]

The bridgehead was to be established through a general line running from Hoedenskerke to Molenberg. Once the bridgehead had been established elements of 156th Infantry Brigade Group were to push north west as quickly as possible. However, this advance was delayed by 24 hours because of the difficulties experienced by 2 Canadian Infantry Division along the isthmus.

The reason the Allies chose the assault to take place from Terneuzen was because of the covered approaches and clear channel across the Scheldt Estuary.

The build-up group was to concentrate in the Rulst area, whence it would be called forward as required to the build-up loading areas. These were in the Ossenisse peninsula, the LCAs and Terrapins were to use a small harbour in the NE corner; a passage of the LVTs was to be cut through the sea dykes in the NW Corner.[25]

The harbour area buzzed with activity while troops readied their vehicles and weapons. From Ostend the LCAs were carried by train as far as Ghent then placed into the canal and sailed up as far as the damaged locks. At this point, the engineers got to work and dammed the canal at Terneuzen in order for the LCAs to get past the damaged locks. By nightfall on 25 October, everything was ready.

Timed to coincide with the Canadian assault across the Beveland Canal, H-Hour had been set for 0445hrs on 26 October.

However, everything about South Beveland was new to 156th Infantry Brigade. They discovered that South Beveland, while being surrounded by dykes and most of the land being below sea level, was also criss-crossed with dykes. They also realised that the beaches they were to land on were made of 'sand six to eight inches under mud and silt, salt marsh and esparto grass'.[26] Indeed, Thompson tells us that the infantry could only negotiate the dykes by crawling between the wooden stakes and that tracked vehicles should only be able to cross them at high tide.[27]

There were two flotillas – A and B. On the right flank was A Flotilla whose task was to assault Green Beach, while B Flotilla was to land on Amber Beach. According to Thompson, 176 LVTs had been assembled for the assault. The 5th Assault Regiment Royal Engineers had 80 LVTs, while 11th Royal Tank Regiment had 76 LVTs. Also, there were 27 Terrapins and 25 Landing Craft Assault (LCA)s ready for use when required, as well as a support squadron of Staffordshire Yeomanry.[28] Depending on how light, or heavy, German resistance was 4/5 RSF were to move on and take Hoedekenskerke while the Cameronians were to continue westward after securing Amber Beach. Behind the two main flotillas was the Follow Up Group, C Flotilla, whose ultimate direction would be decided by the Brigade Commander, but the most likely point they would be directed towards was north and north west of Baarland to seize enemy positions between Hoedekenskerke and Gravenpolder or to advance north west. They had thirty-nine LVTs all told.[29]

In the early morning hours of 26 October, the Royal Scots Fusiliers of

A Group and the 6th Battalion Cameronians of B Group climbed into their Buffaloes ready to go.[30] Finally, at 0245hrs, in the cold darkness the assault force set sail from Terneuzen. Both A and B Flotillas each had two LCAs, one to act as a navigation guide and the other 'as a whipper-in'. The night was clear and the distance across the West Scheldt was only 9 miles, but the sea was rough and the LVTs wallowed and ploughed into the crests and troughs of the waves. Many men were seasick. On the southern shore red marker lights had been lit, acting as navigation aids for the leading craft as they passed by. From the Ossenisse peninsula, Bofors tracer was fired to ensure that the approaching craft did not land too far north, while marker shells were fired onto the beaches from H-Hour - 10 minutes onwards.[31]

As they rounded the coast there was a sense that the night was unnaturally quiet. Save for the occasional burst of shells from somewhere in the south-east corner of Walcheren Island, there was no activity from the enemy. These shells dropped far off the mark, closer to Terneuzen. As they continued they could see the Bofors tracer lazily arcing across the water. The red marker lights were clear. They sailed on.

At 0450hrs, the two flotillas simultaneously touched down on their respective Beveland beaches. On Amber Beach, near Baarland, there was no resistance as a group of Buffaloes carrying troops from 6 Cameronians managed to move quickly up the beach. One company even advanced as far as a mile inland. Although two Buffaloes were bogged down, the rest had better success. Within an hour of landing the bridgehead had been established and leading elements of the Cameronians arrived at the outskirts of Oudelande before the Germans woke up to this new danger.

As the second wave of Buffaloes came in on Amber Beach, the enemy had started harassing the landing parties with mortar fire. A small group of Buffaloes got caught in this enemy fire and floundered in the mud as they tried to crawl up the slopes of the dykes. As dawn approached the Cameronians on Amber Beach had taken ninety prisoners at the cost of eight casualties. By late afternoon the Cameronians had taken Oudelande as the Germans withdrew, increasing the number of enemy captured to well over a hundred. However, in this action they suffered sixteen casualties.[32]

To the north on Green Beach the situation was somewhat different. Thompson tells us that as the Royal Scots landed in their Buffaloes they were met by a hail of enemy fire from mortars and anti-tank guns. The sea wall here prevented the Buffaloes from moving beyond the beach and enemy gun positions were well concealed along the wall. 'The vehicles were too crowded for the ramps to go down, and it was a moment for individual action and initiative.'[33] In one instance a platoon commander took a section over the side of their Buffalo and charged along the sea wall, attacking an enemy position that had been spraying the beach with machine-gun fire. They used grenades and machine guns against the Germans and, while the enemy gun was silenced, the men lost their lives in the process. Across Green Beach, the Buffaloes were stranded as men jumped out onto the mud, charging over the sea wall. Within 2 hours of the landing the enemy guns along the sea wall had been neutralised and the bridgehead was secure. All that remained, in terms of enemy fire, were the mortars firing on the Allies from long range.[34]

Around this time C Flotilla, the Follow Up Group, landed at Amber Beach. Dashing forwards, 7 Cameronians managed to push inland to about 1,000yd before they were stopped, while behind them came the Staffordshire Yeomanry whose Buffaloes became bogged down in the mud flats. All the while, Amber Beach was under fire from German mortars and anti-tank guns. The engineers began building a ramp at the dyke but the Brigade Commander stopped this construction 'as it became cut up, and priority was given to infantry vehicles'. Even as the enemy shellfire continued, the Staffordshire Yeomanry Squadron opened up, providing support fire from their positions on the beach.[35]

Later in the day, the Germans counter-attacked from the north but the Allies, beating off the counter-attacks, managed to push out and expand the bridgehead. As has already been mentioned, 6 Cameronians captured and occupied Oudelande in the afternoon of the 26th, while, in reserve, 7 Cameronians patrolled a line between Oudeland and Baarland. Despite sporadic machine-gun and rifle fire from the Germans throughout the day and well into the night, the bridgehead was now firmly in Allied hands. Both bridgeheads had been linked into one large bridgehead within a few hours of the landings.

By late evening of the first day, the weather had deteriorated. On the Ossenisse peninsula a ferry service of Buffaloes, Alligators and Terrapins had been set up to ferry supplies, ammunition and troops to the bridgehead. But driving, steady rain on 27 October turned the embarkation points at Ossenisse into oozing, slimy mud making it virtually impossible for vehicles to use. Despite this, more than 700 loads were ferried across to the bridgehead in 3 days by the amphibious vehicles. Indeed, two battalions of HLI of C were able to get across during the worst of the weather.

On 27 October, the bridgehead was expanded beyond Oudelande by the Cameronians, while the Royal Scots moved towards Molenberg but were stopped by a further counter-attack from the Germans. In the early hours of 28 October, 5th RHLI, under command of 157th Infantry Brigade, after landing on the beaches joined up with 156th Infantry Brigade which then advanced towards the line running from Molenberg to Ellewoutsdijk. Molenberg was attacked by 5th RHLI but fierce German resistance meant the place was not taken until later in the night. Nevertheless, by the end of the day, five battalions were on the bridgehead that now encompassed Hoedenkenskerke on the right and on the left Ellewoutsdijk.[36]

Further progress was made on 29 October when 4th and 5th Canadian Infantry Brigades crossed the Beveland Canal and advanced into South Beveland. Goes was captured and at Gravenpolder, just south of the main road, 4th Canadian Infantry Brigade linked up with leading elements of 156th Infantry Brigade. At the same time, leading troops of 157th Infantry Brigade advanced towards the German defensive line that ran through Oudelande to Driewegen to S'Heerenhoek. More than 600 prisoners had been taken by midday.[37]

By 30 October the LVTs were no longer needed for ferrying supplies across the West Scheldt from the Ossenisse peninsula as the land route from Antwerp to South Beveland was now open. On 27 October, more than eighty LVTs from II Royal Tanks and 5 Assault Brigade were withdrawn in order to prepare for the invasion of Walcheren Island.

However, the Allied advance across the South Beveland peninsula was halted by the causeway that linked South Beveland to Walcheren Island on 30 October. Arriving at the causeway, 2nd Canadian Infantry Division was pinned down at the eastern end by very heavy German, machine-gun, mortar and anti-tank fire. 'With 157 Infantry Brigade leading, directed on the causeway, 52 (L) Division expanded NW and held the area south of the general line Hoedenskerke –S'Heerenhoek.'[38]

The following day, the east end of the causeway was finally cleared of German resistance by 4th Canadian Infantry Brigade, while 5th Canadian Infantry Brigade managed to get some of their leading elements to within 100yd of the German defenders at the Walcheren end of the causeway before they were driven back by accurate, withering enemy fire. This marked the beginning of the Battle of the Causeway, which is detailed elsewhere in this book.

Across the South Beveland peninsula German resistance crumbled and soon ended altogether. North Beveland fell to the Canadians without a shot being fired. Since 26 October the Terrapins and LCAs had undergone a maintenance programme in the harbour near Ossenisse but because of the tide they were unable to make more than one turn around trip per day. Much of the delay was caused by trying to get the Terrapins off the muddy beaches and onto the solid roads. During the entire operation to clear South Beveland the LVTs and Terrapins had used 27,000 gallons of fuel.

Operation Switchback that encompassed Vitality 1 and Vitality 2 had at its heart the requirement for the Allies to clear out German resistance from the Breskens Pocket and South and North Beveland. Before the Allies could mount any assault against the German forces on Walcheren Island, the Bevelands and the Breskens Pocket had been cleared of enemy defenders. All resistance in these areas had to be overcome and destroyed if the Allies were to mount operations successfully. The Allies had to be sure that there was no way the Germans could attack them from this area once they'd mounted their assault against Walcheren.

At this stage, mopping up operations were all that was left of Operation Switchback. The 7 Canadian Recce Regiment attacked the remaining German defenders in the strip from Zeebrugge to the Leopold Canal. With this complete, Operation Switchback ended on 3 November at 0930hrs. More than 12,500 prisoners were taken by the Allies.

As difficult and costly as this operation had been, the worst was yet to come.

Notes

1. See Thompson, *Eighty-Five Days*, p. 126.
2. Ibid.
3. 21 Army Group Report, Historical Section, Clearing of the Scheldt Estuary, October – November 1944, CAB 106, 1947.
4. Ibid.
5. Ibid.
6. See Thompson, *Eighty-Five Days*, p. 126.
7. See 'Report No. 188', Part IV.
8. Ibid.
9. See 21 Army Group Report, Historical Section, Clearing the Scheldt Estuary.
10. 'Report No. 188', 2 Canadian Infantry Division/C/F, Docket I, 2 Canadian Infantry Division, Historical Officer's Reports, Weekly Summary 22–8 Oct 1944.
11. H.Q. 6 Canadian Infantry Brigade, 23 October 1944, cited in 'Report No. 188', Part IV.
12. H.Q. 5 Canadian Infantry Brigade, 23 October 1944, cited in 'Report No. 188', Part IV.
13. See 21 Army Group Report, Historical Section, Clearing the Scheldt Estuary.
14. Ibid., 24 October 1944.
15. 'Report No. 188', H.Q., 4th Canadian Infantry Brigade, 23 October 1944.
16. See 21 Army Group Report, Historical Section, Clearing the Scheldt Estuary.
17. Ibid.
18. See 'Report No. 188', Part IV.
19. Ibid., 26 October 1944.
20. See 21 Army Group Report, Historical Section, Clearing the Scheldt Estuary.
21. See Thompson, *Eighty-Five Days*, p. 129.
22. Ibid.
23. See Thompson, *Eighty-Five Days*, p. 130.
24. DD tanks were a development of the Sherman tank, which turned it into a swimming amphibious vehicle by using an inflatable floatation screen around the tank. A propeller on the back of the tank, powered by the tank's engine, provided the motive power for swimming. DD tanks were a British invention.
25. See 21 Army Group Report, Historical Section, Clearing the Scheldt Estuary.
26. See Thompson, *Eighty-Five Days*, p. 130.

27. Ibid.

28. Interestingly, 21 Army Group Report states that the two flotillas were divided into groups with A Flotilla Group commanded by 4/5 Royal Scots Fusiliers and B Flotilla Group was commanded by 6 Cameronians. Also, the report states that both groups had thirty-nine LVTs available. See Thompson, *Eighty-Five Days*, p. 131.

29. See 21 Army Group Report, Historical Section, Clearing the Scheldt Estuary.

30. See Thompson, *Eighty-Five Days*, p. 131.

31. Ossenisse is a small village in the Dutch province of Zeeland on a peninsula that juts out into the West Scheldt.

32. See Thompson, *Eighty-Five Days*, p. 133.

33. Ibid., p. 134.

34. Ibid.

35. See 21 Army Group Report, Historical Section, Clearing the Scheldt Estuary.

36. See Thompson, *Eighty-Five Days*, p. 135.

37. See 21 Army Group Report, Historical Section, Clearing the Scheldt Estuary

38. Ibid.

Part 3

Operation Infatuate

Chapter 12

Battle for the Causeway

In his book, *Eighty-Five Days*, Reginald Thompson states that the battle for the Beveland causeway was a nameless operation, that is no official title was given to this battle.[1] Over time it has come to be known as the Battle of the Causeway. It was probably nameless because, up to this point, the Allies had been pushing hard against an enemy that, by and large, had been falling back while putting up a fierce fight. The point is, in the clearing of the Scheldt Estuary, the Allies had not been stopped. So it is likely that no name was given to this operation because the Allies believed it would be a walkover. They were to be rudely awakened.

First the eastern end of the causeway had to be cleared of enemy and the Canadians were steadfastly moving forward towards this objective. Brigadier R.H. Keefler, in temporary command of 2nd Canadian Division, drove his two brigades forward towards Walcheren, 4th Canadian Infantry Brigade moved through to Heinkenszand to the channel at Niewdorp, while 5th Canadian Infantry Brigade advanced along the main axis of road and rail to the causeway.

By the morning of 30 October, 5th Canadian Infantry Brigade had pushed forward and had one battalion within 3,000yd of the causeway leading to Walcheren Island. However, this formation had not yet opened up a clear route along the main highway west of Goes due to extensive minefields, which had caused some casualties during the previous night.[2]

Mines hindered both brigades: 'Mines were found in "verges", mostly tellers with a scattering of AP shut mines. Some French type "Loaf" mines were also encountered laid in the pavements. One of the units reported mines laid under the cobble stones, the stones taken out being replaced and making the mines very difficult to spot.'[3] Yet:

> 4 Canadian Infantry Brigade had made excellent progress and had one battalion on the WEST shore of SOUTH BEVELAND about 2,000 yards SOUTH of the causeway. It was decided to have 4 Canadian Infantry Brigade clear the eastern end of the causeway, as by this time (30 Oct), 2 Canadian Infantry Division had been directed to secure the

crossing of the causeway itself. Previously, the divisional objective had been merely to clear the peninsula of South Beveland.[4]

The advance towards the eastern end of the causeway continued apace until it was held up by more determined opposition. On the left, with 157 Infantry Brigade (British) taking the lead, also directed on the causeway, 51 (Light) Division (British) expanded to the north west and held the area south of a general line between Hoedekenskerke and Heerenhoek.[5]

It was at this stage that Brigadier R.H. Keefler decided that 4th Canadian Infantry Brigade, commanded by Brigadier F.N. Cabeldu, would take out the enemy still defending the approaches to the eastern end of the causeway and that 5th Canadian Infantry Brigade, commanded by Brigadier W.J. Megill, could then be brought in to tackle the causeway itself and force an entry into Walcheren. He recognised that the initial attack to clear the eastern side was more likely to be carried without undue loss if Brigadier Cabeldu were to make his assault under cover of darkness, since the enemy were dug in and unlikely to evacuate without a struggle.[6] The assault, carried out during the early hours of 31 October, was successful. In the words of Brigadier Cabeldu:

In a 'well organized operation', which commenced at 0200 hours 31 Oct, The Royal Regiment of Canada cleared the eastern end of the causeway, taking 200 P.W. and their guns. The enemy position had been rendered untenable by a skillful infiltration movement from the SOUTH, that took the enemy in the rear at the same time that a frontal attack was made from the southeast. By 0700hrs, 31 Oct, the last German was out of SOUTH BEVELAND.[7]

It may be added that:

In Brigadier Cabeldu's opinion the high-light of all operations by 4 Canadian Infantry Brigade on SOUTH BEVELAND was the movement of Essex Scot from KAPELLE, by way of NISSE, to NIEUWDORP, on the WEST coast of the peninsula. This route covered approximately 12 miles and was done entirely on foot. Throughout the operations on the peninsula the rapidity of the advance seemed to leave the enemy stupefied.[8]

At this juncture Allied intelligence reports found that the Germans, 'who put up the minimum resistance in SOUTH BEVELAND, retired to the island disorganized, depressed and worn out, to concentrate in a general area of ARNEMUIDEN – NIEUWLAND – KLEVERSKERKE with the intention of making a getaway by sea from VEERE and VROUWENSPOLDER . . .'[9]

With the eastern end of the causeway now cleared of the enemy, it was time for the Allies to turn their attention to the western end where the Germans were dug in. The causeway was 40ft wide by 1,200yd long. It sat 20ft above a salt-marsh channel of mud, swamp, slime and water that was known as Slooe Channel. The causeway had a single road and rail line running along it. In peacetime, on the northern and southern sides, 10ft above the railway embankment, ran a footpath lined with trees. Unfortunately, those trees were now just splintered stumps and the entire causeway was a mass of wrecked, destroyed and mined paving. The rail line itself was nothing but twisted and broken steel. Craters covered the entire length of the causeway. All the resources of the Allied engineers could not clear the debris and fill in the craters, it was that bad. Perhaps, they could have done if there had been no withering, concentrated, deadly enemy fire that covered every inch of the causeway.

The Walcheren end of the causeway connected to the buttress of the dyke that ran the entire circumference of the island. Behind this, in concrete strongpoints, pillboxes and bunkers, the Germans had placed heavy, medium and light artillery guns, their deadly 88mm anti-tank guns, mortars and heavy machine guns all with their fire concentrated directly on the causeway. Anything that tried to cross along the narrow track would be blasted into oblivion.[10]

The first unit to discover this was the Canadian Black Watch, who had gone on the attack after troops of the RRC had destroyed German strongpoints and gun batteries on the eastern end of the causeway, the South Beveland end, on 31 October. The Germans had waited until the Black Watch were roughly within 100yd of the western end then they opened fire with every gun they had. The subsequent hell that fell onto the Black Watch meant that they could not move forward or backwards but had to stay where they were suffering an onslaught of shells exploding nearby or on top of them while machine-gun bullets smashed into the dirt, into bodies and whizzed overhead. Their only hope was to wait until darkness.

On the afternoon of 31 Oct 5 Canadian Infantry Brigade took over the end of the causeway with R.R.C., which essayed the passage towards the enemy. Their reception was heated in the extreme. They were met with mortars, cross-fire from machine-guns, and shelling, and suffered heavy casualties. The causeway itself was badly catered and impassable to vehicles. A plan to get amphibians across the channel to the north and south had to be abandoned because there was not an efficient depth of water for them to swim all the way to the far bank and too great a depth of mud for wheels and tracks.[11]

R.R.C. were partially withdrawn that evening to enable an attempt at the causeway to be made by Calgary Highlanders. One company of the newcomers tried to get along that heavily registered avenue during the night, only to go to ground under another hail of fire. A second company was committed at 0600hrs on 1 Nov and did succeed in getting to the enemy's end. Here obstacles across the road and more intensive fire held our troops again. During the morning, however, Calgary Highlanders, aided by Spitfires and Typhoons, managed to get a shallow foothold on the island and began to pass their remaining companies over to consolidate their gains. From this lodgement R de Mais were to pass through to exploit. But at about 1730hrs the enemy put in a determined counter-attack and forced the Calgary Highlanders to withdraw all but a small force back into Beveland. Those left behind had orders to hold their ground until R de Mais could reinforce the situation on the far side. But only an hour had elapsed after R de Mais had passed over at 0400 hours, when, in accordance with the decision that the G.O.C. 52 (L.) Division should command the actual operations to capture Walcheren, the order came through for 5 Canadian Infantry Brigade to give place to 157 (British) Infantry Brigade. But the situation both on and over the causeway continued to be so oppressive that Brigadier Megill had to pull the bulk of R de Mais back to our side, leaving only one depleted company at the western end. The process of relieving that remnant by 1 Glasgow Highlanders was not an easy one and could not be completed until mid-after-noon on 2 Nov. Even then R de Mais did not leave the vicinity at once but remained there until late the following morning, in order to gather up its wounded who lay strewn along the causeway, still under fire.[12]

Throughout the evening of 31 October the Highlanders tried to move forwards and as 1 November dawned the soldiers were crawling slowly, inch by inch, around huge craters, in narrow tracks, under intense, lethal enemy fire. Throughout the day the Highlanders gradually pushed forwards and managed to get one company across the causeway. Here they came across an extensive enemy defence, like a road block, that caused them a great deal of trouble in terms of machine-gun fire and sniping. Yet, the Highlanders managed to push beyond this defensive position onto the mainland of Walcheren with some support companies following.[13] By the end of the day, just as night was falling on 1 November, the Calgary Highlanders were forced to withdraw leaving behind those that had managed to get across but were now stuck, victims of a hellish, concentrated barrage of high explosives.

In order to get the rest of the Highlanders out of the killing zone and back to safety the Allies began a bombardment of the German positions at the western end of the causeway. Under this bombardment, the Canadian R de

Mais were able to get to the beleaguered units and enable the remnants of the battered Calgary Highlanders to move back to safety.

At this point, Brigadier Megill decided to turn to his reserve unit, the R de Mais, to try to push across the causeway and establish a bridgehead on the Walcheren side, provided that support was given to the Canadians from 52nd Lowland Division Scots.

The attack by R de Mais began at 0400hrs on the morning of 2 November. They received the same reception of concentrated hellish fire as the Canadian Black Watch had and only D Company was able to get right across and establish a bridgehead, albeit a small one. This bridgehead on the Walcheren side of the causeway consisted of a railway underpass and a house. The rest of the R de Mais only managed to get halfway across under withering intense enemy fire and had to be pulled back to the South Beveland end of the causeway.[14]

Here, the 1st Battalion the Glasgow Highlanders were ready to go. According to Rawling, the Highlanders were part of the 52nd Lowland Division and the spearhead unit for 157th Infantry Brigade.[15] We can only speculate as to what must have been going through their minds as they waited for the signal to go. They had been initially briefed that the passage across would be relatively easy. From the reports coming in they now knew that this would not be the case. They knew the moment they set foot on the causeway they would be stepping into a killing zone, an inferno of shells and bullets that they had not yet experienced. So, were they afraid, terrified, anxious and appalled? Quite probably. However, they were also anxious to go and since the news coming from Flushing was good they also knew that the hell of the causeway would not, could not, last forever. At some point the Germans would have to capitulate, wouldn't they?

At the headquarters of the 155th Infantry Brigade and the Canadian 5th Infantry Brigade a state of desperation was setting in as report after report came in telling of the inability of the Allies to penetrate the German defences. Casualties were mounting up and the Canadians, now stuck on the causeway needed to be relieved before they were all lost. The tiny bridgehead they were holding had to be reinforced and secured but the prospect for this was slim indeed.

On the night of 2 November the Battalion Commander and Intelligence Officer of the Glasgow Highlanders decided to try to make contact with the beleaguered Canadians still stuck on the causeway.[16] There was no moon that night just the inky blackness of an overcast night. Soon after midnight this near pitch darkness was ripped apart by an artillery barrage from both sides that hammered the causeway. The light from the exploding shells made visibility a little easier as the two men crawled along the sloping sides of the causeway towards the Canadians. By 0426hrs they made contact with the R de Mais when the Glasgow Highlander Commander heard the grim news from his Canadian opposite number. It was thought that one company of the regiment was still alive further forward in a small defensive position but completely isolated. The shocking news was that the Canadians had no more than forty men left on the causeway, the rest were dead.

As the Glasgow Highlander Commander moved back as quickly as was possible in the heavily mined causeway, along the sloping side, he realised that the relief of the Canadians was paramount.

An advance across the causeway was still a very unpleasant prospect. At 5.20 (a.m) the commander of 157th Brigade told the Glasgow Highlanders' commanding officer that the relief was to go on, but that his battalion was not to put across any more troops than Le Regiment de Maisonneuve had, 'after deducting casualties'. The Glasgow C.O., having consulted Lt Col J. Bibeau of the Maisonneuves, who told him that he believed he had not more than 40 men alive in the forward area, agreed to relieve the Maisonneuves with one platoon.[17]

He gave the order for his men to do just that at 0520hrs, before daybreak. First to move up was B Company, which dug slots on the side of the south dyke under supporting mortar fire. Gradually, in the black night, they moved forward along the sloping embankment of the causeway, digging in, seeking shelter in the slots, then leaving and moving forwards, digging in again, waiting, then moving forward again. As they did, the remnants of the R de Mais began moving back. 'At half past six o'clock day began to break "grey and drear" with B Company crawling from slit to slit and hole to hole over that sloping embankment. At quarter past seven o'clock the Company Commander was wounded, and the appalling, inescapable fire began to take a steady toll.'[18]

According to Thompson, the Company Commander, instead of withdrawing back to safety to have his wounds seen to, dressed them himself and carried on leading his men forward.

By the time daylight arrived, with the concentrated enemy fire pounding B Company, D Company was trying to relieve them. They moved forward towards B Company with the order to establish at foothold on the island no matter what the cost. In this they were supported by A Company.

Around 0800hrs, over the din of the enemy fire, the men of B Company and D Company heard a welcome sound. It was the roaring engines of rocket-firing Typhoons. The fighters came in low, barrel-rolled into their dives and fired salvos of rockets and cannon shells at the German positions. As they did, D Company moved into the reeds on the flats of Slooe Channel and began to advance. They slogged through the mud and slime as the Typhoons came round again, strafing the Germans with 20mm cannon fire. Finally, it was the soldiers of 18 Platoon the Glasgow Highlanders who made the first contact with the twenty remaining men of the R de Mais. Unable to move forward or to move backwards, they had taken refuge in the cellar of a farmhouse that was now just a shell. Instead of immediately moving back to safety, the Scots and the Canadians held out in the cellar for another 4 hours while the rest of the Glasgow Highlanders tried to move into positions that would enable them to attack the Germans behind their dykes and strongpoints.

At this point, Rawling tells us that the 5th Canadian Field Regiment had a forward observation officer in the bridgehead with the Maisonneuves and he called for smoke from the Field Regiment. It was duly provided and using this cover, at 1400hrs all the Canadians withdrew back along the causeway to South Beveland. From here, the desperately tired 2nd Canadian Infantry Division was withdrawn from the fighting to recuperate and rest. 'Since crossing the Antwerp–Turnhout Canal in late September they had taken 5,200 German prisoners and killed an unidentified number more. Their own casualties amounted to 207 officers and 3,443 other ranks.'[19]

At 1500hrs three snipers from the battalion moved towards the enemy to begin picking off the Germans. One was killed shortly after leaving. 'The battle had reduced itself to the terms of a duel, these three men going out alone into that wasteland to counter-snipe. They went off in the smoke.'[20]

Under the cover of darkness on the night of 2 November, a bulldozer rumbled out from the safety of the eastern end of the causeway to try to repair the worst of the craters. However, the enemy soon spotted the vehicle and hammered it with artillery and mortar fire. Nothing could live on that terrible strip of land. Yet, for the Allies, cracks in the German defences were beginning to appear. Only a few miles from the causeway lay the town of Arnemuiden, which the Germans declared an 'open town'.

They had done this because the town was full of civilian and military wounded, with little food, water, medical supplies or shelter. As a result of this, 18 Platoon and 17 Platoon were slowly gaining a grip on the German right flank near Arnemuiden. Allied stretcher bearers were pulling the wounded from the foxholes and the reeds and taking them to the town. As they did, the Scots moved slowly forward.

The Germans holding out at the western end of the causeway knew that time was running out for them. Only a few miles away, the huge coastal gun batteries that had been blasting the Allied landings were now silent. They knew the Allies were behind them slowly advancing and on the right flank, the Allies had made a foothold that they were slowly securing. To illustrate this we can turn to Thompson who cites the Glasgow Highlander Diary entry at 2359hrs on 2 November – 'Enemy moving along main road to Causeway broken up in disorder by artillery fire.'[21]

To make matters worse for the Germans the Cameronians had done what they, the Germans, thought impossible. During the night they had crossed the Slooe Channel and by dawn of 3 November were moving up the flank towards the Germans, dug in on the causeway. That morning the drizzle and grey overcast conditions had gone, replaced with brilliant sunshine. At this point, with the sun shining, a squadron of Typhoons arrived again and began attacking the Germans with rockets and cannon fire.

The crossing of the Slooe Channel is an interesting story of bravery and challenge in the face of severe adversity and deserves a more detailed examination. Major General Hakewell Smith, commanding the 52nd Lowland Division had a plan. He was in charge of the three-pronged attack against enemy positions on Walcheren Island, the first two against Flushing and Westkapelle were fully committed. The third prong was to be the assault along the causeway but that had turned into a killing ground and he was loathe to commit his troops to a suicidal attack. Another way had to be found to cross from South Beveland to Walcheren. That way was across the Slooe Channel.

At low tide the channel was a mass of creeks, salt marshes, oozing sticky mud, reeds, grass, sand and water. Channels in the mud and slime ran in all directions. In 1940 the Germans had tried to cross it to attack a French armoured division. They failed and lost more than a hundred men. As a result, they were unlikely to believe that anyone could cross and so did not fortify the shore lines as well as they should have done. The Allies would cross via the causeway, they could not come via the Slooe Channel. Or could they?

Hakewell-Smith believed it was possible and spent the days leading up to 1 November studying maps and aerial photographs of the area with his engineers, looking for a way. Scanning through all the material they had, they did find something – a small ridge that ran through the saltings. Only wide enough for men to cross in single file if it was firm enough it might do the trick. It was a chance but one that Hakewell-Smith was prepared to take. He ordered the sappers from 202 Field Company Royal Engineers to work out how to get across using this ridge.[22]

What the General needed was time and he didn't have it. Just prior to 1 November he had been ordered to attack across the Beveland Causeway during the night of the assault, 1 November, by Commander 2nd Canadian Corps. At his headquarters in Breskens, Hakewell-Smith was told by visiting Corps Commander General Foulkes to attack the German defenders along the causeway. For more than an hour the men argued, with Hakewell-Smith stating that a frontal assault against the well-dug-in Germans was untenable, partly because the entire causeway was mined and also because the Allies were totally outgunned and had no armour that could shift the enemy. He argued for a crossing by the Slooe Channel and outlined his plan to Foulkes who finally relented and gave Hakewell-Smith 48 hours for his plan to work otherwise he would have to attack across the length of the causeway and send his troops into that inferno.[23] In addition, Foulkes told Hakewell-Smith that if his troops were not on Walcheren Island within that time period he would be replaced as Commander of 52nd Division.[24]

Havenhuis is a small port not far from the causeway on the South Beveland side, and it is from here that two engineers left during the night of 1 November and began slowly to grope their way across the Slooe Channel in an attempt to prove that crossing this hazardous channel was indeed possible. Lieutenant F. Turner MC and Sergeant Humphrey moved cautiously through the darkness.[25] The point at which they were crossing was 1,500yd wide, and of that more than 300yd of it was a water channel that at low tide seemed to be constantly changing.

Turner and Humphrey had managed quietly to get across the channel onto the firm ground of Walcheren Island to within 200yd of the German positions. Indeed, they could actually hear the Germans talking. Silently, the two men slipped back across the channel following the exact route they'd come and reported that the crossing was feasible. It would have to be done in assault boats and on foot but if they were able to mark the way using tape then behind them the battalion could cross. It would be a dangerous exercise but everyone knew it would be nothing compared to the killing taking place on the causeway.

The Germans had mined the area around Havenhuis making the effort of crossing the Channel even more treacherous. The thick darkness of the night of 2 November masked the operation when Turner, and three other engineers, began clearing the way forward. On the Walcheren side of the channel they laid out marker tapes while on the Beveland side small groups of engineers quietly cleared a way through the mines enabling the first leading companies of the 6th Battalion Cameronians to begin their crossing.[26] Supporting the Cameronians was 4/5th Battalion Royal Scots Fusiliers which remained behind, waiting for the former to cross.[27]

At 0300hrs, the Cameronians began crossing in assault boats, not willing to wait and see if Turner had successfully marked out the route ahead. By 0345hrs they had crossed the channel in their assault boats and reached the muddy, oozing Walcheren side of the Slooe. The leading troops managed to identify the tapes laid down by Turner and pushed forward through the mud and slime finally arriving on the dry land of Walcheren Island. All this had been done under the cover of darkness and as quietly as possible in order to achieve surprise. The surprise was complete and the Cameronians captured sixty Germans 'almost immediately'.[28]

Of course, the Germans were soon alive to the crossing and tried to counter-attack with artillery and machine-gun fire but the bridgehead established by the Cameronians held. At the same time, the Germans, perhaps suddenly aware of what the Allies were trying to do, began shelling Havenhuis.

Not only did the Cameronians have to contend with enemy fire but also, and perhaps worst of all, the oozing, sticky, liquid mud that at points was near waist-deep. Thompson tells us that some of the amphibious vehicles that tried to help out stranded troops became, themselves, bogged down in that slimy viscous material 'like ungainly beetles, their noses poking into the banks of the runnels and the craft slewing, unmanaged as the tide receded'.[29] However, by dawn the dry land of the western shore had been gained by a company of Cameronians. Here they waited, short of food and ammunition, knowing that behind them, strung out across the channel and in the mud before dry land, the rest of the troops were stranded, bogged down and isolated. In one case, soldiers from the Royal Scots Fusiliers found themselves completely held fast by the mud on the saltings. The wind increased, blowing in from the south, turning the sea flowing into the channel into a choppy nightmare. The temperature fell to near freezing but the Allied units clung on.

Indeed, the Cameronians managed to expand the little bridgehead to 1,000yd and began to take prisoners, putting them to good use in laying down palings over the muddy shore for men and vehicles to drive over. Thompson illustrates just how much impact this crossing had in demoralising the Germans.

> All through the night, of the 3rd–4th, the Brigade passed men, food and ammunition across the channel, and contrived to pass prisoners and wounded back. On the morning of the 4th, the right flank of the bridgehead was on Groeneburg, and that afternoon the forward company of the 5th Battalion H.L.I., coming in to support, was smashing the enemy out of the dykes with grenades within sight and sound of the Glasgow Highlanders on the Causeway.[30]

With the Allies now all around them, the Germans, entrenched in their concrete pillboxes and strongholds behind the dykes, knew the game was up. Groeneburg had been the last link between the Cameronians on the western shore and the Glasgow Highlanders on the causeway. The actual link-up took place when a single private charged a German machine-gun post, firing his Bren gun from the hip and killing six of the enemy. Following behind him came more Allied soldiers reinforcing and expanding the link.

However, while the Cameronians had been struggling in the mud to reinforce their tiny bridgehead on the causeway, the Glasgow Highlanders had hung on and gradually started to move forward. The mood was changing and the soldiers of 17 and 18 Platoons were slowly advancing. They could sense victory. Indeed, after 18 Platoon held off a German counter-attack with a force of around 100 men Lieutenant Renwick, commanding the platoon, called for artillery fire. For an hour the shells rained down on the Germans in their concrete shelters, then Renwick forced home an attack on the Germans. Their resistance crumbled and his men took ninety-four prisoners, including three enemy warrant officers and eight NCOs.[31] A further 130 Germans left their dug-outs and surrendered. However, there were still many other enemy soldiers, prepared to fight to the death and, as Thompson states, some actually machine-gunned their fellow soldiers who surrendered.

By nightfall on 3 November the bridgehead was 2 miles wide and 2,000yd deep and 18 Platoon had taken more than 370 prisoners. At the same time, engineers worked on clearing the causeway of mines, but more vehicles and men would succumb to the mines over the next few days and it would be some time before the causeway was actually safe to cross.[32] On the same day, the 5th HLI of C crossed the channel to reinforce the bridgehead while further to the south the HLI had marched beyond the Cameronians towards the causeway dealing with remaining enemy held up in strongpoints along the dykes. The two bridgeheads were securely united the following day.[33]

Dawn on 4 November brought silence from the enemy guns that once covered the Scheldt Estuary. Before no Allied ship could traverse the estuary towards Antwerp without being hammered by the guns on Walcheren Island, now on this day for the first time those guns were silent.

The assault across the Slooe Channel had been a stroke of genius for the Allies, a gamble that worked. The Germans, dug in behind concrete emplacements, pillboxes, strongpoints and so forth at the end of the causeway had been outflanked by the crossing. With the 2-mile wide bridgehead secured the 'Lowlanders advanced the next day until they came to the edge of the inland floods. From here it was water all the way to Middelburg apart from the elevated road and railway running into the city and both of these were heavily mined.'[34]

Three minesweepers began sweeping the estuary for mines, a process that would take several days. They sailed into Antwerp later in the day safe and sound. However, Antwerp along with London was a target for the V2 rockets (Hitler's secret terror weapons) but that is another story. Suffice it to say, the Scheldt was now clear of the guns but not yet of enemy mines.

The Canadian 2nd Corps Intelligence Summary under the date November 4th records briefly that 'the enemy no longer controls the approaches to the Port of Antwerp' and that 'only mines remain to prevent the use of the Scheldt estuary by Allied shipping.' On November 3rd Commander of the British 52nd Division had declared Flushing cleared of the enemy, and on the same day Commander of the Canadian 3rd Division had announced the end of Operation Switchback.[35]

Notes

1. Thompson, *Eighty-Five Days*, p. 194.
2. 'Report No. 188', 2nd Canadian Infantry Division/C/D, Docket I, fol. 4, Account by Brigadier Keefler.
3. 'Report No. 188', H.Q. 4th Canadian Infantry Brigade, 30 October 1944.
4. See 'Report No 299', Account by Brigaider Keefler.
5. See 21 Army Group Operations Clearing of the Scheldt, p. 13.
6. See 'Report No. 188', 4th Canadian Infantry Brigade/C/D, Docket I, fol. I, Account by Brigadier Cabeldu; AEF/2 Canadian Infantry Division/C/D, fol. 4, account by Brigadier Keefler.
7. See 'Report No. 188', 4th Canadian Infantry Brigade/C/D, Docket I, fol. 1, Account by Brigadier Cabeldu.
8. Ibid.
9. 'Report No. 188', First Canadian Army/L/F, Docket I, Vol II, October 1944, 15–31 October, Intelligence Summary No. 122, 30 October 1944.
10. See Thompson, *Eighty-Five Days*, for a more complete description of the causeway, pp. 195–6.
11. 'Report No. 188', H.Q. 5th Canadian Infantry Brigade, 31 October 1944.
12. Ibid., 1–3 November 1944; W.D., G.S. Ops H.Q., First Canadian Army, November 1944, Appendix 4, 1 November 1944, Serials 54, 55, 70, 75, 80, 83, 2 November 1944, Serials 15, 18; AEF/5 Canadian Infantry Brigade/C/D, Docket III, Account by Captain J.L. Field.
13. See Rawling, *Cinderella Operation*, p. 80.
14. Ibid., p. 81.
15. Ibid.
16. Ibid., p. 195.
17. From the 'Canadian Official History of the Walcheren Operation', cited in Rawling, *Cinderella Operation*, p. 81.
18. Thompson, *Eighty-Five Days*, p. 196.
19. See Rawling, *Cinderella Operation*, p. 82.
20. See Thompson, *Eighty-Five Days*, p. 198.
21. Ibid., p. 199.
22. See Rawling, *Cinderella Operation*, p. 83.
23. See Thompson, *Eighty-Five Days*, p. 200.
24. See Rawling, *Cinderella Operation*, p. 84.
25. Ibid.
26. Ibid., p. 85.
27. Ibid., p. 201.
28. Ibid., p. 85.
29. See Thompson, *Eighty-Five Days*, Operation No Name, p. 201.
30. Ibid., p. 202.
31. See Thompson, *Eighty-Five Days*, Operation No Name, p. 203.
32. Ibid.
33. See Rawling, *Cinderella Operation*, p. 86.
34. Ibid.
35. See Thompson, *Eighty-Five Days*, Operation No Name, p. 204.

Chapter 13

Assault on Walcheren – Flushing

While the Canadians fought to clear the Breskens Pocket and take the Bevelands, planning for attacking the island of Walcheren was well underway. For example, the preparations for the Allied amphibious landings on the island were moving quickly. Then there were the operations by the RAF, specifically Bomber Command, which used 1,000lb and 4,000lb weapons that reshaped the Walcheren landscape by bombing the dykes. Lancaster heavy bombers lead by Mosquito pathfinders smashed gaps in the dykes in four different places. The first was the dyke at Westkapelle where 247 Lancasters dropped 1,274 tons of bombs on 3 October. On 7 October, the next raid, by fifty-eight Lancasters, hammered the dyke at Noledijk west of Flushing with 348 tons of bombs. To the English, Vlissingen was known as Flushing, and this is the name that will be used in this book.

Also on 7 October another group of sixty-three Lancasters dropped 384 tons of bombs on Ritthern, east of Flushing. The final gap was created on 11 October when a group of sixty Lancasters pounded Oostwatering north west of Veere with 374 tons of bombs.[1]

The raids were flown during the day to allow for the best accuracy. And accuracy they achieved. With the gaps in the dykes blown open the sea was allowed to flood inland. Within a few days the area around Flushing was under more than 3ft of water and in some cases the flood waters reached to more than 10ft high. Prior to the bombings the RAF dropped leaflets telling the people of Walcheren Island to leave their homes and seek high ground wherever they could. The civilian casualties on the days when the bombs were dropped were much less than they could have been as many heeded the warnings and moved to higher ground around Middelburg. Yet, there were civilian casualties. Some 198 people were killed, less as a result of the flooding and more due to the bombing.

The sea moved quickly through the four gaps made by the bombing. At the gap at Westkapelle the movement of the sea increased the breech from the original size of 100yd to more than 350yd. The result of the floods, according to Richard Brooks, was that the island was divided into three sections, 'the coastal dunes, Vlissingen and the high ground to the east, connected only by road embankments between them'.[2]

While the Germans tried unsuccessfully to build a secondary line of dykes inland of the gaps, they were able to keep their communication lines open up until they surrendered. However, the flooding had submerged most of their gun batteries and cut off their reserves.

The softening up process of the remainder of the German defences was only partially successful. For example, at the end of October, the RAF mounted a 3-day bombing campaign on a wide variety of targets, flying 649 sorties and dropping more than 3,000 tons of bombs. Yet, out of those sorties only 167 were against the coastal gun batteries not affected by the flooding. Against the gun batteries that directly affected the beaches where the landings would take place, W11, W13 and W15, only ninety-five sorties were flown. A report written after the operations at Walcheren were finished suggested that had the bombing concentrated on the main batteries at W13 and W15 'three quarters of the guns at Walcheren could have been destroyed'.[3] When the amphibious landings took place, all these big guns were still in action and caused the Allies considerable difficulties.

While the fighting in South Beveland and the Breskens Pocket continued the amphibious forces for the assault on Walcheren were pulled together. The force, known as T Force, assembled on 27 October at Ostend but without the Bombardment Squadron or the minesweepers. Three days prior to the launch of the operation a maintenance base was established at Ostend that could berth up to 100 landing craft of various types, along with accommodating more than 400 officers and men. A large amount of stores and equipment was brought here ready for the landings while radios were also installed in the vessels.

Not far from Ostend, at a place called de Haan, 4 Special Service Brigade was training hard on the sand dunes that were similar to those on Walcheren. While they were based at this seaside resort, 4 SS Brigade worked out drills for attacking German batteries and their bunkers. Most of the big German gun batteries were encased or mounted in concrete and had concrete bunkers for the gun crews. The men of 4 SS Brigade trained with abandoned bunkers the Germans had left behind as they withdrew. The general training regime saw the assault groups from 4 SS Brigade following the crest of the dunes where they worked their way through simulated enemy positions and strongholds closely followed by supporting mortar fire. Using the ruins of Ostend as their backdrop, 4 Commando, which was to land at Flushing, trained for house-to-house fighting. In the absence of the necessary equipment for a full-scale rehearsal aerial photographs were studied, sea walls were climbed, exercises at commando level were carried out, which included integrated support from tanks and amphibians. Despite the lack of a run through, live firing during training was carried out and was so robust that four marines were killed during this phase of the preparations.

Time was running short and the Allies had not had the chance to reconnoitre the beaches painstakingly as they had with the Normandy landings. Maps had been created by the Canadians that showed the island and the German defences in great detail but true information for the landings was not as available as it could have been.

However, 4 Special Service Brigade did try probing the German defences in the Westkapelle gap. The reconnaissance section, Keepforce, made several night-time attempts between 15 and 27 October to get through the gap. The code-name for these attempts to investigate the defences was Tarbrush. A motor torpedo boat would transport the team near the beach where the Tarbrush party would try to land, then using rubber dinghies the reconnaissance teams would float towards the shore.[4] They were attached to a dory some 100yd away. Despite being as quiet as they could be each time they were spotted, the Germans fired off flares, switched on their searchlights and then peppered the approaching marines with small arms fire. This meant that each time the reconnaissance teams had to turn back before they could learn anything really useful for the landings.

The machine-gun posts that lined the seafront at Flushing made any close reconnaissance of the area virtually impossible. It was also difficult to tell whether the beach itself was a practical landing point. However, on D-Day, a Tarbrush party was sent in prior to the assault group from 4 Commando to check the viability of the landing site. If it wasn't suitable, 155 Brigade was to be diverted to Westkapelle.

In the end the landings at Flushing took place. Indeed, the Allies decided to land at Flushing because the less heavily defended beaches were unsuitable, being on the wrong side of the Flushing–Middelburg Canal as well as being flooded. The landing site, code-named Uncle, was in the dock harbour area near the Oranjedijk mill, south east of the town centre. 'This was 110 yards wide and 250 deep (100 x 220m) with a rubbish dump at the inland end likely to provide firm going for vehicles.'[5] Groynes stretching almost 10ft high ran the length of the beach on either side and included steel rails built in concrete along with rows of stakes for defensive purposes. A natural bridgehead beyond the beach was defined by different patches of water and the ground around them that the Allies could hold while they consolidated their positions. West of the beach were the Fishermen's and Merchants' docks, or the Western Harbour, while to the north was the Schelde Shipyard's dock and Binnenhaven, also known as the inner harbour.[6]

The strength of Flushing as a fortified port had at first seemed to preclude the possibility of a head-on assault from the sea without the virtual razing of the defences by air and artillery bombardment beforehand. As the expected weight of attack from the air proved to be impossible, the success of the amphibious operation is the more remarkable, and can only be assessed as one of the most brilliant and fortunate of the war. As 4 Commando was afterwards to report:

Conditions were imposed upon the operation, which, if they had been observed, would have prevented its performance. It was first laid down that FLUSHING must have had at least one very heavy attack from the full might of Bomber Command before an assault could be contemplated. Next, it was stipulated that the assaulting Commandos be preceded by a small recce party from the Special Boat Section and that this party should be responsible for getting ashore and calling in the Commandos if there was no opposition. As at first envisaged, therefore, the landing at FLUSHING was to be carried out only after the heaviest bombardment had reduced the garrison to the point of surrender, and, if it was found that the garrison, in spite of the bombing was still capable of resistance, it was proposed to call the landing off rather than risk the annihilation of the assault force. Finally, it was decided that the landing should definitely take the form of an assault, and that the recce party should be retained to assist in the resolution of some of the difficulties in finding a landing point. Heavy aerial bombardment was promised, certainly once prior to D Day, and also immediately prior to H Hour if weather conditions permitted. Artillery support from the mainland was on a vast scale, and consisted of a Basic Fire Plan supplied by five field Regiments and three Medium Regiments – of which one was on call to No. 4 Commando through an F.O.O. – with increments from Heavy and Super Heavy Regiments. All targets along the water-front were to be subjected to bombardment and four additional Medium Regiments were to be held available for counter-battery work. Every known or potential target area was carefully registered and allotted code numbers, and it proved that the Artillery Fire Plan was equal to every situation that arose throughout the battle for FLUSHING.[7]

To this testimony may be added that of Lieutenant General Daser, the German commander, who claimed that all the coastal artillery guns on the south shore were destroyed either by flooding or bombing or counter-battery fire, and that there were only machine guns and a few of his Czech land defence guns available to deal with the landing force.[8]

70 Infantry Division at Flushing and on both sides of Westkapelle the enemy landed with forces of altogether about one infantry brigade and several armoured units. He succeeded in penetrating Flushing and, on both sides of Westkapelle in gaining ground with tanks toward the Northeast and southeast. . . . The enemy advance in northeasterly direction along the coastal road Westkapelle – Domburg has reached the area 1 km SW Domburg. In the northern quarter of Flushing the enemy has pushed forward to the bridge across the canal. A counter-attack at 1800hrs forced the enemy to fall back across the narrow part of the canal . . . The three anti-aircraft batteries around Flushing have only one single barrel left ready for use, the port battery Flushing one gun fit for action to some degree. As Walcheren cannot be reached by sea or land the length of the fighting there depends entirely on the steadfastness of the garrison which cannot possibly receive support from the outside.[9]

Canadian experience in the combined operation at Dieppe, another fortified port, had sufficiently indicated the necessity of preparing the way for the assaulting troops by heavy bombardment, and everything possible had been done in this case to ensure that those committed to the hazards of such a landing would receive all possible support. But 24 hours before the operation was due to begin, political considerations were added to the many other complications in the matter, and General Simonds, commanding First Canadian Army, was informed that the carpet-bombing required as a matter of military necessity could not be carried out. With his forces concentrated and everything ready, General Simonds had been faced with a serious situation. He decided, however, that the operation could not be called off, and although the German positions were attacked from the air, they were more leniently treated than he had intended them to be.[10] During the night of 31 October/1 November 2 Tactical Air Force reported that: '35 out of 37 Mosquitoes attacked defensive positions on WALCHEREN throughout the night. Poor visibility prevented observation of results but 1 gun emplacement was silenced and a large explosion seen in the FLUSHING area.'[11]

To the commandos, who from their concentration area in Breskens could see Flushing and its forest of cranes clearly visible across the water, there seemed very little hope that the one element on which they must now rely, that of achieving surprise, could be realised. Their report affords an impression of their own somewhat dismal assessment of their chances.

There seemed very little hope of obtaining surprise in this operation anyway. The strategic situation made it plainer than a pikestaff that the freeing of the great port of ANTWERP must be the dominant consideration for the Allied Supreme Command at this time, and it was clear that an assault on WALCHEREN was an essential prerequisite to the use of the SCHELDT.

The clearing of the BRESKENS area must have suggested the direction of the coming attack to the Germans on the island, and it seemed impossible that the concentration of artillery and, latterly, of L.C.A., in and around this little town should have passed altogether unobserved. The main hopes of achieving a modicum of surprise lay in the chance that the enemy might appreciate that our attack on WALCHEREN was coming only from across the SOUTH BEVELAND CAUSEWAY. In any event, it was anticipated that the opening of a sudden artillery barrage on FLUSHING, more violent and concentrated by far than anything hitherto experienced in this town, would show the enemy pretty clearly what was to be expected. This danger was provided for in the planning by asking for the heavy bombers to continue to make dummy runs over FLUSHING after the actual bombing was over and while the artillery barrage was opening up. It was calculated that to a man cowering in a deep shelter and already much shaken by the bombing attack, all explosions would sound very much alike, particularly if aircraft were still overhead. By the time the Germans had realised that they were under shell fire only, and had drawn the logical conclusions from this, we hoped to be well ashore.

As it turned out, the heavy bombers were unable to come over at all and consequently an increased artillery barrage was put down on FLUSHING, and was opened at H60 instead of at H15. So far from forfeiting surprise this concentration gained almost complete surprise for us. The whole affair was an excellent example of how very different the enemy's appreciation of a situation is from what we think it must be. To anybody on the British side it seemed that the enemy must have been expecting an attack at the time and place we had chosen, but the FLUSHING garrison Commander was later to confess that the preparatory artillery bombardment was the first real indication he had that the town was about to be assaulted, and that by then it was too late to take any special measures.[12]

The full strength of the Commando Group committed to this daring and apparently suicidal attack amounted to only 550 all ranks, among whose complement of attached troops and units was a light section of 6 Canadian Field Dressing Station (FDS). These were embarked at Breskens on 20 LCA in the early hours of 1 November. The dreary circumstances of their setting out and the more hopeful opening of the assault are thus described by their intelligence officer:

> It was cold, and very wet, with a steady drizzle, which limited visibility very considerably, and heavy low cloud. We knew by now that the bombing programme had to be called off and that the increased artillery fire plan was to take its place. As we filed down to the harbour a Mosquito was circling overhead, and swooping over FLUSHING to strafe at regular intervals.
>
> Loading was completed by 0415hrs, and at about 0440hrs the landing craft slipped and passed the harbour mouth. At almost the same moment the artillery barrage commenced, and the mainland was from now on silhouetted against the flickering muzzle flashes of three hundred guns. We gazed anxiously over to FLUSHING, straining our eyes for the answering flashes of the German artillery, but all that we could see were the sudden bright pin points of light all along the waterfront which were our own shells exploding, and one glow somewhere in the town where the Mosquitoes had started a fire. Sometimes our shells struck the steel anti-landing stakes, and then there was a shower of red sparks reminiscent of a firework display. But the German guns remained silent.
>
> . . . Gradually the fire in the town was gaining hold, and suddenly the unmistakable silhouette of the windmill – the ORANJE MOLEN – was thrown into relief against the glare. We could have had no clearer indication of our chosen landing point.[13]

At 0545hrs the reconnaissance detachment closed the beach, the barrage having lifted in that place just before they did so, and 'a landing was effected', without casualties. The actual landing place had only been decided upon after a searching study of air photographs and a thorough interrogation of Dutch civilians and river pilots who knew the port well. The most prominent feature of the waterfront, the Oranjemolen, is a huge brick windmill, marking the promontory to the east of which lies a bay, the relic of a small harbour of earlier days, called the Ooster of Dokhaven. It was decided that the first landing must be attempted on the promontory itself, and that the Ooster of Dokhaven would be the main landing beach for stores and follow-up troops.

> The Commandos' objectives were obvious from the start – the defile between the promenade and the Sput of Binnenboezem, and the gap between the inland side of that basin and the shipyards where a large liner lay under construction on the stocks. The first objective was given the code name 'DOVER', the second 'BEXHILL'. Once seized, they

would place the main part of the town within our control, for there no enemy troops could either enter or leave without our mandate.[14]

The plan to get in was a simple one. When the landing place had been reconsolidated by No. 1 Troop, the main force was to pass through and go for 'DOVER' with No. 3 Troop, followed by No. 5 Troop, and for 'BEXHILL' with No. 6. The beachhead force would then debouch into the town, and clear the Arsenal Barracks and the area directly to the west of the harbour along the Engelsche Kaai. No. 2 Troop would then attack the enemy's positions eastward on the spit enclosing the Verbreed Canal and the inner harbour. The streets west of the Engelsche Kaai were to be left to No. 3 Troop on completion of its primary task. For the reinforcement by 155 (L.) Brigade, the first battalion 4 King's Own Scottish Borderers (4 K.O.S.B.) was on 40 minutes' call, with one of its companies ready to come in earlier if the need arose.[15]

At 0200hrs troops from 4 Commando slowly made their way through drizzling rain down to the harbour at Breskens. The silence of this early November morning was shattered suddenly when all along the seafront more than 300 Allied guns began shelling German targets. The area under the artillery barrage spanned east of the gap in the dyke at Nolle Point right down the seafront to the harbour. Over the heads of the commandos the shells hurtled towards Flushing and as each one found their targets they added to the glow on the horizon.

Finally, at 0440hrs the first of the landing craft cast off and set sail for Flushing. The fires caused by the bombing and artillery barrage lit up the windmill on the left side of Uncle Beach making navigation in the drizzling gloom much easier.

Members of the Keepforce reconnaissance teams in two patrol craft guided the first of the LCAs to the beach 'followed by a section of 1 Troop under Captain Dennis Rewcastle'.[16] Once the first of the landing craft had touched down the beach clearing party jumped out and began preparing the beach for the rest of the force to come in. They cut wires and taped out specific areas of the beach. The beach party commander ran to the end of the promontory and set up a lamp pointing out to sea to guide in the rest of the flotilla. Both of the first two landing craft that came in carried elements of No. 1 and No. 2 Troop 4 Commando.

As the Keepforce teams set about their tasks the commandos from No. 1 troop stormed ashore, their objective to secure the beachhead. As they moved from the beach onto the sea wall, one section under Colour Sergeant Major (CSM) Lewis, moved quickly towards the Oranjmolen area taking twenty frightened German prisoners when they entered a German strongpoint. These prisoners were the crew of a 75mm gun that was now out of action. At the shore end of the promontory some of Captain Rewcastle's men overran an underground shelter where they found the crew of the beach searchlight and took them prisoner. In order to block the entrance to Oranjestraat, Captain Rewcastle left a patrol in place to cover this area while the rest of his men moved into the streets north of Oranjemolen, code-named Seaford, where they began clearing the streets of German defenders. 'They were well on their way to securing the western approach to the beach.'[17]

Elsewhere men from No. 2 troop, under Lieutenant John Hunter-Grey, moved eastwards along the shoreline overrunning several enemy strongpoints. One section smashed their way into a pillbox only to find several startled Germans who had been manning a 50mm anti-tank gun.

> it was not until the RN Beach Group was rounding the mole that the enemy opened fire. The defences soon came to life and there was 20 mm and MG fire on the main body of LCAs as they came in, but none were stopped. One LCA, carrying 3-inch mortars and W/T sets, ran on to an anti-landing stake and sank, but it was close enough to the shore to enable the occupants to salvage the contents . . . The main body landed without many casualties, and the Commando cleared the immediate waterfront, including the Arsenal Barracks.[18]

The next two landing craft came in carrying the rest of No. 1 and No. 2 troops 4 Commando. Once the craft had touched down, the ramps opened and Lieutenant King's section jumped out, moving quickly up the beach along Oranjestraat to the Willelm II Barracks, which they found empty. At that point, two German machine guns began firing at the approaching landing craft, and Lieutenant King immediately ordered his section to attack the enemy positions. Quickly overpowering the German machine-gun crews King's men took ten prisoners. The Germans, at first taken by surprise, began firing at the approaching landing craft as another machine-gun post opened up from the promontory area, code-named Brighton. While this machine gun was firing across the harbour King decided to split his section. He ordered one half to return fire while he took the rest of his men towards Seaford to join up with No. 1 Troop already there.

Back on the beach, in the second wave Lieutenant Albrow and his men landed safely and quickly took up their positions covering the advance along the shoreline of Hunter-Grey's section. In the area code-named Troon, No. 2 advanced quickly encountering little resistance and managed to capture seven defensive positions before the Germans had time to react. Both the captured anti-tank guns and the 75mm guns had been taken from their gun pits and placed in positions where they could be used to engage German targets. The British gun crews that were quickly thrown together for manning these guns learned on the spot how to use these captured weapons and soon the 75mm gun was aimed at targets across the dock where two machine-gun posts and an anti-tank gun were hit and put out of action. The area of the promontory code-named Falmouth was quickly sealed off by Lieutenant Albrow and his section.

By this juncture the Germans had not yet mounted a determined resistance to the landings and the commandos had managed to establish a small beachhead. The approach to the town had been sealed off and the area east of the beach was now secure. Those Germans who were caught by surprise had surrendered and been taken prisoner. The flanks of Uncle Beach had also been secured.

With Nos 1 and 2 Troops ashore and achieving most of their objectives, the third wave, No. 3 Troop, came ashore in their landing craft. Just as they touched down a German 20mm cannon opened up. Fortunately, as the men scrambled out of the landing craft onto the beach the enemy fire was inaccurate and the shells whizzed overhead. No. 3 Troop was commanded by Major Gordon Webb, and as they assembled beyond the dyke he lead his men forward towards their first objective, code-named Braemar, Bellamypark. This was in the town centre and to get to it Webb took his men swiftly along Gravestraat then onto Wilhelminastraat. As they reached the harbour, Webb could see it was under fire from the enemy pillbox, Brighton. Not wanting to get tangled up with it he pushed his men ahead, diverting them away from the harbour down Nieuwstraat. The streets were dark from the early morning drizzle and grey low clouds. As they ran along they occasionally encountered a sniper or machine-gun fire but they continued moving. Only one casualty was taken by No. 3 Troop.

The Second section of No. 3 Troop, as they entered Bellamypark, suddenly encountered an active enemy pillbox that was laying down a determined rate of fire. A decision was taken for most of the section to bypass the park area by fanning out, thus avoiding the fire, while Sergeant Jackson was detailed to lead an assault on the German position. It was all over very quickly and the German defenders managed to get off a few bursts before they were overrun. Unfortunately during this short melee Private Laux was killed. The section lost another man as they began clearing the houses around the edge of the park. Despite very limited resistance, Lieutenant Nicholas Barrass was killed during these operations. While this was taking place, Captain Murdoch McDougall, leading No. 1 Section of 3 Troop, took his men towards the naval barracks on the seafront. McDougall took his men through the back streets and alleys behind the barracks as the main approach, the Boulevard de Ruyter, bristled with enemy pillboxes and strongholds.

As dawn approached and the dark drizzle of the night gave way to grey drizzle of early light, the Germans were waking up to the fact that Allied troops were landing. McDougall continued, pressing forward, leading his men and as they rounded a corner they suddenly came face to face with a group of very surprised Germans. After a brief moment, small arms fire erupted and in the short firefight the commandos accounted for ten enemy dead with a loss of only one trooper. Realising that things were heating up, and that the enemy was now aware of their presence, McDougall lead his men away from the streets into the backyards of houses, down alleyways, over sheds and garden walls to avoid the snipers and machine-gunners that he knew would soon be everywhere.

At the harbour, the pillbox code-named Brighton continued its harassing fire on No. 1 Section and MacDougall, realising he would have to be prepared for a German counter-attack, ordered sentries to be posted in houses along the line of his section's advance to cover this eventuality. However, by doing this it left him with not enough men to clear the naval barracks, his primary objective. Instead, he decided to limit the German's movements within the barrack complex as much as he could by sending in a few men who slowly worked through the many rooms in the barracks where they set up lookout posts to cover the exits.[19]

Meanwhile, No. 3 Troop continued to press on. They had achieved most of their objectives but they were thinly stretched. Realising the danger, Major Webb radioed a request back to headquarters for more men but everyone else was committed. Webb knew he would have to wait until nightfall.

By this time the Germans had finally begun firing accurate mortar and machine-gun fire on Uncle Beach just as No. 5 Troop's LCAs were coming in. As they did their run-in, intense fire from heavy machine guns riddled the water and hit the first LCA. Enemy shells pounded the engine compartment and the coxswain, wounded from the barrage, was no longer able to keep control of the craft. It rammed into the pier. As it sank, the commandos were able to disembark under heavy fire. The second LCA also came under attack from German machine guns and mortars. Confusion reigned as the craft suffered hit after hit, Captain Alexandre Lofi and his men jumped into the water at shoulder depth and began to wade towards the shore.

Once on the beach, the men from both LCAs assembled quickly and began moving along Oranjestraat, Emmastraat and Wilheminastraat. One section, commanded by Lieutenant Paul Chausse was stopped by heavy enemy machine-gun fire in Gravestraat. After a short firefight, Chausse decided to use his 2in mortar teams to suppress the fire from the Germans. Several mortar rounds were fired at the German positions, which were then quickly overrun by the commandos.

Meanwhile, No. 2 Section, commanded by Lieutenant Pierre Amaury was heading down Breestraat after crossing Bellamypark in order to set up a defensive position in Groote Markt. As Amaury's men moved slowly into the market square they were suddenly greeted by heavy machine-gun and sniper fire. Diving into shops and houses for cover, they slowly moved from doorway to doorway around the square, answering the enemy fire with their own. Realising what they were facing, the Germans withdrew from their positions in the square and retreated to the barracks on the seafront which were subsequently attacked by Lieutenant Chausse and the rest of his section.[20]

Prior to the attack, Chausse decided to move forward to work out the safest approach against the barracks. As he did, however, stick grenades thrown by the defenders landed close by and exploded, wounding him. As he lay on the ground two sergeants, Messanot and Paillet, ran out under heavy fire and managed to drag Chausse to safety. The approach to the barracks, for the time being, was too much for them to handle. With Chausse wounded the section moved back to Groote Markt, where they consolidated their position with the rest of No. 5 Troop and waited for reinforcements.

A major crossroads, code-named Bexhill, was situated at the northern end of Flushing between the shipyards and an inland lake Binnenbozem. It was the task of Captain Vourch, commanding No. 6 Troop, to seize these crossroads to stop any German attempt at reinforcing their positions in the centre of the town. Any troops they sent would have to traverse this junction. 'On the left, No. 6 Troop, led to its objective by the Dutch Chief of Police, 'made splendid haste to BEXHILL, and were in position there at an extremely early hour . . . They kept a firm hold on this important bottle-neck throughout the battle'.[21]

The support of a captured 37 mm gun helped No. 2 Troop on the right to make the area between the dry dock and the marine sluice by 0930hrs, while No. 3 Troop pushed on and fought its way to Bellamy Park. Reinforced by 4 K.O.S.B., the invaders had consolidated on the near end of the spit, in the town immediately north-west of the landing beach, and at 'BEXHILL' by 1000 hours.[22] Though casualties so far had been surprisingly moderate, the battle was now being heavily engaged on both the flanks by an enemy who had become aware of the assault too late to do anything but seek desperately to retrieve the lost advantage of a strongly defended sea front. So far as we were concerned, the worst was over. Tactical surprise, seemingly unattainable, had been gained.

Not yet ashore, this thought along with many others must have been going through Vourch's mind as they headed for the beach. Just at their LCA touched down the enemy opened up with machine-gun fire, strafing the vessel as they disembarked. Fortunately, casualties were light but the machine-gun section that was supposed to be with them could not be found. Assembling behind the dyke, Vourch ordered his men to move as quickly as possible and then lead them off the beach.

The post office at Steenen Beer was a strongly held German position and also Vourch's first objective. When Lieutenant Jacques Senee lead his section on a charge at the enemy positions most of the Germans in the post office surrendered and for the diehards that held out, a few grenades were thrown into the building by Senee and his men, which dealt with the hold-outs. Pressing on, Vourch lead his men along Walstraat towards the Bexhill crossroads. As they moved through the streets many local Dutch people began to come out of their houses. The Dutch section with Vourch were a godsend as they communicated with the local people as they went forward. Fortunately, one of the Dutch section leaders, Hendrik van Nahuys, had been a Flushing police officer who was captured by the Germans. He'd managed to escape and was back with the Allies guiding them forward using his local knowledge.

At 0745hrs the troop reached the strongpoint known as Bexhill. Vourch moved his small headquarters across Coosje Buskenstraat while the lead section took up positions covering the crossroads. Suddenly, as the commandos moved across the street, the pillbox, code-named Dover, situated on the sea front opened fire. Shells bounced off the pavement kicking up dust at the feet of the commandos as they ran to take up sheltered positions.

The strongpoint contained a 20mm flak cannon, which was now being used as a close-range defensive weapon. Every time the commandos tried to move into the open it's devastating fire would answer. Vourch now had the street and the strongpoint under watch but his troop was split into two. On the one hand, one of his sections had taken seven German prisoners when they captured a school that overlooked the junction. The commandos consolidated their grip on the crossroads by turning the school into a defensive position while lookouts that Vourch had positioned in key places around the junction had spotted a large section of German soldiers moving along Badhuisstraat in the Bexhill direction. In order to stop these new reinforcements the commandos quickly set up a defensive firing position and opened up on the advancing troops. They scattered the moment the commandos began firing on them.

At this point, the commandos held the crossroads and Vourch knew that he had to hold it for as long as he could even though his troop was split. West towards the seafront, Lieutenant Nahuys had led one subsection by mistake and quickly found himself and his men cut off by German troops who had come in behind him. East of the crossroads, Lieutenant Guy de Montlaur had tried to enter the shipyard gates and capture the shipyard only to be repulsed by accurate enemy fire from the machine-gun post in Aagje Dekenstraat. Captain Vourch ordered his men to form a tight defensive perimeter and when it was done they sat down to wait for reinforcements. Vourch wondered just how long that wait would be, especially how long he would have to wait for the machine-gun section that had been left behind on the beach.

Back on the beach, the Support Weapons Group No. 4 Troop began their run-in to the shore. As the LCAs came in closer, they were suddenly sprayed by heavy enemy fire from two pillboxes. Just before it came ashore the LCA carrying Captain Knyveth Carr and his men rammed an iron bar which brought the craft to a dead stop. Under heavy enemy machine-gun fire the men clambered out of the stricken vessel and began a quick salvage job of their equipment, which included mortars and other light arms. A second LCA that carried the medium machine-gun section arrived on the beach safely as Carr's men headed for the cover of the sea wall. Once they were assembled there Carr took two of his best men and moved quickly back to the LCA stuck on the iron bar and retrieved another mortar with several cases of bombs. Half an hour later the mortar was ready for action.

The machine-gun section was the one that Vourch was waiting for and they arrived 15 minutes behind schedule at Bexhill. In order to make contact with Captain Vourch the machine-gun section commander, Lieutenant Kelly, braved heavy German fire and ran across the junction. However, on his way back he was not so lucky as a bullet from an enemy sniper found its mark. Kelly was hit in the chest. Braving the sniper fire, Kelly's batman dashed out to the wounded officer and managed to drag him into the shelter of a nearby shop. The plan was for the section to cross the junction and support Vourch, but as the first crew tried to cross Lance Corporal Lambert was hit by sniper fire. As Corporal Lambert lay wounded in the street, all was quiet. Realising that Lambert needed urgent medical attention, Private Stoddart ran into the open street towards Lambert. A single shot was fired and Stoddart lay in the street having been mortally wounded in the head.

It was clear to Carr that they couldn't cross the junction at this point so he decided to move further down Scherminkelstraat for a safer crossing point. Ordering smoke to be layed down and supporting fire from the Bren guns in his section, Carr managed to lead his men across the street towards the junction safely. Lambert and Stoddart would have to be picked up later when it was safe to do so.

By ignoring isolated groups of Germans and moving quickly to key strongpoints the commandos had taken, and now held, key positions in the town. Indeed, by 0830hrs a tight perimeter had been established by the commandos in the old town by No. 4 Troop. Behind the seafront to the west of the town Nos 3 and 5 Troop had set up a defensive line while 'NO 6 Troop held "Bexhill" junction with assistance from the support troop.'[23]

By this point radio contact with the sections in the north and west of the town had not yet been established and Lieutenant Colonel Robert Dawson was anxious to know what was happening so he could make further plans. Without the radio he fell back on an old tradition of using runners to gather the information he needed. One runner made contact with Nos 3 and 5 Troop and reported back to Dawson that they were under heavy and determined fire from the German defenders. Another runner told him that No. 4 Commando had a firm control of their positions but they would soon need reinforcements if they were to continue to advance. Dawson began to formulate his plans accordingly.

In his excellent book, Andrew Rawson says that the 4 KOSB landed in five waves using twenty-six LCAs. As they approached Uncle Beach, C Company, the first to touchdown, did so without any trouble. Behind them came B Company and as the men scrambled off the landing craft they quickly joined the men of C Company, who had assembled behind the dyke. The time was 0800hrs. The battalion suffered its first casualty when Captain James Bennett moved forward towards No. 4 Commando's Headquarters. Approaching Bellamypark, he was shot in the back by a German sniper.

Back at Uncle Beach, the remaining landing craft carrying 4 KOSB began their landing approaches. Where the first two landing craft beached without suffering any enemy fire it was not so now. The German machine guns opened up, strafing the landing craft with bullets. Mortar shells began hammering the beach as the craft touched down. Fortunately, casualties were light but the radio and other equipment were hit and badly damaged by shrapnel. Communications between the units on the beach and the mainland were now cut and the battalion's main control radio was also put out of action.

With Bennett now seriously wounded, Lieutenant Colonel Melville headed for the headquarters of No. 4 Commando in Bellamypark. After a brief discussion he returned and ordered C Company to move to Bexhill along with two carrier companies which left the rest of the men in reserve.

The junction code-named Bexhill had rapidly become a killing zone and by the time C Company arrived, around 1000hrs, the situation was such that any movement by Allied troops in the streets would be met by accurate 20mm cannon and machine-gun fire. Captain Colville, commanding C Company, knew that they did not have the heavy weaponry to take on the German 20mm cannon so he ordered C Company to find cover while sending a runner back to Melville for heavier reinforcements.

Lieutenant Colonel Melville, after hearing Colville's report, decided to find out for himself just how bad the situation was and leading B Company he set out for Bexhill. On arrival he led B Company along Walstraat and was fired on by an enemy machine-gun post at 'the end of Badhuisstraat'. This heavy concentrated fire forced the men of B Company to take cover wherever they could, in shops, crouched in doorways, down side streets. Realising that they would not get far in the current situation, Melville ordered his men to use gardens, houses, alleyways whatever means they could for pushing on away from the killing zone of the junction. His objective was to reach the school on the far side of Coosje Buskensstraat so Melville decided to use smoke to cover the crossing. Ordering the carrier sections forward he waited while the smoke slowly began filling the streets obliterating the German's ability to see. It was now, under the cover of smoke, that the men of B Company ran across the street and took cover in the school. Only one platoon got across before the smoke began to clear.

However, slowly but surely, the Scots were tightening their grip on Bexhill. Some 3in mortars were brought up and their fire was concentrated on the German machine-gun post at AAgje Dekenstraat while across the estuary, Canadian artillery guns began pounding streets behind Bexhill. Yet, despite this, German snipers and machine-gun crews targeting Bexhill stayed at their posts and fired on anything that moved in the junction. It was a stalemate and something had to be done to break the deadlock.

Realising there was little more he could do at Bexhill, Lieutenant Colonel Melville returned to his headquarters in Gravestraat. A working radio set finally arrived enabling Melville to communicate with Battalion Headquarters. Reporting to Brigadier McLaren, Melville outlined the situation. The battle for Flushing could not move forward because of the stalemate at Bexhill. All of 4 KOSB was tied up either at Bexhill or fighting alongside 4 Commando pinned down at the strongpoint code-named Dover. Melville believed that the battle could move forward only when 5 KOSB arrived and took over.[24]

According to Rawson, the situation on Uncle Beach was deteriorating as 5 KOSB was getting set to land. 'The Germans targeted the area with every available mortar and gun.'[25] As the LCAs moved into the shore they ran into a storm of lead. Shrapnel and machine-gun shells flew all around them. If they tried to land they would be cut down by this hail of fire. It was decided that the LCAs should return to Breskens.

On Uncle Beach the men ready to help the LCAs unload waited and waited under fire for the LCAs to return. It would only be under the cover of darkness when the LCAs carrying 5 KOSB would return to Uncle Beach.

In the meantime, Lieutenant Colonel Melville made good use of the afternoon to take stock of the situation. On the far side of Coosje Buskenstraat C Company was bogged down but they held a secure perimeter. After capturing a German cook, Captain Colville ordered that his men should be fed with German rations so not all was lost!

At the Dover strongpoint, 4 Commando's attack had been reinforced by D Company but they still had not been able to reach the German bunker. They could only get as close as 50m from the German position before they were forced back by enemy fire. 'Even then, the troops would be forced to emerge via a small window, one at a time,' writes Rawson.[26]

As the afternoon wore on an artillery barrage from 155 Brigade's heavy guns across the estuary pounded the Dover position in an attempt to dislodge the defenders. The attempt failed. While the barrage was taking place 4 Commando with D Company 4 KOSB had moved back from the strongpoint. When the barrage stopped they moved forward only to be met by a hail of gunfire from the Germans still entrenched in Dover. Under the cover of darkness 4 Commando and D Company secured a perimeter around Paarden Markt as well as Groote Markt to reinforce their hold on the area. They would attack Dover again early the next morning.

The De Schelde shipbuilding yards had been entered by A Company, which moved into the offices and workshops of the dockyard but they were held back by intense enemy fire at the dock gates. Evening came and with it information that the Germans had sabotaged several buildings in the dockyard and planned to blow them up during the night. Hearing this intelligence, Lieutenant Colonel Melville ordered A Company out of the area and then sent in a small team to find the booby traps and disarm them.[27]

Down at Uncle Beach, 5 KOSB had finally landed when night fell and pour visibility prevented the Germans from targeting the landing craft. With the Scots now ashore they would be able to renew the attack on the town early in the morning while 4 KOSB would hold their positions. An artillery barrage was to precede the attack.

At Lieutenant Colonel Melville's headquarters some disturbing news was received late in the evening from the head of the Dutch Resistance. On this first day of the Allied assault on Walcheren Island, as the town of Flushing had been attacked, several civilians had been killed or wounded in the fighting. There was a hospital at the south-west corner of the De Schelde aircraft factory and it was here that most of the casualties had been taken, along with people who had gone there to shelter from the artillery bombardments. 'The resistance leader estimated there were over one thousand men, women and children in the area.'[28]

Melville's choices were limited. In his book, Andrew Rawson states that Lieutenant Colonel Melville assured the Resistance leader that he would do his best to ensure that the heavy guns would not target the hospital.[29] He also stated that by first light he would endeavour to get as many civilians out of the battle zone as possible but he wanted something in return. He told the Resistance leader that before the battle began he must get the Dutch people to persuade the Germans to surrender with a promise of fair treatment. All he could do at this stage was wait until morning.

Having now got our grip on the town, we spent the rest of the day in tightening it, building up our strength, and slowly expanding the bridgehead, though not without some hard fighting, particularly at the western corner of the town. 'The situation by nightfall was that the main town area was firmly in our hands, and that the possibility of reinforcement by the enemy was stopped, though some strong points still remained to be mopped up.' The landfall and ferrying cost us about eight L.C.A., and three L.V.Ts., sunk or damaged by gunfire and mines. Most and heartening assistance was given by the R.A.F., for with the weather still poor but improving, aircraft flew in, despite all difficulties, and attacked the enemy throughout the day. In addition to the Mosquitoes, which were busy before first light, 104 sorties were made by Typhoons in immediate support and 48 by Spitfires on pre-arranged targets, a great contribution to the success of the enterprise.[30]

By midnight, Brigadier McClaren had landed on the island and he went straight to 4 Commando Headquarters to meet with Lieutenant Colonel Dawson. Here he ordered that at first light the commandos were to attack the enemy strongpoints Brighton, Worthing and Dover and clear the surrounding areas of enemy defenders.[31]

Fortunately, in the early hours of the morning a message came through from the Canadians that Lieutenant General Daser, the German officer commanding 70th Division, was willing to surrender. He had broadcast the message on the Canadian frequency. It seems Melville's message to the Resistance may have got through to the Germans.

McClaren broadcast a cautious note back to Daser that the white flag of surrender would be respected but that if it was used as a decoy by those Germans prepared to fight to the last they would be dealt with summarily.

While the news of the German willingness to surrender was welcome the Allies were cautious.

Notes

1. Richard Brooks, *Walchern 1944, Storming Hitler's Island Fortress*, Osprey Publishing Ltd, Oxford, 2011.
2. Ibid., pp. 27–8.
3. Army Operational Research Group Report No. 299, 21 Army Group, as cited in Brooks, *Walcheren 1944*, p. 28.
4. Ibid.
5. See Brooks, 'The Walcheren Campaign, Infatuate 1: The Landings at Vlissengen', *Walchern 1944*, p. 31.

6. In Dutch the Fishermen's and Merchants' docks were known as Vissershaven and Koopmanshaven respectively. See Brooks, *Walchern 1944*, p. 31.

7. See 'Report No. 188', Attack on Flushing by 4 Cdo, 1 November 44, p. 8.

8. 'Report No. 69', Special Interrogation Report, Lieutenant General Wilhelm Daser.

9. See 'Report No. 69', The Campaign In NorthWest Europe, Information From German Sources, Part 3, p. 32.

10. See 'Report No. 188', Personal Diary, Major W.E.C. Harrison, 1 November 1944.

11. W.D., 'G' Air Branch, H.Q. First Cdn Army, 1 November 1944.

12. See 'Report No. 188', Attack on Flushing by 4 Commando, 1 November 1944, pp. 11, 12.

13. Ibid., p. 14.

14. Richard Brooks, *Walchern 1944*, p. 7.

15. Ibid., p. 13.

16. Andrew Rawson, *Walcheren: Operation Infatuate*, Pen & Sword, Barnsley, 2003, p. 45.

17. Ibid.

18. 'Report No. 188', 21 Army Group Clearing of the Scheldt, p. 21.

19. Rawson, *Walcheren*, p. 51.

20. Ibid.

21. AEF/4 CDO/C/D, Docket II, Attack on Flushing by 4 Cdo, 1 November 1944.

22. AEF/21 Army Gp/C/F, Docket III, Clearing of the Scheldt.

23. Rawson, *Walcheren*, pp. 45, 57.

24. Ibid., pp. 54–60.

25. Ibid., p. 60.

26. Ibid., p. 61.

27. While Andrew Rawson doesn't mention it in his excellent book, presumably this information came from the Dutch Resistance who were in regular touch with the Allied forces during the assault, *Walcheren*, p. 61.

28. Ibid.

29. Ibid., p. 62.

30. See 'Report No. 188', C.O.H.Q./Y/3: C.O.H.Q. Bulletin Y/47, April 1945, Combined Operations against Walcheren and 'Report No. 188', 21 Army Group, Clearing of the Scheldt, p. 23.

31. Rawson, *Walcheren*, p. 62.

Chapter 14

Commandos Attack Westkapelle

While the assault and capture of Flushing was taking place, the assault on Westkapelle was also well under way. Now ashore, 41 Commando, under the command of Lieutenant Colonel E.C.E. Palmer Royal Marines, began organising itself. A small headquarters was established and B Troop moved quickly towards the western edge of Westkapelle where they took up a position at the edge of the dyke. Meanwhile, along the dyke P Troop had moved to a position covering the northern edge of the village. Here they encountered enemy fire and quickly captured the gun battery at W15 with small arms fire. S Troop had not been idle, and had established a covering position at the south edge of Westkapelle at the church tower situated at the opposite end of the main street. From this vantage point they would be able to attack any German fire that was laid down from the village onto the gap where the rest of the landings would take place.

Coming in close behind 41 Commando was the armour of 79th Armoured Division in four LCTs 'manned by troops of the 1st Lothians and Border Yeomanry and the Royal Engineers'.[1] In the four LCTs the armoured assault groups had four different code-names. They were Bramble, Cherry (LCT 650), Apple and Damson (LCT 513). Both Bramble and Cherry had 1 command Sherman tank each, 2 flail tanks, 2 AVRE tracked vehicles and 1 bulldozer. The other two groups each had, respectively, 1 bulldozer, 2 AVREs and 3 flail tanks.[2] Their jobs were relatively straightforward. They were to provide fire support for 41 Commando by bringing fire onto the German positions in the village and their other key task was to provide fire support for 48 Commando heading into the south dunes area. In addition, they were to attack German troops who had been bypassed by the commandos and neutralise their positions.

It was decided that all the LCTs carrying these four assault groups would beach at the same time, but later decisions were made that saw the landing craft organise into two waves of two landing one behind the other. The reason for this was to avoid any underwater obstacles that could stop the assault in its tracks if one or more of the LCTs hit them. In the front of one of the landing craft of the first wave an AVRE was moved up, while in the same position in one of the landing craft of the second wave a flail tank was positioned.

The plan was for the AVRE to smash through any obstacles such as stakes that were sticking up from the bottom but if it failed to do so then the Flail tank from the other craft would blast its way through. The first wave was formed by Damson and Cherry. Damson was about 40yd ahead and was the first to be hit by enemy fire. Shells howled overhead and one hit the bridge of the bridge-laying AVRE, exploded and blew the bridge onto the flail tank in front of it. Another shell exploded on the fascine of the other AVRE and set it alight, while further shells pounded the rest of the vehicles in the craft and blew a hole in the vessel itself. In all, the landing craft received six direct hits from the gun battery at W15. Casualties were relatively light with 'one naval rating being killed, and three wounded, three of the four protective section from 10 Commando were also wounded. There were no casualties to the tank crews.'[3]

We turned around and lay offshore, flooding and on fire. All hands rigged fire hoses and extinguishers. The burning Fascine threatened disaster to H.E. charges. Tank crew contrived to jettison HE and fought flames. Crew of this tank under command L/Sergeant J. Black very brave. Craft put about to go alongside hospital ship. Many craft burning and mines all around us.[4]

With the stricken craft beached the troops disembarked and moved off equipment that was still operating, while Apple moved across to help fight the fires. All the flail equipment on the flail tanks was damaged from enemy fire and could no longer function. Only one gun was working, the waterproofing around the tanks was damaged and the bridge-laying AVRE had lost its bridge. The fascine AVRE had lost its fascine and its waterproofing and its petard on top of the turret was no longer operating. The only equipment still serviceable was the bulldozer. 'The craft was then ordered to transfer its casualties to a hospital LCI(S) [Landing Craft Infantry (Small)] and return to Ostend. During the transfer of casualties further damage was done by the blast from the mines struck by other craft.'[5]

Enemy fire from the battery at W15 now raked Cherry as it sailed in towards the beach. No serious damage was sustained from the first two direct hits but two more hits on the stern of the landing craft killed one naval rating and wounded three others just as the craft was about to touch down on the beach. It was immediately ordered out and as it turned around and sailed away more hits from enemy fire struck her.

Red Beach had become too hot and Bramble was now ordered to steam into White Beach and unload its troops and equipment there. It did so expecting the same reception as at Red Beach but it landed safely without being hit. Cherry tried a second time to touch down at Red Beach but it quickly came under fire as it approached with several shells striking the bridge of the bridge-laying AVRE. Finally giving way, the damaged bridge crashed onto the flail tank in front of the AVRE. The other flail in the craft was hit as well but luckily sustained no serious damage. The commander of the landing craft ordered his crew to swing the vessel to the right and head for White Beach away from the enemy fire. This vessel quickly moved out of range, heading for the alternate beach where it touched down on the right side of Bramble and began unloading.

Seeing the problems at Red Beach, the commander of Apple also decided to steam into White Beach and landed his craft on the left side of Bramble at 1100hrs. This was 1½ hours past H-Hour and 50 minutes after the first landings had taken place.

On White Beach, unloading was partially successful. The weather was atrocious with a constant drizzle that made the clay on the beach soft and boggy. Four vehicles managed to disembark from Bramble but the crew of the first AVRE found themselves stuck fast in the clay as they disembarked. They did manage to land both flail tanks, the command Sherman tank and the D7 armoured bulldozer without any difficulty. As the second AVRE was disembarking it came under heavy fire and the bridge it was carrying was shot away, which jammed the vehicle. Once on the beach, they moved off towards the village of Westkapelle. However, not all the vehicles got off the beach, as Rawling states. Many of the heavy tracked vehicles such as the tanks and AVRES were bogged down 'well below the high water mark'.[6]

The AVRE, command Sherman, a flail tank and the D7 bulldozer all disembarked safely from Cherry and they all reached the village except for the D7 bulldozer, which became bogged down on the beach. In the landing craft, the second flail tank was now trapped under the bridge that had been shot away from the bridge-laying AVRE.

However, the disembarkation process from Apple proved to be a small disaster. Nothing left the beach. For example, the first flail tank reached the beach and got ashore with no problems but the second got bogged down and as the first flail turned back to help the second one it too became bogged down in the wet sticky clay. The craft moved out and steamed a little down the beach in order to land again in a better place. It was to no avail as its third flail managed to land without problems but it was soon bogged down in the soft oozing clay. The bridge-laying AVRE from Apple managed to disembark and lay down its bridge. It crossed without having any problems but as it rolled off the bridge it was immediately bogged down in the oozing slime, as was the second AVRE from Cherry. At this point the commander of the landing craft decided to move off leaving the fragile party on the shore.

The total number of vehicles that were able to reach the shore on that day amounted to 2 command Sherman tanks, 3 flail tanks, 2 AVRES and 1 D7 bulldozer. As has been seen, the rest of the heavy vehicles landed were stranded in the soft clay and eventually drowned by the high tides.[7]

The second wave of landings was supposed to touch down at White Beach 5 minutes after H-hour, with the third wave coming in at H+25 minutes. Elements of 48 Commando were in each wave with objectives in the south dunes area. The second wave included B, X and Y Troops with A and Z Troops in the third wave. The remaining elements of the second and third waves were to land on the gap at the north shoulder. In the second wave there were elements of 41 Commando A and X Troops with Y Troop and 10 Inter Allied Commando in the third wave.

On the run-in to the beach the LCTs containing 48 Commando, under Lieutenant Colonel J.L. Moulton, were shelled but luckily weren't hit. The shelling was coming mostly from the south and also covered the beach. However, 48 Commando were able to touch down at 1010hrs north of the Westkapelle gap. Disembarking, they split into their troops and headed for their individual objectives. For example, B Troop was to attack the low pillboxes on the south shoulder of the gap but when they did they were found to be empty of the enemy. Within 10 minutes of landing X Troop had moved swiftly towards its objective, the radar station at W154 and it was also empty of the enemy. Fanning out, they quickly cleared the area of any enemy troops they found and took them prisoner.

X Troop was then ordered to move to strongpoint W285 and mount a quick and sudden attack. Overrunning it, they took more than a dozen prisoners. For a brief few moments the commandos rested here, allowing those troops coming up behind them to pass through their position before moving onto their next objective.

The third wave beached 18 minutes after the second, and also experienced enemy shellfire. As the shells rained down one struck its mark and hit LCT (serial 13) damaging vehicles and forcing the men to manhandle them ashore. As the LCT pulled out it hit a mine and quickly sank. Even though the beach was being shelled and one or two amphibians were knocked out the advance was moving along smoothly with limited opposition.

The third wave also carried elements of 48 Commando, which by 1115hrs had managed to achieve its first objective, which was to secure a footing on the south dunes. They were then ordered to advance towards the Battery W13 and destroy it.

At about 1030hrs that day the large gun battery at W13 had stopped firing inexplicably. It had been one of the main batteries responsible for so much devastation of the support squadron. Now it lay silent. The Weasels of 48 Commando had been unable to keep up with the troops on foot, which meant that the equipment they were carrying for communications and other stores could not get to the leading troops. Lieutenant Colonel Moulton was unaware that Major de Stacpoole, his troop commander, had launched an attack against the silent battery hoping for a quick victory. Unfortunately, the fact that the guns were silent did not mean that the enemy personnel, some seventy odd men, were silent as well. They put up such stiff resistance against the commando assault that the attack was repulsed and de Stacpoole was killed.[8]

The reason why W13 had stopped firing was because it had simply run out of ammunition. The flooding now prevented the Germans from resupplying the battery. In light of this information, one could say that this lack of ammunition had a profound effect on the outcome of the Battle of Walcheren. That, however, is speculation. What is sure is that the enemy soldiers in the garrison at W13 would not surrender. Indeed, they fought back with an intensity that resulted in the three leading troops being mortared and suffering severe casualties. 'In one troop everyone above the rank of corporal was killed or wounded, in another troop the commander was mortally wounded and the Royal Artillery Forward Observation Officer, who could call in fire from HMS *Roberts*, was killed along with his orderly.'[9]

Lieutenant Colonel Moulton decided the only way to attack the enemy gun emplacements was to bring more firepower to bear on the battery. He managed to scrounge a radio set and radioed the Canadian artillery positions across the Scheldt to open fire on W13. He also arranged for an air attack to be made on the battery by rocket-firing Typhoons. This attack took place at 1545hrs when the Canadian artillery opened up and pounded the battery and the area around it for several minutes. With the smoke from the bombardment still in the air, the Typhoons arrived and hammered the target with 500lb bombs and rockets. Finally, as the afternoon was drawing to a close and darkness was falling W13 was taken by the Allies.[10]

Meanwhile, elements of 41 Commando, A Troop, Commando Headquarters and Y Troop had landed on the north shoulder of the gap at 1018hrs. Once the two landing craft touched down, the troops quickly disembarked and dashed across the beach to the dyke where they split up and headed for their objectives. A Troop's first task was to mop up any enemy resistance on the southern edge of the town, which they did quickly. However, at the east end of the village, the enemy were in the tower W268 and they began firing at A Troop. Pinned down by the fire from the tower, all that A Troop could do was return the fire. Calling for amour, they waited in their positions until the tanks arrived.

On the beaches things were not going well for the Royal Engineers. They landed in four LCTs carrying a variety of equipment and vehicles that included bulldozers, flail tanks and AVRES. Their job was to clear away any obstacles and build passages that would get the vehicles off the beaches, onto the dykes and into action. There were eight bulldozers in all. Unfortunately, three of the four LCTs beached in the wrong place so that when the bulldozers were disembarked they immediately went into oozing slimy mud and were stuck fast. This mud was below the high-water mark and out of the eight bulldozers only two managed to get through the mud onto the dyke. When the tide came in the marooned bulldozers were drowned. In addition to the bulldozers, four AVRE tanks and three flails were also stuck in the mud and drowned.

However, the two remaining bulldozers did not fair that well either. One had been landed on the wrong side of the gap and the other on the right side of the gap. The one on the right side fell into a submerged crater as it moved slowly through shallow water. It too was drowned. That left only one bulldozer for the Royal Engineers and it was on the wrong side of the gap in the dyke. The LVTs or Buffalo and Weasel tracked vehicles were also lost. Of the five vehicles carried by the LCTs only one managed to get ashore, the rest either being hit by shellfire or damaged and destroyed by mines.[11]

When A Troop of 41 Commando put their call through for armour to knock out the tower in the village of Westkapelle only one Sherman was able to move into range, and it began firing on the roof of the tower. Shells from the Sherman's guns pounded into the tower, setting it on fire. Clouds of dust and debris were thrown into the air as the shells exploded, badly damaging the building. The Germans not killed or wounded in this attack, realising that there was nothing they could do, ran out into the street surrendering as showers of bricks and masonry fell all around them as the tank continued firing.[12]

Meanwhile, X Troop operating behind A Troop had been ordered to clear the main street of enemy soldiers, and this was achieved. A reconnaissance mission was set up to check on whether batteries W14 and W22 were still operative. As the commandos moved closer to the batteries they realised that they were both under water and out of action. Clearing the remainder of the town had fallen on to B Troop's shoulders.

At 1035hrs three more LCTs arrived at the beach and began unloading their troops and equipment. However, one craft was unable to lower its ramp because it had run into an iron stake which had caused serious damage. Wallowing in the water, for 10 minutes the crew and troops of the craft tried desperately to free the ramp but to no avail. Finally, the commander ordered that everyone should leave the landing craft as quickly as possible and take what they could with them. They had to manhandle some of the amphibians into the water while the rest, up to their necks in water, began to wade or swim ashore, soaking wet.

All in all, they managed to salvage three Buffaloes and four Weasels by 1115hrs.

From the other two craft that had landed safely, 5 Troop and Y Troop of 41 Commando managed to get ashore and were held in reserve until they received the signal that the town was clear of the enemy. Of the these three landing craft the one that had struck the iron stake was hit ten times by direct enemy shellfire and eventually sank while another hit a mine on the way out after unloading and sank.

In order for more landings to take place on the south edge of the Westkapelle gap the Allies needed to establish a position on the north dunes to ensure the approaches and the beaches would be free from enemy fire. Troops assigned to gain this northern position included elements of 41 Commando and 10 Commando as well as First Platoon 510 Field Company Royal Engineers.

The village of Westkapelle was finally cleared of enemy positions just before noon on the first day of the assault. However, small arms fire from the gun battery at W15 along with its 3in gun had P Troop pinned down. With the Allies in control of the village, the Germans began shelling it from gun positions beyond it. The main one was from W17 whose 150mm field gun began pounding the village. For the Allies to move forward from Westkappelle to the rest of the island, and join up with the Flushing assault group, they needed to deal with the enemy gun batteries.

By the time the Allies had captured the town of Westkapelle there was not much left standing. It had suffered several raids from the RAF, an artillery barrage from across the Scheldt as well as a hammering from the Bombardment Squadron that had fired on it from off the coast. The town was so smashed and ruined that the roads could not be made out clearly. They were 'completely unidentifiable and their course could only be conjectured by assuming that they had previously existed as intervals between the lines of shattered ruins that had once been buildings'.[13] The Westkapelle Tower was also in ruins after being shelled by the Sherman tank. The roof of this solid structure had been utterly destroyed by the tank fire.

By this time, Lieutenant Colonel E.C.E. Palmer, commanding 41 Commando, was on the scene and decided that an attack on the coastal gun battery W15 was necessary. Y Troop, laying down smoke, began the assault from W15's flank using small arms and mortar fire just after 1200hrs. Within 30 minutes it had overrun the German position, put the gun out of action and taken 120 prisoners. With this position now silenced and secure, Y Troop continued their advance forward and attacked German positions in and around the lighthouse. The enemy resistance crumbled quickly and more prisoners were taken. Across the northern approach to the village, 10 Commando had established a secure position. At the lighthouse Y Troop had been told to stay where they were and wait for further orders, as had 10 Commando. Before any further advance could take place, the enemy gun battery at W17 needed to be silenced.

The quickest way for the Allies to silence the guns at W17 was with air support. At 1300hrs the commandos put in a call for just that, while Brigade Headquarters, now ashore and established in the village, ordered the advance on Domburg, the next major obejctive, to begin. This advance fell onto the shoulders of 41 Commando while 10 Commando, along with A and S Troops of 41 Commando, stayed behind in Westkapelle to ensure the village remained secure and could be used as a base for continuing the assault to clear Walcheren. Meanwhile, in the concrete gun housing at W15, 10 Commando had established its headquarters.

The air support arrived 3 hours after the call went out. Each loaded with a single 500lb bomb, twenty-four Spitfires flew over Westkapelle towards the enemy gun battery at W17. From the ground, the commandos watched the Spitfires peel off into their dives, release their bombs on the target and climb away, circling round again for another attack. A total of eighteen bombs smashed into the battery sending shrapnel and debris flying in all directions. The Spitfires came in again, strafing the German position with 20mm cannon and .50 machine-gun fire. From different directions the fighters attacked, firing their guns and cannon at the hapless enemy below. In all, 2,096 rounds of 20mm cannon and 3,290 rounds of .50 machine gun were fired at the battery.[14]

The result was that the battery at W17 was now silenced, as was the battery at W283 which had also been bombed and strafed by the Spitfires. Amid the smoke, flames and dust the Germans in both batteries slowly came out to surrender impeding the last part of the advance into Domburg. By 1815hrs it was becoming too dark to advance further and with the main crossroads in Domburg now in Allied hands a decision was taken to halt and wait for daylight. In the centre of the town, P Troop had taken up a covering position while Y Troop covered their right flank all the way down to the point where the ground was flooded from the gaps blown in the dykes. Further back in reserve was B Troop. However, in the dunes the commandos still faced a determined enemy dug in on one of the highest dunes. Here X Troop decided to contain the enemy until they could attack the following morning.

Finally, as dusk fell on the first day, D-Day, after W17 had been put out of action, enemy fire on the landing beaches ended.

Examining the first day of the assault on Westkapelle, it is worth considering some of the other elements that were in action that day. Fire support and armour deserve a mention here. Indeed, it will be shown how effective armour was in the days to come after D-Day.

Regarding fire support, 41 Commando was accompanied by 68 and 71 Forward Operating Bases (FOB) and a Forward Observation Officer (FOO).

The FOO was able to call on the fire of 155mm batteries of 1, 51, and 59 Heavy Regiment Royal Artillery (HY Regt RA). 1 HY Regiment records that at 1016hrs the FOO reported he was established ashore, at 1020hrs began calling for fire, continued shooting for the rest of the day, and at 1840hrs was established in Domburg.[15]

Interestingly, around 1245hrs 68 FOB contacted HMS *Warspite* calling for fire support on the lighthouse area but at that time the positions of Allied troops were not known so *Warspite* didn't start shelling. In fact, this request for fire support was later cancelled and that FOB did not call for fire on any other targets.

As far as armour is concerned, the tanks that had managed to land were able to get off the beach and into the main street with a certain degree of difficulty. Their objective was to find a position where they could provide fire support to 48 Commando in the south. Headway was slow because of the craters and flooding but two flail tanks managed to find suitable positions from which they could provide fire support if needed.

The armoured vehicles had left the beach by destroying the beach obstacles and making a lane through them. Leaving the beach was one thing but getting around the craters was something different. Houses had to be demolished and the rubble bulldozed into a lane for the armour to move through to get past the craters. Elsewhere, trees had to be ripped up in order to bypass large craters, making the going very difficult. So it was not until dusk that the tanks managed to take up their positions at the tower. Unfortunately, those tanks still on the beach at high tide were drowned.

The approach, the bombardment and the successful landing, which the sacrifice of the Royal Navy made possible, were thus described to the House of Commons by the First Lord of the Admiralty:

In daylight, the time of assault being dependent on tidal conditions, the Westkapelle force approached the coast and when close inshore was heavily engaged by the coast defences, all known batteries going into action against them. The gun support squadron composed of converted landing-craft of various types manned by Bluejackets and Marines, under command of Commander K.A. Sellar, Royal Navy, stood close inshore and engaged these batteries at pointblank range, while tank-landing craft carrying the Royal Marine Commandos beached in succession and discharged their vehicles.

This process was slow as they could only beach two at a time in the gap in the dyke previously breached by the R.A.F. By their determination and gallantry, the landing-craft support squadron drew most of the enemy's fire, and the Marine Commandos were landed successfully without heavy casualties. Once ashore, however, Commandos came up against tough opposition at nearly all the enemy batteries and strong points, which they cleared in succession with utmost resolution. As the weather improved during the forenoon close air support was afforded by the R.A.F. in increasing degree and air spotting became available to the bombarding squadron during the afternoon.

The gallantry and determination of landing craft crews and of the Royal Marine Commandos were equalled by that of the naval beach party, which had to work under gun and mortar fire throughout D-Day, and for a large proportion of D-plus one, during which enemy fire could still be brought to bear on the gap in the dyke. Difficulties were experienced in landing stores for the force because of this, and later the weather worsened and prevented supply by sea. Stores were dropped by air on D-plus four and these and rations captured from the enemy enabled the Commandos to complete the clearance of the western half of the island . . .

The great success of these operations, which had perforce to be undertaken under difficult and somewhat unfavourable conditions against a desperate enemy, was not achieved without relatively heavy casualties to craft and personnel. Of the total of 25 support craft engaged, nine were sunk and eight damaged, and of their crews 172 officers and men were killed and 200 wounded.

Of 47 other major landing craft engaged, four were sunk and others damaged. The casualties in these craft and in the attack on Flushing were 21 officers and men killed and missing, 81 wounded. The Royal Marine Commandos suffered 37 officers and men killed, 77 missing, 201 wounded.[16]

Notes

1. See Rawling, *Cinderella Operation*, p. 125.
2. Army Operational Research Group Report No. 299.
3. Ibid.
4. An excerpt from a report by Lieutenant Sloan, an army officer who was onboard while this action took place, as cited in Rawling, *Cinderella Operation*, p. 126.
5. Army Operational Research Group Report No. 299.
6. See Rawling, *Cinderella Operation*, p. 127. Rawling states that accounts differ as to the

details of the vehicles that were stranded but it seems that somewhere between '9 and 13 AVREs, Flails and bulldozers were abandoned to the rising tide and were drowned'.

7. The figures in this paragraph come from the Army Operational Research Group Report No. 299 but Rawling also agrees with these figures.

8. See Rawling, *Cinderella Operation*, p. 129.

9. Ibid.

10. Ibid.

11. Ibid., p 131, cited from the Combined Operations Headquarters Bulletin.

12. It is interesting to note that Rawling states that only one Sherman was able to open fire on the tower yet the report from the Army Operational Research Group No. 299 states that there was more than one tank involved in this. Perhaps another AVRE? Ibid., p. 132.

13. Ibid.

14. Army Operational Research Group Report No. 299.

15. Ibid.

16. Ibid., 'Report No. 188', *The Times*, 16 November 1944.

Chapter 15

Support

While continuing with the narrative of this book it is worthwhile detailing the support the commandos received on the first day and throughout the operations to clear Walcheren Island. For without this support, it is highly likely the operations could not have been a success. In the previous chapter, the First Lord of Admiralty described the operations on Walcheren to Parliament and in that address he mentioned the support from the Royal Navy and the RAF along with elements of the British Army, such as the Royal Engineers, supporting the troops attacking the Germans.

D-Day for the assault was 1 November 1944. In support of the main landings was the air campaign, although:

> at dawn, on 1 November, weather conditions at the aerodromes prevented the aircraft from leaving the ground . . . off WALCHEREN, conditions were fair. The sky was overcast but appeared to be clearing, and later the sun shone in the gaps which appeared in the clouds . . . Sea conditions were favourable and so in the hope that air conditions would improve, the expedition closed the island and the big naval guns opened fire . . . At H-hour, the first Typhoons appeared and from that moment the air programme went ahead.[1]

Actually, though the 'cabrank' rocket-firing Typhoons flew over on time:

> it was apparent that the touchdown was to be behind schedule, they were held up for a few minutes until the LCT(R)s had discharged their rockets. When these had been fired the Group Captain, Air Controller, on HQ ship, gave them the 'all clear', and the Typhoons pressed home a determined attack just as the LCTs were about to land. There is no doubt, that the determined action of the Typhoons had a profound effect on the operation at a time when the support squadron was not only suffering

severe casualties from the still active batteries, but had also received some involuntary discharges from the rocket craft.[2]

Commander K.A. Sellar, RN, of the Support Squadron had a word to say later in appreciation: 'I have no doubt that the landing was materially assisted by Rocket-firing Typhoons, which plastered the strong-points close to the Radar Station on the southern shoulder of the Gap about H-5.'[3] The importance of the intervention of the Typhoons was thus signalled from the control ship: 'Timely and well instituted sp by RP Typhoons undoubtedly vital factor in turning scale to our advantage at a time when 80 per cent support craft out of action due to enemy fire.'[4]

According to the Army Operational Research Group Report No. 299, the plan was for the landings to take place in waves. For the first wave B, P and S Troops of 41 Commando, carried in three LCI(s), were to land at Red Beach at the north end of the Westkapelle gap at 0945hrs. They were to be supported by an armoured assault group from 87 Assault Squadron Royal Engineers and 1 Lothians in four LCTs.[5]

To cover the landing craft the Royal Navy decided to wage a separate battle with the shore batteries while the landing craft slipped into shore with comparative immunity from the shattering cannonade opened up by the still capable and very active enemy gunners.

The Support Squadron led the advance, sailing on a final course set due east to arrive off shore at H-20 minutes, the leading groups of landing craft being astern of them. Firing from the shore was first observed at 0715hrs, coming from the batteries at Domburg, which appeared, however, to be firing at Flushing. HMS *Warspite* and HMS *Roberts*, part of the Support Squadron, opened fire at 0820hrs, but without the benefit of spotting aircraft. At 0848hrs the squadron passed a point 5 miles off the beach and deployed. The battle was joined 2 minutes later. All craft were now being heavily fired on by every German battery from the north of Westkapelle, about 5 miles south of the gap. The ensuing action is briefly outlined in the Naval Force Commander's report:

From this time until 1230, the craft of the Support Squadron were continuously engaged with the enemy batteries, firstly in support of the Commandos advance to the south. Their losses were heavy but they stuck to their job of engaging the enemy, thereby drawing the enemy's fire and enabling the landings to proceed . . . A number of direct shoots were carried out by all ships both before and after H-Hour, both at pre-arranged and opportunity targets. Spotting aircraft could NOT take off from their airfields in the United Kingdom until NOON. Air O.P. were sent but proved ineffective due to poor communications. Immediately that air spotting and F.O.B. became available p.m., some effective shoots were carried out. Bombarding ships withdrew to the southward at dusk, HMS WARSPITE returning to the United Kingdom.[6]

It may be remarked that:

HMS EREBUS and HMS ROBERTS returned to the area at 0700 on D-1. A number of shoots in answer to call for fire were carried out. Good visibility and air spotting enabled effective shooting to be carried out. They were sailed for the United Kingdom at 1730, after receipt of signals from C.C.R.A., 2nd Canadian Corps and Commander 4th S.S. Brigade, that they would NOT be required the following day.[7]

As a testimony to the devotion with which the crews of the support craft sailed in to meet almost certain annihilation the following passage in the Force Commander's report is worthy of record:

Meanwhile L.C.G.(M)s [Landing Craft Gun (Medium)] 101 and 102 with their supporting L.C.S.(L)s [Landing Craft Support (Light)] had been ordered in to beach at previously specified points on the northern and southern shoulders of the Gap respectively. Each had their pre-selected targets of pillboxes close to and commanding the approaches of the positions on which L.C.I.(S)s and L.C.T.s were later to beach to unload. Keeping well up tide which was known to be extremely strong (possibly up to 6 knots on the beam of their approach course) these two craft and their attendant L.C.S.(L)s went in at maximum speed against heavy opposition. Though it was not known in the case of the L.C.G.(M) 102 what damage was sustained before beaching, both craft were seen to beach in their correct position at H Hour, continuing to fire at their target. L.CG.(M) 102 was seen to be on fire though this was apparently got under control only to break out again later. She was last seen burning apparently on the beach or possibly broached to near it [*sic*]. L.C.G.(M) 101 remained beached and firing until 1003 when she un-beached and came out at best speed and under fire, only to sink by the stern abeam of L.C.H. 269 some minutes later. I cannot speak highly enough of the courage, determination and devotion to duty of L.C.G.(M)s 101 and 102 and their supporting L.C.S.(L)s particularly Lieutenant S.N. Orum, R.N.V.R. who led in the southern three L.C.S.(L)s at point-blank and what proved to be suicidal range of the strong-points on the southern shoulder of the Gap. All three L.C.S.(L)s on the southern side were seen to be on fire, beached or close to the beach. An L.C.P.(L) was sent to make smoke and to pick up all the survivors she could. At the time of writing this Report no survivors have been contacted from L.C.G.(M) 102 and L.C.S.(L) 252. One survivor has been reported from L.C.S.(L) 258, but no report is yet available. That these craft accomplished their mission is I think reflected in the fact that shortly after landing, the Colonel Commanding 41 Commando made a signal saying he was ashore and casualties had been very light.[8]

The decision to maintain close action under enemy fire was a deliberate one, made by Commander 'Monkey' Sellar, with the intention of attracting the fire of the German guns away from the commandos onto his Support Squadron for as long as he could sustain the resultant losses to his craft and still continue to give effective support to the troops ashore. The following extract from his report is of great interest:

It was early realised that we were up against formidable opposition and that losses and damage were to be expected in craft engaging shore batteries at close range. The test of whether the maintenance of close action was justified was considered to be the progress of the Commando landings. It was evident from signals received that progress of landing and uploading was continuing satisfactorily and it was known that casualties in what may be termed the 'Trade' forces were light. I, therefore, considered that so long as the Germans made the mistake of concentrating their fire at the Support Squadron, close action was justified and losses acceptable. In fact, I decided that if there were signs of batteries selecting incoming loaded L.C.T.s as their primary target even closer action would be ordered so as to force the Germans to fire at the Support Squadron. Accordingly, no withdrawal was envisaged until about noon by which time the advancing Commandos were reported to have captured (W286) adjacent to (W13). It then became difficult under the prevailing conditions to fire accurately at (W13) without fear of hitting our own troops next door in strong-point (W286). By about 1230, it was known that only L.C.G.(L)s 9 and 10 and L.C.S.(L)s 254 and 259 remained fit for action and it was clear that the Support Squadron was no longer able to close to the desired range for continued support to the advance of the 48 Commando, (W11) and (W13) being still most active and apparently unfired at. I, therefore, considered that further support must come from the heavy ships, at all events, until the two heavy batteries had been engaged, neutralized or knocked out by heavier metal than we had at our disposal.[9]

Commander Sellar's comments on the significance of this battle of batteries versus craft further illustrates the nature of this problem as it was originally posed at Headquarters First Canadian Army:

> It was again evident that the old historical principle established after experience in action between a well-sited fort and an attacking ship, the odds are bound to be on the fort. This Operation proved no exception. It is submitted that although, in this instance, the battle was ultimately won – at a cost – losses and casualties would have been lighter in the Support Squadron if the active batteries could have been successfully bombed or shelled during the assault and throughout the forenoon. Even then, this bombing or shelling would not necessarily have had the effect of knocking the batteries out as it was once again proved that only a direct hit on a strongly emplaced gun will knock it out, but it would probably have had a disturbing effect on the accuracy and rate of fire. In fact an observer, just returned, has stated that no large gun in either (W13) or (W11) had received a direct hit from a heavy gun though there were many near misses. It is gratifying that this Officer reports, however, that he found one of the emplaced guns in (W13) where a 4.5" shell – presumably from an L.C.G.(L) – had entered through the slit and burst on the rear concrete wall. This observer also stated that in his opinion, these defences of WALCHEREN were 'much stronger than those at DEN HAAN'. It may be added that they have also been described with authority as 'some of the strongest defences in the world'.[10]

Notes

1. Operation Infatuate, 4 SS Brigade's Assault on Walcheren, 1 November 1944, p. 7.
2. 'Report No. 188', 21 Army Gp/C/F, Docket III, Clearing of the Scheldt, p. 22.
3. Ibid., Operation Infatuate, Naval Commander, Force 'T'.
4. Ibid., Air Branch, H.Q. First Canadian Army, 1 November 1944.
5. Army Operational Research Group Report No. 299.
6. Ibid.
7. 'Report No. 188', Operation Infatuate II, Naval Commander, Force 'T', Section One, pp. 2, 4.
8. Ibid., Appendix 'E', p. 6.
9. Ibid., p. 8.
10. Ibid., pp. 9, 10 and C.O. H.Q./Y/3, Bulletin Y-47, April 1945, Combined Operations against Walcheren.

Chapter 16

Domburg and Beyond

The following morning, D+1, at 0800hrs, the Germans began withdrawing along the dunes towards the north east of Walcheren Island. Brigade Headquarters was ordered to hand over to 10 Commando and return to Westkapelle 3 hours later. Then 10 Commando began the march to Domburg, with 4 Troop arriving at 1530hrs and 5 Troop half an hour later. Enemy sniping at Domburg was increasing in intensity at this time so B and X Troops, from 41 Commando, were put under the command of 10 Commando. To deal with the sniping problem, fire support from armour was called for and by 1800hrs tanks from 1 Lothians and 87 Assault Squadron Royal Engineers arrived and began pounding enemy positions. While enemy small arms fire ceased very quickly throughout the night of D+½, enemy shells and mortar bombs continued to be fired at the advancing Allies. By 2000hrs 41 Commando had moved back to Westkapelle.[1]

On D+1 HMS *Roberts* provided fire support throughout the day on five different enemy gun batteries. Using spotting aircraft to pinpoint the targets, the firing was north of Domburg on batteries W18, W19 and two other batteries on the north coast. The first firing took place at 0837hrs when the pilot flying the spotter aircraft provided rough coordinates for firing on W18, however, only eight rounds were fired as the pilot was unable to provide exact coordinates to the artillery fire team. At 0910hrs three shells from the ship's guns ripped into the German gun battery W19, each one a direct hit. The same battery received another battering a little more than an hour-and-a-half later when HMS *Roberts* again opened fire, sending thirteen high-explosive shells hammering into strongpoints, slit trenches, bunkers and gun emplacements around W19. In the spotter aircraft, the pilot ordered more fire to be brought to bear on the batteries and the gun crews on HMS *Roberts* fired fourteen rounds, the shells hammering and exploding with direct hits on the battery. From his aircraft the pilot could see the shelling had caused a lot of damage and that activity had stopped, but the guns themselves were still intact. Later in the afternoon, at 1450hrs the Germans fired flak at the spotting aircraft and the pilot relayed the coordinates of the flak position back to HMS *Roberts*. A few minutes later, the enemy flak position was plastered with shells from HMS *Roberts'* 4in guns, many of which were direct hits.

According to the Army Operational Research Group Report No. 299, 'The Westkapelle Assault on Walcheren', the following day, D+2, there was no fire support from either the RAF or the navy. The main event that day was when 10 Commando captured 211 prisoners after advancing about a mile or so beyond Domburg. In this case, fire support was from the Sherman tanks and the commandos lost only one killed and four wounded during the advance. Elsewhere, 87 Assault Squadron's last remaining bulldozer was lost when trying to haul some of the commando vehicles out of the mud. The bulldozer ran over a mine and was put permanently out of action.

While all this was taking place, 48 Commando situated in the south dunes area, had captured the batteries and strongpoints W154, W285 and W286 with virtually no opposition from the Germans. However, they were now approaching W13, which they knew, was heavily defended.

At 1140hrs Y troop attacked but was quickly repulsed by enemy machine-gun fire. At this point, 48 Commando had no other weapons available for support and had to make do with what they carried. During D-Day for 48 Commando, the tanks from 1 Lothians were still moving through the village and so were not yet available to provide fire support as reported by 66 FOB. However, 67 FOB had been in contact with HMS *Roberts* for several minutes and ordered the ship to stop firing on W13 because 48 Commando was somewhere in the vicinity. Just after midday, four rocket-firing Typhoons arrived overhead and immediately attacked W13. Rolling into their dives, they fired their rockets and strafed the enemy gun battery with 20mm cannon fire. In all, the aircraft fired 30 rockets at the emplacement and more than 1,700 rounds of 20mm ammunition. However, in the report the diarist does not indicate what the results of this attack were.

At 1310hrs, fire was called on the German gun battery at W287 from HMS *Roberts*. Aboard the ship, the gun crews hammered home five rounds into their guns and fired them in quick succession, scoring three direct hits on the enemy gun battery. The gun crews on HMS *Roberts* were active once again 17 minutes later, this time firing another barrage of shellfire onto the battery. However, the first two rounds landed short of the target. A few minutes later, the controller at 67 Forward Observation Base and his telegraphist were killed when German mortar fire from the battery at W13 found their positions. Something had to be done to silence this gun battery.

A plan was quickly formulated to put this battery out of action. Artillery from Breskens and fire from HMS *Roberts* would start, followed by an air attack. At 1545hrs the barrage began and lasted 15 minutes. As the barrage died away, eight Typhoons, armed with two 500lb bombs each, attacked the battery, pounding it with bombs and strafing the installation with cannon fire. The pilots reported two direct hits on a concrete building while the forward observation officer reported that one of the gun casemates was torn apart by a bomb that also destroyed the gun and killed the gun crew. There is some controversy over where the bomb came from. The navy claimed that this destruction was the result of naval shellfire. However, as only six unobserved naval shells were fired between 0930 and 1000 it is unlikely that this damage was a result of naval gun fire.[2]

Once the air attacks by the Typhoon fighter-bombers was over, and the fighters left the area, the ground assault on W13 began. At 1610hrs, Z Troop led the assault with A Troop providing fire support. Unfortunately, Z Troop was caught by mortar fire and pinned down. To keep up the momentum of the attack, B Troop took over assaulting the battery. As they moved forward among the rubble and debris from the bombing attack, they quickly took the battery command post then moved on towards the second gun. Here, thirty Germans surrendered and were taken prisoner. The big guns of the battery were now finally silent. But at the far end of the battery enemy rifle fire continued to take shots at the commandos and an enemy Oerlikon gun in the same vicinity as the rifle fire remained active. Y Troop moved through the battery past the first gun that had been destroyed by the bombing raid, where the crew lay dead, to the second gun that had been spiked by the Germans making it unusable. They swept through the battery, dealing with the rifle fire at the far end and then consolidated their position. Only the Oerlikon on a mound near the far end of the battery remained in enemy hands.

The following morning, D+1, the commandos woke to find the Oerlikon at the far end of the battery now quiet. Moving cautiously towards it, expecting it to open up at any moment, they suddenly stormed the position only to find the enemy had melted away during the night. With W13 now completely in Allied hands preparations began for the assault on Zouteland and the clearing of the dunes south of that town. HMS *Roberts* and *Erebus* had returned to provide fire support for the advancing commandos. *Roberts* was to cover W18 and W19 as directed by 68 Forward Observation Base along with a spotting aircraft, while *Erebus* was tasked with firing on the batteries at W288 and W11 as directed by 65 Forward Observation Base. The spotter aircraft for HMS *Erebus* was a Spitfire.

The advance on Zouteland began at 0915hrs by 48 Commando and A Troop quickly captured the battery at W287 taking twenty prisoners. As the commandos moved forward the spotting Spitfire roared overhead, directing fire from HMS *Erebus*, whose guns pounded W288 and W11. The ship's guns spoke twenty-six times, sending shells hurtling through the air to smash W288.

However, W11 was worst hit. In all, the ship fired ninety-nine times directed by the Spitfire and the Forward Observation Base onto the gun casemates of W11. This took place between 1026 and 1640hrs. But when the installation was reached by the commandos it was found that the fire from *Erebus* had had little effect. The guns had been destroyed by the retreating Germans. By 1015hrs the commandos of A Troop reached the outskirts of Zoutlande and began their assault. An hour later, the Germans in the town surrendered. While 48 Commando consolidated their positions and secured the village, 47 Commando passed through Zouteland and pressed on. Other than the shelling from HMS *Erebus* during this advance the only other fire support came from 4 rocket-firing Typhoons that attacked the battery at W4, firing 24 rockets and more than 1,300 20mm cannon rounds.

By 1320hrs 47 Commando, continuing their advance, captured the gun battery W288. However, as they approached the German strongpoints W238 and W237 they were attacked by the German defenders dug in behind the concrete emplacements. Realising the Germans could not be dislodged without help, 47 Commando called in air support. At 1615hrs a formation of ten Typhoons arrived overhead. Rolling into shallow dives, the aircraft attacked both batteries, firing a total of 75 rockets and more than 4,000 rounds at the installations.

While the gun battery at W11 was eventually captured it was at a heavy cost for the Allies. A report from the forward observation officer for 47 Commando sums up the action that took place.

W11 was given four stonks (artillery bombardment) along the top of the dunes up to and including the objective. Three regiments engaged the fire plan – two on the first stonk and one on the second, followed by two on the second and one on the third, and so on, finishing with three regiments on the last stonk, which was the objective itself. Fire commenced at 1655 hours and was lifted to the next stonk, every 10 minutes. Fall of shot was very good except for one troop, which during the whole of the fire plan fired on the northern end of the first stonk, causing some casualties to our troops. The commandos found that they had underestimated the resistance and the sand dunes, for they could not cover the 100 yards in the two minutes that they had asked for. However, W11 was captured, but the casualties had been so heavy, and the situation was so confused, that the forward troops had to be withdrawn to a more firm base for the night, and the enemy re-established himself in the southern end of W11. Just prior to darkness, some enemy mortar positions were engaged and recorded. During the night HF fire was brought down on these and on the southern end of W11.[3]

By 1845hrs that evening the commandos captured the strongpoint at W238 and an hour later the first troops silently moved into the perimeter of W11, quietly dealing with enemy soldiers that they came across. Finally, at 2200hrs 47 Commando was able to report to headquarters that the battery, W11, had been captured and that they had consolidated their position just short of the battery due to the heavy casualties they'd taken. Because of these casualties one troop had to be formed from two depleted ones and this troop was attacked during the night by determined German resistance. The Germans called on the commando troop to surrender. Instead, the commandos attacked and the situation, which could have been very unpleasant for the Allies, was saved.

According to the report, 3 November, D+2, 4 Commando had completed the assault and capture of Flushing and was now ready to join up with the rest of the units from 4 SS Brigade across the Flushing gap.

> Artillery support on the 3 November consisted of Mike targets every two or three hundred yards down the dunes in support of the final attack on and capture of W11. The response to these Mike targets was extremely slow. A fair example is that of a correction of N200 which took nine minutes from receipt at RHQ to rounds on the ground. Many took longer than this. Harassing fire was also called for, to be engaged by another regiment on stretches of the dunes about 1000 yards beyond the commando's immediate objectives. This proved very effective. After the capture of W11 all resistance was weak, and no artillery fire was called for. When the commandos reached W4 all artillery fire NW of Flushing was stopped as the Air Op was engaging our forward troops, taking no notice of the yellow smoke that was put up. At W3 the commando was held up by small arms fire, but the commander of the garrison asked for and was given a parlay, at which he surrendered.[4]

Another report from 4 SS Brigade details further action that took place on D+2.

> The engineers had been working hard for 47 Commando during the night and at first light Brigade HQ moved to down Zoutelande [Zuidland] from where it could better direct the battle. 412 Commando had also crossed the Westkapelle gap at first light and were to be in Zoutelande by 1000hrs. The advance of 47 Commando was continued at 0830hrs. By now, excellent artillery support was available from the opposite side of the Scheldt and opposition from small arms weapons was not sufficient to prevent the commando from capturing W11 complete by

1230hrs. Before W3 could be taken on, there was W4 which consisted of 3x75mm HAA guns in concreated emplacements. These were backed by an anti-tank ditch that formed the outer defence line of Flushing and which was heavily infested with mines. It was established that some 200/300 troops held this 'Stuzpunkt'. Beyond this formidable barrier lay W3, consisting of 4x105mm coastal defence guns. The width of the dunes made it impossible for more than two troops to attack at one time. There was a gale blowing so it was impossible for 4 Commando to cross the Flushing gap at present, and it was decided that 47 Commando should continue as far as possible with 41 Commando in reserve.

Nothing daunted by their losses of the previous day, 47 Commando tackled their final task with grand determination, and passed through the W11 position, 41 Commando moving up and being prepared to take over if required. By 1530hrs, 47 Commando was held up at 088255 but a quarter of an hour later reported the capture of 200 PW and at 1610hrs that all resistance appeared to have ceased. This was, in fact, true. It transpired from the interrogation that the rapid advance and determination of this commando had completely taken the enemy in W3 by surprise, and by 1830hrs 47 Commando had reached the edge of the Flushing gap. The main task in the assault of Walcheren had been accomplished.[5]

To all intents and purposes both Flushing, Westkapelle, Zuidland and Domburg now lay in Allied hands. But the last few days of the battle for Walcheren were as grisly and ferocious as any part of the first day was. For the Germans, the battle for Walcheren was lost. That the Allies would take the entire island was inevitable. All the Germans could do was to continue to fight, continue to die and take some of the Allied soldiers with them. Their insistence on holding out was just senseless bloodshed. It was, to coin a phrase from Thompson, simply 'evil'.[6]

As mentioned at the beginning of this book, hindsight makes it easy for a historian to speculate. The only real reason for the Germans to continue to fight to the last man was because they had been ordered to do so. But that is something that can only be guessed at. It is known that the lives of soldiers' families back in Germany were held in the balance and that if they surrendered, the Gestapo would surely kill their families. But at this stage of the war Germany was in chaos, mostly in ruins from the round the clock heavy bombing campaign by the USAF and the RAF. They were running out of everything such as food and fuel. It is likely that many of the families of the soldiers fighting on Walcheren had melted away into the rubble. Order was breaking down. And yet, the soldiers on Walcheren continued to fight. It is to be wondered whether they were told about what was going on at home – did they know? It is doubtful. So they fought on.

By the evening of 4 November the situation was that Middelburg still remained in German hands. This was the town where General Daser, overall commander of the German garrison, had his headquarters. Middelburg stood silently above the grey water all around it. With the exception of a heavily mined bridge and approach to the town it was isolated, grey, remote and silent. Yet inside the town's population had been augmented by 20,000 refugees who had poured into the town since the beginning of the fighting.[7] They were running out of food and water, they lived on rooftops and the threat of disease was very high.

At this point in the battle, there were a little more than 3,000 armed Germans in the garrison of Middelburg.[8] On the island as a whole, there were little more than 5,000 Germans still at arms. Many were in the north of the island, in the woodlands 'lining the dunes of the north-west coast'.[9] Many were stranded and waited for the Allies to come and get them. However, others were fanatically suicidal, prepared to fight to the death rather than surrender. Die they would.

Notwithstanding the danger from the remaining, heavily armed Germans, there was another danger, one more insidious and unseen. The entire 9 by 9 mile island had been heavily mined by the Germans, and under the flood waters these mines lay with wire and obstacles all at varying, unknown depths. Any Allied amphibious vehicle that crossed these waters when touching upon an embankment or small piece of land or hitting a submerged polder, building or obstacle might easily set off a mine that would spell death and destruction.

The gap west of Flushing was crossed by 4 Commando in Buffalo amphibious vehicles on 4 November and, once they reached Zoutelande, came under the command of 4th SS Brigade. Advancing towards Domberg were 41st and 10 (IA) Commando while 5th KOSB attacked across the Middelburg Canal against strong resistance. Also moving forward was 4th KOSB, although progress was slow as their route along the canal banks to Middelburg was heavily mined. It was a lengthy slog.

In the north of the island the coast was lined with large sand dunes while inland there were wooded areas running parallel from Domburg to Fort de Haak. It was here that 41 Commando and 10 (Inter-Allied) Commando fought a fierce battle against fanatical Germans intent on holding out to the last man. Dutch, French, Belgian and Norwegian personnel made up 10 Commando, as well as some British being attached later after the loss of their Weasel vehicles. These men were Royal Artillery observers or liaison officers.

On the evening of 3 November, a small armoured group of the two remaining Sherman tanks and two AVRE tanks were attached to 10 Commando.

Under the command of Major D.R.R. Pocock these tanks proved to be invaluable in the battles to come. The tanks arrived in Domburg that evening to support the commandos and immediately opened fire on a German machine-gun post and observation post in the Domburg water tower, completely destroying it.

At this stage the Allies were in control of most of the island and most of the gun batteries were either destroyed or captured. Not so in the north. On the edge of the woods near Domburg, the Germans had positioned W18, a heavily fortified gun battery that was part of a larger defensive position to the north which dominated this installation. This position, just north of W18, was known as the Black Hut. 'The whole area was thickly mined and booby-trapped and defended by the toughest troops on Walcheren.'[10] The firepower that the Germans could bring to bear on the commandos was impressive – Oerlikon cannon, machine guns, flamethrowers and mortars. However, supported by the Sherman tanks firing 75mm and the AVREs firing Besa rounds the commandos charged through the minefields attacking the enemy positions.

The first assault was by 10 Commando which launched an attack on the gun emplacements at 1500hrs. Sherman and AVREs tanks moved forward slowly, keeping up a steady, deadly, stream of fire. An enemy Oerlikon cannon near W18 was hit and destroyed with sixty prisoners being taken. Adding to the bombardment by the tanks were three Typhoons that arrived overhead, rolled into their dives, firing their rockets and strafing the enemy with cannon fire.[11] However, the enemy gun battery remained active.

The following day, the Allies tried again. This time 41 Commando attacked W18 on the left flank while 10 Commando attacked on the right. Bad weather made air support impossible so, once again, the Shermans and AVREs were pressed into providing fire support for the attacking commandos. Mines and oozing mud made the progress slow. An AVRE rolled over a mine and had its track blown off. The crew abandoned their vehicle in the minefield and gingerly made their way to safety.

The tanks rained fire upon a target near W18 that turned out to be filled with ammunition for a Nebelwerfer gun.[12] The ammunition blew up, rendering the gun useless. When they moved into W18 that afternoon they found that:

a number of pillboxes and Ops in the dunes to the North were shot up and further rounds put into the Black Hut area and the large concrete emplacement. A wooden screen had been put across the slit but this was soon destroyed and both WP and HE delay put through the slit at 2,000 yards. The Nebelwerfer was not firing.[13]

Gradually, the defenders were worn down, battered by continual attacks from the commandos, from the air, from the sea and the virtual continuous and accurate firing of the tanks. What it must have been like for the German defenders, as fanatical as they may have been, in their bunkers under regular fire for hours on end can only be guessed at. The battery at W18 fell on 6 November and the commandos took the surviving 300 men prisoner.[14]

With W18 silent the only stronghold left in the north of the island was the Black Hut gun emplacement, a strongly fortified gun battery in concrete casemates with pillboxes, barbed wire and other out buildings. This gun covered the approaches from the dunes and had to be silenced. However, the commandos knew that commanding this garrison was one of the fanatical German commanders ready to fight to the death rather than surrender. It would be a difficult battle.[15] The Shermans turned their attention to a large concrete emplacement in the Black Hut area and began firing on it.

06 November opened by 41 Commando advancing towards W19 but finding the going very treacherous due to minefields. In fact, they were unable to push on until they had cleared a suitable route for supplies. On their right, 10 Commando were also finding progress difficult through the woods which were thick with enemy snipers. Consequently, it was decided to delay the attack on W19 until the following day with zero hour at 1000 hours, depending on the availability of air support. By midnight however, we were able to report 10 Commando holding the high ground, the Belgian troops having advanced skillfully through the woods and 4 and 48 Commando having moved up from Zoutelande and established themselves in Domburg. Brigade HQ was also in Domburg at this time.[16]

The following day, 7 November, the Allies decided another attack on the enemy positions around the Black Hut area was warranted. The day was clear enough for air support so before the ground assault began eighteen Typhoons mounted several sorties against enemy gun positions in the area. They fired 144 rockets and 7,415 rounds of cannon fire at different enemy targets. On the ground, the combined mortar teams of 4 Commando and 41 Commando, as well as the Sherman tanks and the AVRE, provided close fire support. However, one AVRE was blown up in a minefield as it headed for the Black Hut area. Unfortunately, three fatal casualties occurred in this incident.

Two Nebelwerfers were found destroyed in the spot at which we had been firing and a 50mm in the big emplacement. There was a hole in the gun, the marks of two HEs on the inside rear wall and plenty of blood on the floor. A number of other pillboxes that had been engaged were badly knocked about.[17]

Nevertheless the battle continued and for more than three hours commandos from 10 and 41 Commando attacked the German defensive positions, charging through the minefields, cutting their way through barbed wire all the time supported by fire from the Sherman tanks that poured a steady stream of 75mm shells onto the defenders. 'When at last the "Black Hut" caved in the whole of the ground was "slippery with blood" and the last gun was out of action. One hundred and fifty Germans surrendered, and that was the end of the last real fight on Walcheren, north, south, east or west.'[18]

The Allies also attacked W19, another battery in the Black Hut area, and the last stronghold of resistance. The attack began with eight Typhoons screaming down on the enemy installation firing their rockets and cannon fire. The fighter-bombers sent 63 rockets and more than 1,100 rounds of cannon fire hurtling into their targets. On the ground, the commandos reported that two rockets directly smashed into a pillbox while ten more hit the gun emplacements. In the afternoon, another formation of 8 Typhoons attacked W19 again, this time with 62 rockets and more than 3,800 rounds of 20mm ammunition. The pilots, watching their rockets pepper the ground and the enemy positions, saw a series of flashes as an ammunition dump exploded causing a large fire. 'The map reference given was well out to sea but if the casting given is assumed correct the target could only have been W19 or perhaps some suspected ammunition dump just south of it.'[19]

W19 was attacked again by sixteen Typhoons in the afternoon. The pilots fired 125 rockets and 4,610 rounds of 20mm at the enemy gun battery with 2 salvos of rockets being direct hits. It was reported that a further salvo of rockets entered the embrasure of a gun casemate.

On 8 November, D+7, further attacks by the Allies were planned on the German defenders still fighting. By this time, heavy artillery had been brought across to Walcheren from South Beveland. During the night of 7 November these guns had opened a concentrated fire on enemy positions, most notably those in the woods providing the most difficult resistance.

Poised to attack, the commandos waited for the go signal to advance, while artillery and armour fired on the enemy. But the signal never came. By 0830hrs 4 Commando sent a signal down the line that all fire support was to stop and 41 Commando moved into W19 while 4 Commando arrived at Fort de Haak. The fight had gone from the Germans.

In this phase of the fight for Walcheren Island, the Shermans and AVREs had made a huge difference, without them it would have been a much longer, bloodier, hard-fought battle. The Shermans alone fired off more than

1,400 rounds of 75mm as well as more than 30 boxes of Browning machine-gun ammunition, while the AVREs had fired more than 46 boxes of Besa ammunition.[20]

Sadly, however, one LVT that was transporting a patrol of 48 Commando was on its way to Veere to meet up with elements of 52 Light Division when it ran over a large mine and was blown up with almost all the occupants casualties, the majority of them fatal. 'This mine caused more casualties to one troop of 48 Commando than had been suffered by the whole assault force in any day since D+1 when W11 was captured.'[21]

The effectiveness of armour in these operations is summed up in a report from 1 Lothians.

> Between 03 November and 08 November the two Shermans fired over 1,400 rounds of 75mm and 30 boxes of Browning and the two AVREs 46 boxes of Besa. Throughout the operation the going along the dunes was extremely difficult and the AVREs did yeomen service path-finding and track-making. Reports from prisoners indicated that the presence of tank support materially assisted the rapid collapse in the North. They had been prepared to stand behind their MGs as long as they only had infantry to assault them. The presence of tanks also had a great moral effect on the commandos, who, owing to losses in landing, were short of support weapons, and the only artillery available were the Heavies and Super Heavies which, at 12 miles, were not sufficiently accurate to give close support.[22]

Notes

1. Army Operational Research Group Report No. 299.
2. Ibid.
3. Report from 47 Commando FOO cited in Army Operational Research Group Report No. 299.
4. From the report by Forward Observation Officer, 15 Medical Regiment, Royal Artillery, attached to 47 Commando, cited in Army Operational Research Group Report No. 299.
5. This quote is from a report by 4 SS Brigade cited in Army Operational Research Group Report No. 299.
6. Thompson refers to these last five days as hideous, grisly, senseless and evil. Thompson, *Eighty-Five Days*, p. 206.
7. Rawling, *Cinderella Operation*, p. 141. Interestingly, Thompson, *Eighty-Five Days*, states that the total population of Middelburg with the refugees was a little over 40,000.
8. See Rawling, *Cinderella Operation*, p. 141.
9. See Thompson, *Eighty-Five Days*, p. 207.
10. Ibid., p. 211.

11. Army Operational Research Group Report No. 299.

12. The nebelwerfer was a series of weapons for the German Army in the Second World War that could be used to fire high-explosive rounds, smoke rounds and was even developed to fire rockets.

13. See Army Operational Research Group Report No. 299.

14. See Thompson, *Eighty-Five Days*, p. 212.

15. Ibid.

16. Taken from 4 SS Brigade report cited in Army Operational Research Group Report No. 299.

17. 1 Lothians report on the results of the close-fire support by the Shermans during this operation as cited in Army Operational Research Group Report No. 299.

18. See Thompson, *Eighty-Five Days*, p. 212.

19. Army Operational Research Group Report No. 299.

20. See Thompson, *Eighty-Five Days*, p. 212, for these statistics. However, elsewhere in this book there are more detailed statistics on the battle.

21. See Army Operational Research Group Report No. 299.

22. 1 Lothians report on the results of the close-fire support by the Shermans during this operation as cited in Army Operational Research Group Report No. 299.

Chapter 17

Last Days on Walcheren

In hindsight it is easy to look at past battles and criticise the reasons or the outcomes of this or that battle. But the fight for W18 and the Black Hut was, from the German perspective, completely unnecessary. The men were sacrificed and, in reality, died for nothing. Their deaths are even more pointless because by the time the Black Hut battery had capitulated, the German commander General Daser, headquartered in Middelburg, had already surrendered.

Unlike the bitter fighting that raged on the island around Middelburg the town fell to the Allies without a shot being fired. On the morning of 4 November a Dutch doctor who had managed to escape the Germans in Middelburg arrived at 155 Brigade Headquarters with some interesting news. General Daser would almost certainly surrender to a tank force but not to an infantry force.[1] The veracity of this statement has to be examined as it is highly likely that the German commander knew that the approaches to Middelburg were not accessible by armour because of their defensive positions. The most direct line of approach to the town was from the north along the Middelburg Canal from Flushing. However, this route was heavily fortified with pillboxes and concrete strongpoints along the top of the route while the canal banks had also been heavily mined.[2] True or not, this statement gave the Allies a chance to end the fighting and save lives.

Tentative signals were sent to the Germans but they were ignored. There was an urgency to liberate Middelburg and try to push for a peaceful surrender. The population of the town had doubled since the battle began with refugees flooding in and food was scarce. Fresh water was running out, sanitation very poor and the threat of disease very real. If the Allies entered into a long, drawn out stalemate things would get much worse.

By this time, the only armour left on the island were the two Shermans still in the north and so far no reinforcements had arrived from South Beveland so the overtures from the Allies for Lieutenant General Daser to surrender continued.[3] A more intensive effort other than sending signals was made when Major Dawson of 7/9 Royal Scots left Brigade Headquarters with an intelligence officer and brigade civil affairs officer to make contact with the Germans. The three men received no reply and managed to get back to their headquarters without incident. Middelburg remained silent, brooding.

While most of the rest of his forces were in the process of being destroyed and capitulating Lieutenant General Daser remained isolated and strong, knowing that he could hide behind his protective wall of refugees. Because the town was so full of people, mostly civilians, Daser knew that the Allies would not bombard the town. He also knew that the approach from the west, over flood water was impossible for armour and that all the bridges leading into Middelburg were mined. For as long as their supplies held out, Daser knew that they could keep on fighting, or at least keep the Allies at bay.

The Allies devised a bold plan to force Daser to surrender and call his bluff. He said he would surrender to a tank force so a tank force would go to Middelburg to accept his surrender. Only the tank force would be Buffaloes 'pretending to be tanks'.[4] They would swim over the flooded western approaches while the infantry struggled along the fortified Middelburg Canal, heavily defended roads and mined bridges leading into the town. In the east a dummy attack was to be staged as a diversion to keep Daser's men occupied. General Hakewell-Smith, the Divisional Commander, approved the plan that had been devised by 52nd Divisional Headquarters.[5] The plan initially called for 15 Buffaloes to be used carrying 250 troops. The Buffaloes were tracked vehicles that could possibly pass for tanks in the distance but, more importantly, because of their tracks they sounded like tanks.

The Allies believed that the west was the one direction from which the Germans would least expect an assault, largely because 'that way lay floods of varying depths covering fields, polders and even complete villages where only roof-tops and church spires poked above the empty desolation of an inland sea all the way to Zoutelande and Westkapelle'.[6]

In the end only 8 Buffaloes could be found to represent this 'tank' force and they were manned by 120 men from 7/9 Royal Scots with a few specialist machine-gun teams from the 7th Battalion the Manchester Regiment. This force, under the command of Major Johnson of the Royal Scots, assembled in Flushing and then sailed a slow route of nearly 12 miles, passing over submerged villages, past people sitting on their rooftops waiting for rescue, over submerged strongpoints obstacles and mines. It was a tense and difficult time for surprise was vital. Danger lurked everywhere. A well-placed enemy sniper or mortar team would have been able to reign fire down on the little flotilla, virtually stopping the advance in its tracks. Major Johnson knew this and he also knew that under the grey water lay the possibility of touching off one of the mines or a booby traps that the Germans had sown so liberally over polders, dykes, buildings and canal banks. Touching just one of these would mean destruction for the amphibious vehicle and likely death for the troops it was carrying. The worry that must have filled Johnson's mind during this trip can only be guessed at, especially when one of the leading Buffaloes did, in fact, set off a mine and promptly disappeared into the murky, grey flood waters. Now Johnson had only 100 men and 7 Buffaloes. They ploughed on.

While this was taking place, on the direct regular routes into the town the KOSB moved slowly along the banks of the Middelburg Canal. A maze of foxholes and strongpoints and filled with mines, the banks were a very dangerous place to be, as Thompson recalls.[7] Many prisoners were taken and the Scots even had to pull some out of foxholes but the going during the day was virtually impossible and by night only slightly better. By the end of the first night the Scots had advanced no more than 150yd and by the end of the second day they'd covered even less ground, but they kept moving forward inch by inch, yard by yard.

The Cameronians, having broken out from the causeway, were now north east of Middelburg attacking enemy positions, drawing mortar and machine-gun fire in their diversionary assault across the Middelburg–Veere Canal.[8] Fanatical enemy suicide fighters held out in strongpoints all around Middelburg making the advances by the Cameronians and the Scots deadly slow. Heavy casualties were taken.

By 1600hrs on 6 November, the small force of Buffaloes were approaching Middelburg from the west. They could hear the noise of the battles taking place in the east but where they were all was quiet, except for the rumbling engines of the Buffaloes slowly taking them forwards. The men were alert, tense, waiting for enemy shots to ring out that could so easily have scuppered the entire operation. The force finally reached Middelburg and entered the town through a breach in the walls. Switching over from the propellers that pushed them through the water to tracks that drove them over the ground, they rumbled over Middelburg's cobbled streets, making as much noise as they could, opening their throttles so their engines would roar. They were doing their best to sound like tanks even though they didn't really look like tanks.

Within fifteen minutes of their arrival, happy excited throngs of civilians wildly cheering englulfed the little force as they slowly moved through the streets. When they reached the main square it was filled with mostly Dutch faces. According to Gerald Rawling, they pulled up outside the town hall and Johnson then set up his headquarters in the burgomaster's house and 'sent his Intelligence Officer, Captain Jones, and a lieutenant, to demand the surrender of General Daser'.[9] The two men, the only officers he had, made their way through the throngs of people, and groups of armed German soldiers congregating in the main square and found Lieutenant General Daser at his headquarters at 1640hrs.[10]

It was a tense time. The German soldiers were still armed and for the moment remained cowed but that could change very quickly. The two British officers met with General Daser and his staff and demanded his surrender, but the general stalled. He would not surrender to a junior officer. It was beneath him to do so. 'A German General, it seemed, would surrender only to an officer of equal rank or to a Staff Colonel at the very least.'[11] The meeting was not going well and the British officers knew that it could turn at any moment but Daser was unsure. Unsure of themselves, the two British officers decided to return to their headquarters and seek advice from Major Johnson. The situation suddenly changed dramatically when five officers from Daser's staff handed over their weapons and wanted to be treated as prisoners of war. The five officers accompanied the British back to their headquarters leaving a shaken Daser behind them. He too had handed over his pistol to the British but he had not relinquished his command. According to Thompson, quoting from the war diaries of the 7/9 Royal Scots and 155 Infantry Brigade, Daser was unrelenting in his refusal to surrender to Captain Jones. By this time, the Buffaloes had moved into positions in each corner of the main square which was now filling up with armed German soldiers. Indeed, these soldiers 'were lolling about, apparently docile but potentially dangerous'.[12]

Having a little more than 100 men at his disposal and with thousands of civilians and more than 2,000 armed Germans in both main squares, Major Johnson realised that the situation could turn very nasty, very quickly. When the two British officers returned to their headquarters with their five prisoners they found Johnson beset from all sides, with voices from the Dutch Resistance telling him how he should be dealing with the situation. It was pandemonium. Johnson knew he had to act so he silenced all the advice coming at him from all directions and boldly strode across the square and entered Daser's headquarters. Some scholars and historians have suggested that just prior to this Johnson had given himself a local acting, temporary promotion to brigadier or full colonel.[13] After several minutes of arguing with General Daser, Johnson achieved the outcome he wanted. Finally, the German commander relented and surrendered to Johnson. However, this version is based on Thompson citing the war diaries in his book. Rawling also states that the temporary local promotion may or may not be the truth. What is certain is that Daser did finally relent and surrender his command to Major Johnson.

What were his motives? That would have to be speculation but it is likely that he wanted to save himself, while still holding a certain amount of respect and prestige. However, he also knew that the town had huge numbers of Dutch civilians that far outnumbered his own men and the British. German mistreatment of the Dutch has been well documented. There was no love lost between the Germans and the Dutch. Daser knew that if the Dutch took control of the town they would begin retribution. 'If they did, he was likely to find himself hanging from the nearest lamppost.'[14] According to Rawling, Daser decided to pin his hopes on the British holding the town.

By 1830hrs Johnson had returned to his headquarters where members of the Dutch Resistance were demanding that the charges on the bridges leading into the town should be cleared as quickly as possible in case the Germans changed their minds.[15] One of Daser's more fanatical officers, his Chief of Staff, was detailed to round up parties of German prisoners and clear the bridges of demolition charges.[16] To ensure this officer's cooperation, he was ordered by the British to stand in the middle of each bridge while his own people removed the charges under his orders. All of this took place under the watchful eyes of a British guard party.

While the square was filled with people and the still armed, but docile Germans, the sounds of fighting from the east drifted into the town. Johnson knew he was still on a knife edge and that the Germans could change their minds as they listened to the sounds of battle from the east. He was desperate for reinforcements as well as supplies, mostly food and water. The civilians were hungry, expecting the Allies to provide them with food. The longer they waited, the more restless they would become. Johnson needed a relief force and needed it quickly. According to Rawling, Johnson began sending a series of signals back to Brigade Headquarters asking for just that.[17]

Hour by hour slowly rolled by when at 2100hrs Johnson received a radio message from Brigade informing him that HLI of C were held up 1 mile east of Middelburg facing stiff and fanatical resistance at an anti-tank ditch that was heavily defended.[18] An hour and a half later Johnson received another radio message with what was good news. The Royal Scots Fusiliers were on their way and should be arriving at any time. However, they did not arrive. With no sign of the Fusiliers Johnson, now very anxious knowing that time was against him and that the armed Germans in the square could change the situation at a moment's notice, sent a message to headquarters complaining that he was sitting on a powder keg. Johnson could only hope that it didn't explode.[19] It was at this time he was told that elements of KOSB were on their way. Their Buffaloes were sailing up the Middelburg canal towards him.

Finally, after many anxious hours the first of the reinforcements arrived at 0330hrs on 7 November. They arrived at almost the same exact time with the KOSB coming in from the south and the HLI of C coming in from the east.[20] Johnson and his meagre force could now breathe much more easily. For more than 12 hours, the 100 British troops had held the town of Middelburg against more than 2,000 docile armed Germans who could easily have overwhelmed them.

By late afternoon of that day, the German prisoners had been disarmed, counted and evacuated out of Middelburg. In all, 2,030 prisoners had been taken in Middelburg.

The battle for Walcheren Island was officially over. However, pockets of resistance still held out. In the afternoon of 7 November the Cameronians accepted the surrender of German forces at Veere, where they captured 13 officers and more than 620 men. Once the prisoners had been taken the British discovered they'd enough ammunition to hold out for much longer.

Finally, on 8 November, the end of all organised resistance was announced by 52nd Division Headquarters. Over the next few days on Walcheren, after 8 November, rescue parties from 52nd Division sailed the flood waters, picking up any remaining prisoners or stranded civilians. The dying, however, would continue, as people and vehicles would roll over mines and booby traps. The engineers did their best to clear these in the days that followed but people continued to die. One single incident illustrates the continuing danger faced by Allied troops as they traversed the island. A single troop of twenty-eight soldiers from 48 Commando were sent out in a Buffalo to link up with elements of 52nd Division near Veere. Only 3 miles short of the town the Buffalo sailed over a mine and was blown up. Nineteen soldiers were killed outright with the remainder being wounded. This was one of many incidents that took place after the fighting was officially over.[21]

Army engineers working together with the Dutch engineers managed to drain the island of water and clear away the booby traps and mines in eighteen months. The salt water that flooded into the land when the dykes were breached by the RAF bombing campaign killed all the submerged trees. According to Thompson, in 1947 the Dutch planted new trees.[22]

Notes

1. Thompson, *Eighty-Five Days*, p. 206.
2. Rawling, *Cinderella Operation*, p. 141.
3. Ibid., p. 142.
4. Thompson, *Eighty-Five Days*, p. 214.
5. See Rawling, *Cinderella Operation*, p. 142.
6. Ibid.
7. See Thompson, *Eighty-Five Days*, p. 214.
8. See Rawling, *Cinderella Operation*, p. 143.
9. See Thompson, *Eighty-Five Days*, p. 215.
10. Rawling, *Cinderella Operation*, p. 144.
11. Ibid.
12. Ibid.
13. Whether he did this or not is the subject of debate. Both Rawling and Thompson do not state that this is true. However, official reports do state that a junior officer was given a

temporary local promotion to either colonel or brigadier, depending on the report, in order to negotiate with Daser.

14. Rawling, *Cinderella Operation*, p. 145.
15. See Thompson, *Eighty-Five Days*, p. 216.
16. Ibid., p. 145.
17. Ibid.
18. Ibid., p. 217.
19. See Rawling, *Cinderella Operation*, p. 146.
20. Ibid.
21. Ibid., p. 147, for more detail on this event.
22. See Thompson, *Eighty-Five Days*, p. 219.

Chapter 18

Legacy

Eight days after the Allied forces invaded Walcheren Island, the Germans surrendered, completely subdued. The Allies, against many obstacles, natural and manmade, and suffering severe casualties had managed to invade from the isthmus and effect successful landings in the teeth of enemy fire. The defensive capability of the German garrison had been virtually destroyed, their morale broken and the Allied troops saved from what could have been a long, drawn-out resistance that might have cost many more lives. There is enough evidence from the commandos themselves and from the defeated enemy to know that that statement is true. Indeed, the following excerpt from No. 4 Commando's report on the action is most convincing:

> The whole situation was governed by the flooding of the island. Apart from the original gap at Westkapelle the Royal Air Force had blasted further breaches in the sea walls northwest of Flushing town, east of Flushing harbour, and just north of Veere, and the inundations had got so completely out of control that by the end of October there was only a strip of high dunes around the Western and Northern coasts and an area around Nieuwland to the southwest of the causeway to South Beveland that remained above water. There was even water in the streets of Middelburg and Flushing. It was frequently debated whether this violent and extensive flooding might not be playing into the enemy's hands by limiting the possible avenues of advance to narrow strips upon which a considerable volume of fire could be concentrated with ease. In the event, however, the Germans never seem to have considered the water as a potential ally. The fantastic flooding mesmerized them into a fatal inactivity, destroyed their communications, and sapped their morale to an incredible extent. Prisoners, and particularly the more senior officers, repeatedly cried 'The water – without that terrible water you would never have beaten us' in accents of despair and frustration, and there could have been no better or more eloquent tribute to the higher

planning of the operation than that paid to it by the Germans themselves.[1]

The following statement also shows just how much the flooding had affected the Germans. It also shows that the suffering of the Dutch people was not in vain. The detailed Allied planning had worked.

> The Garrison Commander, Colonel Reinhardt, together with the Naval Commander and their respective staffs had been captured early the same morning in the Royal Scots attack. At about 1000 hours a long line of dishevelled and badly shaken German officers was standing miserably on the parade ground outside the Arsenal Barracks. Colonel Reinhardt was brought into a shelter for interrogation, but was far too much upset by his recent experiences to be coherent about anything. He was obviously very much the worse for the bombardments he had endured, and was also greatly distressed because he had surrendered his command. During the interview he both wept and urinated freely. His Adjutant, who was subjected to a much more exhaustive examination, proved equally uninformative but by no means uninteresting. He gave the impression of being a somnambulist, so utterly dazed was he after the bombardment and the trials the floods had brought in their train.
>
> Throughout his interrogation he was shaking violently and uncontrollably, and when he did speak, he poured out hysterical curses at the destruction wrought by water everywhere on the island. All the officers testified to the havoc the water had played with all forms of communications and to the appalling effect it had on morale. To anyone who spoke with these officers there could be no question but that the flooding policy had been a decisive success.[2]

With the operations to clear the Scheldt finally over, General Simonds stated that 'Antwerp can now be used as a base for a knock-out blow against Germany'.[3] And so, three weeks after the German capitulation on Walcheren Island, on 28 November 1944, the first Allied minesweepers began the voyage up the Scheldt to the port facilities at Antwerp, entirely unmolested by enemy fire from anywhere along the approaches. The first minesweeper to tie up at the quayside was the Canadian-built *Fort Cataraqui*.[4]

> Some part of the huge total of British and American imports pouring into France and Belgium and taxing the capacity of road and railway, truck and barge, from distant base to forward maintenance area, could

now enter at a point within two hundred and fifty miles of Nijmegen or Aschen – that first great German city to fall into our hands before the onslaught of First U.S. Army on 28 Oct. Hitherto the pressure upon the extended line of our communications had been measured by the arrival every week by sea of some 48,000 men between 9,000 and 10,000 tons of vehicles, more than 40,000 tons of petrol, and over 275,000 tons of supplies.

Three days after the arrival of the convoy, on 1 Dec, 10,000 tons of stores were unloaded on to the docks at Antwerp. This world port, by volume of seaborne freight comparable to Hamburg and considerably larger than Montreal, had now become a vent through which a vast tonnage was soon to flow in for the winter offensive.[5]

Montgomery, in a message to General Simonds, dated 3 November 1944, stated that:

The operations were conducted under the most appalling conditions of ground – and water – and the advantage in these respects favoured the enemy. But in spite of great difficulties you slowly and relentlessly wore down the enemy resistance, drove him back, and captured great numbers of prisoners. It has been a fine performance, and one that could have been carried out only by first class troops.

The Canadian Army is composed of troops from many different nations and countries. But the way in which you have all pulled together, and operated as one fighting machine, has been an inspiration to us all.

I congratulate you personally. And I also congratulate all commanders and troops serving under your command. Please tell all your formations and units how very pleased I am with the splendid work they have done.[6]

In the view of the Supreme Commander when the war was over, in these operations First Canadian Army produced its greatest climax. 'The end of Naziism', he said, 'was in clear view when the first ship moved unmolested up the Scheldt.'[7]

The number of prisoners taken by the Allies throughout the operations amounted to 38,820 from 1 October to 8 November 1944 with another 2,223 being evacuated through the medical channels bringing the grand total of prisoners taken from 23 July to 8 November to 112,521. German casualties, those that were killed or wounded, were heavy while Allied losses were 703 officers and 12,170 other ranks killed, wounded or missing. From this number, as reported by General Simonds' Headquarters, 355 officers and

6,012 other ranks were Canadian.[8] The operations were summed up by General Simonds, while he was Acting Army Commander, in a letter he wrote to General Crerar:

> The Army's operations had been carried to a successful conclusion under the most difficult conditions of ground and weather, and against an enemy who exploited every defensive opportunity that offered. By flooding or saturating the areas in front of his positions, he was able to deny us all the advantages which we would normally possess in the offensive. He could concentrate his fire power on narrow fronts, keep his own positions concealed and dispersed, and make the most effective use of mines and obstacles. In the Breskens bridgehead, as in South Beveland and Walcheren, the approaches had to be made along single strips of road bordered by impassable fields and fully covered by the enemy's fire. Hence, by distracting the enemy's attention and drawing off his forces, the assault landings were of decisive importance in bringing this phase to an earlier conclusion than would otherwise have been possible. The invaluable support provided by the Royal Navy and the Royal Air Force gave further demonstration of the effectiveness of combined operations. The persistence and determination of all troops under command in wearing down the enemy were worthy of the high commendation bestowed on them by the C.-in-C.[9]

General Crerar's view of the operations can be seen in a message he sent to Simonds on 4 November in which he stated: 'My sincere congratulations to you on the great ability and drive with which you have carried out your recent very difficult responsibilities to a most successful conclusion. As a result, the battle reputation of First Canadian Army has never stood higher.'[10]

Montgomery, already busy regrouping and restructuring his forces for the next major offensive, the capture of the Ruhr, fully intended to 'have the Second British Army facing east along the Meuse with its left about Middelaar, whilst First Canadian Army faced east and north from the river at that point through the Nijmegen bridgehead to the sea at Walcheren'.[11]

With Antwerp now fully operational, the Scheldt completely clear of the enemy, the Allies turned their attention to Germany itself and, ultimately, Berlin.

Notes

1. 'Report No. 188', p. 2.

2. Ibid., pp. 39, 40.

3. Ibid., 2 Canadian Infantry Division, Lecture by Lieutenant General Simonds, 6 November 1944.

4. Ibid., First Canadian Army, General Crerar's Despatch, 31 January 1945.

5. 'Report No. 154', Historical Section War Cabinet: Chiefs of Staff Committee Weekly Resume (No. 274) 23–30 November 1944 and Historical Section, C.M.H.Q., paragraph 57.

6. See 'Report No. 188', First Canadian Army, November 1944: Appendix 'A'.

7. Address by General Eisenhower to Canadian Club, Ottawa, 10 January 1946, quoted in 'Report No. 154', Historical Section, C.M.H.Q., paragraph 58.

8. 'Report No. 188', First Canadian Army Report by Lieutenant General Simonds, 22 November 1944.

9. Ibid., paragraph 60.

10. Ibid., covering Letter to Minister of National Defence, 22 November 1944.

11. Ibid., General Crerar's Despatch, 31 January 1945.

Appendix 1

The Air Campaign Against Walcheren

01 November 1944:
8 aircraft attacked a Radar Station at Westkapelle and direct hits with rocket projectiles were seen on the cylindrical tower of the station. The target was then strafed with cannon fire. Rocket ships were seen firing and landing craft were seen approaching the shore under heavy fire.[1]

During the last fortnight of September 1944 the RAF had already begun operations against the German defences of Walcheren Island. The targets were mostly gun batteries and the approaches at Domburg. Three attempts at bombing these targets had taken place but were unsuccessful because of the unpredictability of the weather. Indeed, poor weather throughout the entire period of air, land and sea operations at this late point in 1944 caused the Allies no end of concern. However, on 23 September 1944, the RAF mounted a fourth attack on the same targets, particularly on Domburg. In this attack, Bomber Command despatched fifty aircraft which managed to attack their targets, dropping 174.4 tons of high explosive and 10.2 tons of incendiary bombs.[2]

However, during this period targets on the gun emplacements around Walcheren were:

on a much lighter scale than was usually demanded for the preparation of military targets. Comparative targets were attacked by Bomber Command during September preparatory to the seizure of Le Havre. Between Sep 5th and Sep 11th 2508 aircraft dropped a total of 9614.8 tons of high explosive and 174.6 tons of incendiaries on objectives in this area. Of this weight 6929.8 tons of high explosive was directed specifically against 'Coastal Batteries, Guns, Pill-boxes and Strong Points'. The remainder was directed against 'Troop Concentrations' (first attack) and 'Defended Area' (Final attack). On September 17th, the same day that Bomber Command despatched 100 aircraft to attack three objectives on Walcheren Island, 762 aircraft were despatched to attack Boulogne in support of Army Operation WELLHIT, and delivered 3347.2 tons of high explosive and 44.0 tons of incendiaries on that area.[3]

Of course, the allocation and size of these air attacks were beyond the remit of an Army Headquarters. There were procedures that needed to be followed. At the Army Headquarters, the tactical importance of targets such as gun emplacements or troop concentrations were worked out jointly through discussions with the Air Staff Officers of 84 Group and then referred to Headquarters 2 Tactical Air Force. At Army Headquarters Operations (Air) Staff could make requests for air operations directly to Headquarters 21 Army Group to then be considered by the Group and the Tactical Air Force. In order to reduce the enemy's coastal defences by air attack staff at First Canadian Army Headquarters would put together the strongest case possible in order to ensure the enemy's gun emplacements were put out of action with maximum destructive power. However, factors such as the methods of attack, availability of aircraft and the unpredictable weather were beyond the Army's control and it was up to other arms and services to deal with these.

The army's concern over these issues can be clearly seen in the Air Plan published by 84 Tactical Group HQ on 27 October 1944:

> Assuming that flooding would be successful, the Army have listed the defences which would be unaffected by flooding and which would require to be put out of action to enable seaborne assaults to be likely to succeed. The light scale of equipment of the forces used and their vulnerability to shore defences coupled with the need to capture the island quickly makes the thorough destruction of these defences a necessity.[4]

The Air Plan highlights more of the army's issues:

> We have to rely therefore on air bombardment for the necessary destruction of the defences before D Day. Some of this bombardment is being undertaken by aircraft of 84 Group. Many of the defences, however, are concrete gun emplacements and heavy pillboxes which cannot be put out of action by the weight of attack this Group is able to deliver.[5]

It continues:

> It can hardly be expected that all the defences attacked by Bomber Command will be completely destroyed and some may be effective or be repaired after bombardment but before the Assaults. Some of these defences that have come to life again may vitally jeopardize the Assault, particularly the guns near FLUSHING and near WESTKAPELLE.

Should this happen, it is most desirable that Bomber Command should be requested to attack these individual targets again when possible, up to the agreed times of last bombing for each Assault.[6]

03 November 1944
1205hrs: 4 aircraft attacked a strongpoint on Walcheren Island. Several direct hits with rocket projectiles and many cannon strikes were seen. A proportion of buildings were demolished and left burning. [7]

Although much of the Allied artillery was concentrated in positions behind Breskens, the Allies knew that the only guns that could fire across the Scheldt Estuary and achieve any kind of accuracy on the targets would have to be heavy and super heavy cannon. Naval guns firing at enemy positions from the sea in support of the landings at Westkapelle were dependent upon the weather in the same way that air attacks were. From the military perspective it was crucial that the German batteries sited on the dunes and along the coast near the Westkapelle and Flushing landings were knocked out. The urgency and importance of these requirements were passed onto and emphasised for consideration and implementation by the RAF.

More air attacks took place over ten days in October, based on a schedule of targets created at Army Headquarters.[8] It is during this period that the bombing of the dykes took place. This had been hotly debated since the question of flooding was put forward. The results of this bombing campaign were tensely awaited by everyone especially the troops and officers on the ground who would have to deal with the consequences of these attacks. In the event, the bombing of the dykes was hugely successful and, as Field Marshal Montgomery stated, it was 'an operation of truly magnificent accuracy'.[9] On 3 October, the first of these raids took place at Westkapelle.

The target was a small section of sea-wall approximately 330 ft x 200 ft in area. A total of 237 4,000 pound bombs and 1742 1,000 pound bombs were used in the attack, as well as a smaller number of 500 pounders. The sea-wall was successfully breached, four gun emplacements were drowned, and seven other batteries were surrounded by flood waters as the sea spread inland during the next three or four days. The sea-wall was again successfully breached near Flushing on Westkapelle on October 17th deepened the breach in that area and completed as far as possible the flooding of the island.[10]

With the bombing campaign against the dykes finished by the end of October, Walcheren Island 'resembled a saucer filled with water'.[11] Indeed, further investigation of the effects of the campaign illustrated that several four-gun batteries, W2 with 150mm and 120mm guns, W1 with 105mm guns and W22 with 75mm guns, had been put out of action. This left only W17, a four-gun 220mm (8.7in) battery, W19, a four-gun 105mm (4.1in) battery on the northern tip of the island, and three batteries W11, W13, W15 all thought to be 150mm (5.9in).[12]

The flooding had substantially reduced the Germans' strength and numbers of artillery and defensive gun batteries. The flooding also had a considerable effect on the enemy garrison in terms of alarm and subsequent drop in morale, which quickly became apparent to the commandos when they came ashore.

An excellent indication of the role of air support during Operation 'Switchback' can be derived from the battalion war diaries. During October there were repeated references to aerial attacks. Early in the operation, on 8 October, when the Canadian Scottish were engaged in a fierce struggle to expand their small bridgehead, the battalion war diarist found cause for optimism. 'If a gun position still gives us trouble [after artillery counterbattery fire] he is attacked by Typhoons. That makes the gun members wish they had no Feuhrer! [*sic*]'[13]

Throughout October Bomber Command's attacks on enemy positions were not confined to Walcheren Island. Several strikes were made in the Breskens Pocket in support of gruelling Allied ground operations to clear this area of the southern shore of the estuary. 'Gun emplacements still above water at Flushing were heavily bombed on October 11th, but an attack on the batteries at Fort Frederick Hendrik on the left bank of the Scheldt near Breskens, scheduled for the same day, had to be abandoned because of unfavourable weather. The batteries at Breskens were successfully attacked on October 12th.'

On 28, 29 and 30 October, Bomber Command carried out the major attack on enemy positions in the Breskens area.

The direct results of the air support were quite substantial. Towns such as Breskens, Ijzendijke, and Oostburg were destroyed largely by air attack. R/P Typhoons were responsible for the destruction of enemy HQs, forward artillery batteries, observation posts, and various other defensive positions. In particular, the fighter-bombers were quite successful in their attacks on Fort Frederik Hendrik and the heavy artillery that was shelling the Breskens area from across the Scheldt in Flushing.[14]

Later investigations by No. 2 Operational Research Section detailed the results of these attacks:

> There is nothing remarkable in the results. In view of the fact that the majority of the principal guns were in casemates, only direct hits or very near misses could have been expected to have any effect, and this proved to be the case . . . The density of craters around the targets is in accordance with the weight of attack. The total damage done to the principal defences was:
>
> 2 guns out of action out of a total of 26
> 1 casemate destroyed (but unfortunately empty)
> 1 command post destroyed
> 1 radio location set destroyed.

Within the limits of error occasioned by such a small sample, the rate of destruction accords well with what would be expected from the crater densities that were measured. Photographic interpretation by A.P.I.S., 21 Army Group, of the damage was largely correct, but was optimistic as to the extent of probable damage by near misses. The interpretation left no ground for supporting that the principal defences were not substantially intact.

Damage to line communications was considerable, but in some cases there had been time to improvise new lines and there was evidence that advantage had been taken of the time. Weather conditions did not permit any bombing on either 31 Oct or 1 Nov or more damage could have been inflicted. It is considered that only a very large effort (at least 1000 Heavy Bombers) as soon before H-hour as possible could have produced a really substantial success. Such an effort could materially have increased the destruction of view of morale. The evidence of P.W. showed that they had been upset by the attacks that did take place, but had time to recover sufficiently to man their guns. It may well be impracticable with the methods available, to put on so great a weight in one attack on a precision target: the possibility of sending in successive smaller attacks is likely to depend on flak conditions.[15]

Conversely, the same report also indicated that from the bombing campaign on coastal batteries the crater density around the target areas averaged around 9 to 10 craters per acre for every 1,000 bombs dropped: 'The average density achieved in the Westkapelle attacks was therefore twice what would be expected on experience up to that time and approaching the best any bomber force had achieved.'[16] However, the same report confirmed that: 'In our case targets containing 26 guns in all were attacked with average loads of 390 bombs per target. We should therefore expect 2.17 guns to be hit. Two actually were hit. Thus the number destroyed is in accordance with what would be expected from the weights of attack.'[17] The report stated that as the bomb load for each aircraft averaged 13 bombs, in order to achieve 1 chance in 2 of destroying up to 6 guns in a single battery encased in concrete, more than 720 aircraft would need to attack that single enemy position.

> Such an effort on the remaining day before D-day was possible for Bomber Command had the weather been good, but was not in fact intended. It is also unlikely that the high density of craters obtained in the WALCHEREN attacks could have been sustained with such a large number of plans on one target. Any effort which could deal with other batteries as well, or could give an appreciably greater chance of destruction even of one battery was outside the power of Bomber Command to produce.[18]

Therefore, this detailed study of the plan to reduce the German coastal gun positions by bombing alone concluded that it could not succeed without more resources being made available for such a huge commitment. Poor flying conditions because of the weather further contributed to limiting the bombing campaign on the day preceding the actual amphibious assault on the island including the actual day itself.

> 07 November 1944
> 1345hrs: Gun casements on the North West of Walcheren were attacked by 8 aircraft. The gun casements were facing seawards with smaller gun casements at the rear point south. 2 salvoes of rockets were direct hits but many rockets were seen to bounce off. Good cannon strafing from sea to land and many strikes were seen in and on the casements.

> 1550hrs: 8 aircraft repeated the previous attack, attacking this time from a shallow angle. One salvo scored a bullseye right through the aperture of one gun and flames were issuing from the casement.[19]

Further restrictions affecting both 21 and 12 Army Groups operating on a wider front limited the Allies' ability to deal effectively with the German coastal defences as decisively as they wished to. Brigadier Mann, Chief of Staff at Army Headquarters, made some notes on this subject.

While we were busy clearing the Scheldt prior to assaulting Walcheren, Second British Army had to deal with a counter thrust in the Meuse pocket to the west of Venlo. While this operation was done successfully, and did not unbalance us, it had the effect of diverting a proportion of our air effort and other resources. Farther to the South the thrust of the left wing of 12 US Army Group, directed on Cologne, was NOT being developed with the power which was desirable owing to the long front over which that Army Group now stretched, and due also to the fact that certain US formations had to be allotted temporarily to 21 Army Group.

The assault on Walcheren took place on 1 November as planned but for the reasons just mentioned, very much less preliminary bombing of the heavy batteries had actually been carried out than was intended, and although there was no question that it was essential to proceed with the operation, the result was that the Royal Navy's losses in landing craft, and their crews, largely Royal Marines, were very heavy indeed.[20]

02 November 1944:

1145hrs: Target Blockhouse on the pier 126237 attacked by Typhoons. Several direct hits with rocket projectiles and numerous cannon strikes observed. The target was left smoking.[21]

Notes

1. Operations Record Book, No. 164 Squadron, AIR 27, TNA.
2. AEF/First Cdn Army/S/F, fol. 18: Bomber Command Attacks, September 1944, Report No. 188, Historical Section, Canadian Military Headquarters, Canadian Participation in the Operations in North-West Europe 1944, 7 April 1948.
3. Ibid.
4. AEF/84 Group RAF/C/I, Operation 'INFATUATE', Air Plan, reproduced as Appendix 'G' as cited in Report No. 188, Historical Section, Canadian Military Headquarters, Canadian Participation in the Operations in North-West Europe 1944, 7 April 1948.
5. Ibid.
6. Ibid.
7. Operations Record Book, No. 164 Squadron, AIR 27, TNA.
8. Between 11 and 31 October, Bomber Command flew 941 sorties and dropped 4,871 tons of bombs. This was in addition to the effort against the dykes. Between 28 and 31 October, 654 Spitfire sorties and 150 Typhoon sorties were flown against pre-selected targets, gun positions, dual purpose AA guns and Radar sites (21 Army Group Report, Clearing of the Scheldt Estuary, October–November 1944, p. 17, para 71. W.D., G.S. Ops, H.Q. First Cdn Army, October 1944: Appendices 'Y'–'Z', 'AA'–'PP', fol. 99 *et seq*, and fol. 120 *et seq*: Pre-Planned Air Targets (Revised), 22 October 1944, reproduced as Appendix 'K' to the present

Report as cited in Report No. 188, Historical Section, Canadian Military Headquarters, Canadian Participation in the Operations in North-West Europe 1944, 7 April 1948.

9. Normandy to the Baltic, p. 204, cited in Report No. 188.

10. AEF/First Cdn Army/S/F, fol. 19, Bomber Command Attacks, cited in Report No. 188.

11. Normandy to the Baltic, p. 204, cited in Report No. 188.

12. AEF/21 Army Gp/C/F, Docket III, fol. 3, p. 12: Report No. 299, The Westkapelle Assault on Walcheren.

13. Michael Bechthold, *Canadian Military History*, Vol. 3, Issue 2, Article 6, 'Air Support in the Breskens Pocket: The Case of the First Canadian Army and the 84 Group Royal Air Force', p. 58.

14. See Bechthold, 'Air Support in the Breskens Pocket', p. 56.

15. First Canadian Army, No. 2 Operations Research Section, Report No. 25, 'Effect of Fire Support on Defences of Walcheren, 24 December 44'.

16. 21 Army Group, A.O.R.G. cited in Report No. 299, p. 64.

17. Ibid., p. 65.

18. Ibid., pp. 65, 66.

19. Operations Record Book, No. 164 Squadron, AIR 27, TNA.

20. First Canadian Army, 'The Campaign in N.W. Europe from 7/8 Aug to 31 Dec 44', cited in Report No. 188.

21. Operations Record Book, No. 198 Squadron, AIR 27, TNA.

Appendix 2

First Canadian Army/84 Group RAF Operation
Infatuate Target Schedule

This appendix contains Report No. 188, Historical Section, Canadian Military Headquarters, Canadian Participation in the Operations in Northwest Europe, 1944, Part VI: Canadian Operations, 1 Oct–8 Nov, The Clearing of the Scheldt Estuary. It was written in April 1948 and while it is a Canadian Government Document, it appears to be an open source document and is available on the worldwide web.

```
REVISED EDITION NUMBER 3                    Appx A to

(replacing target list                     17/1/9/Ops  (First Cdn Army)

issued as Appx A to Revised                84G/TS 76/3/Ops (84 Gp RAF)

Edition No. 2 dated 2 Oct 44)               22 Oct 44



                    FIRST CDN ARMY/84 GP RAF              Copy Number



                        Op "INFATUATE"



                        TARGET SCHEDULE



                    for Pre-Planned Air Targets

                    prior to D-Day.  OUTSIDE

                    Resources of 84 Gp RAF



Btys affecting minesweeping and/or

deployment of naval bombardment ships
```

Target No	Type of Target	Description	Map Reference	Photo Reference	Results and Remarks
W11	Gun posn LCB	Bty 16. 4 gun 150 mm LCB 4 casemates 50' x 55' spaced about 85 yds apart 2 more casemates now under construction. Seem to be RADAR and OP sites. About 12 huts to SE, 1 SL nearby to NORTH. Sec armament; 2 20 mm AA guns Estimated max range 24000 yds	DO71278	R16/1145 Print 3017 R4/788 Print 3106/7 NOT annotated R4/860 Print 3080	NO definite damage to casemate visible from bombing attack. NOT affected by flooding. (APIS 21 A Gp 16 Oct.) Casemates on dunes NOT flooded - No bomb damage. (1 Cdn APIS - 24 Oct 44)[1]

```
          1    Annotations added to original schedule for information of the
               Chief of Staff.
```

1   Report No. 188

Target No	Type of Target	Description	Map Reference	Photo Reference	Results and Remarks
W13	Gun posn MCB	Bty 12. 4 gun 150 mm MCB 4 casemates newly constructed 35' x 41'. Remainder open emplacements 35' diameter seem to be shelters. About 10 huts and shelters in shelters in rear. Sec armament; 1 on each flank. Estimate max range 24000 yds.	D034318	R16/1145 Print 3012 R4/788 Print 4106 Not annotated R4/860 Print 4102	Attacked by Bomber Comd RAF on 17 Sep No. 1 casemates hit on front. Nos. 2 and 3 casemates possibly hit No. 4 undamaged huts on posn damaged. NOT affected by floods. (APIS 21 A GP 16 Oct) NO change (1 Cdn APIS 24 Oct 44)[2]
W17	Gun posn HCB	Bty 5. 4 gun 220 mm HCB emplacements open concrete octegonal 30' across 2-3000 rounds amn stored at each site. Arc of fire 360 degrees. Concrete magazines on either side of emplacement ramp below ground level and with roofs 16' thick. Str believed between 200-250 men. Sec Armament 2 150 mm guns 1 47 mm A tk, 4 20 mm AA guns. Estimated max range 25000 yds.	D055376	R16/1145 Print 4025 R4/860 Print 3211	Bty cratered by bombs. No. 3 gun probably damaged by near misses. No. 1 emplacement NO damage. No. 2 emplacement damaged by two near misses. No. 3 NO damage. No. 4 emplacement two near misses. (APIS 21 A Gp 16 Oct.) NO change (1 Cdn APIS 24 Oct 44)[3]
W15	Gun posn MED ARTY	Bty 15. 4 gun 150 mm gun posn. Established max range 24000 yds.	D018349	R16/1145 Print 3174 3008	Attacked by Bomber Comd RAF 17 Sep. NOT damaged. NOT affected by floods. (APIS 21 A Gp 16 Oct.) NO change (1 Cdn APIS 24 Oct 44.)

[2] Annotations added to original schedule for information of the Chief of Staff.

[3] Same as #2.

```
REVISED EDITION NUMBER 3              Appx A to

(replacing target list               17/1/9/Ops (First Cdn Army)

issued as Appx A to Revised          84G/TS 76/3/Ops (84 Gp RAF)

Edition No. 2 dated 2 Oct 44)        22 Oct 44
```

FIRST CDN ARMY/84 GP RAF

Op "INFATUATE"

TARGET SCHEDULE

for Pre-Planned Air Targets
prior to D-Day.   OUTSIDE
Resources of 84 Gp RAF


```
Fixed coastal, med and fd btys capable of
firing onto SOUTH bank of WEST SCHEDULE
```

Target No	Type of Target	Description	Map Reference	Photo Reference	Results and Remarks
W6	Gun posn LCB	Bty 23. 4 gun 105 mm LCB Guns in casemates 45' x 38' on dyke WEST of fort. Casemates face WEST. Estimated max range 19000 yds.	D130239	R4/860 Print 3062	Attacked by hy bombers Bomber Comd RAF 11 Oct No. 1 casemate undamaged. No. 2 badly damaged. No. 3 near misses. No. 4 undermined by five near misses. Comns damaged Bty 50% effective. (1 Cdn APIS 15 Oct.) NO change (1 Cdn APIS 24 Oct 44)[1]

---

[1]   Annotations added to original schedule for information of the Chief of Staff.

1

Target No	Type of Target	Description	Map Reference	Photo Reference	Results and Remarks
W7	Gun posn LCB	Bty 24. 3 or 4 gun LCB, 2 casemates 125238, 1 at 122238 and 1 at 123237. Casemates are 30' x 35'. 8 new bldgs at 123239. Amn 2 large cam mounds at 125238.	D125237	R16/1145 Print 4014 R4/860 Print 3040	Now considered to be a normal strong pt and NOT at it coastal bty (LCB) (APIS 21 A Gp 12 Oct) Reported active however by CBO 2 Cdn Corps 19 Oct. Casemates here possibly hold lt gun firing on beach immediately to WEST. LAA (37 mm) posn on top of casemates probably firing in dual LCB role. NO bomb damage or flooding (1 Cdn APIS 24 Oct 44.)[2]
W16	Gun posn CD	3 lt guns estimated max range 13000 yds. New lt bty in open emplacements.	D048372	R16/1145 Print 4025	NO flooding NO bomb damage. 2 emplacements of 4 gun posn are seen to be occupied (1 Cdn APIS 24 Oct 44.)[3]
W19	Gun posn CD	4 gun 105 mm posn. Estimated max range 19000 yds. In casemates. RADAR strong pt at 110406.	D104404	R4/788 Print 4184/5/6	NOT affected by floods. (APIS 21 A Gp 16 Oct 44.) NO change (1 Cdn APIS 24 Oct 44.)[4]
W21	Gun posn CD	Bty 14. 4 gun 105 mm gun howitzers. Deep crescent layouts. Open emplacements 35' diameter spaced 35-98 yds apart. Estimated max range 13000 yds.	D075301	R4/860 Print 4113	No. 2 emplacement destroyed. Damage to Nos. 1, 3, 4 emplacements 23 Sep. NOT flooded. (1 Cdn APIS 15 Oct.)
		(Now completely flooded - 1 Cdn APIS 24 Oct 44.)[5]			
W26	Gun posn CD	4 gun 150 mm howitzers. Open emplacements. Estimated max range 14500 yds.	D227291	R4/854 Print 4177/4178	On ZUID BEVELAND ISLAND. NOTE: there are 10 dummy btys on these islands and this target may be a dummy.[6]
		(NO activity, probably dummy posn - 1 Cdn APIS 24 Oct 44.)[7]			
W27	Gun posn CD	4 lt guns in open emplacements. Estimated max range 13000 yds.	D428243	R16/1155 Print 4093/4	On ZUID BEVELAND ISL NOTE: there are 10 dummy btys on these islands and this target may be a dummy
		(Cancelled by Op "VITALITY".)[8]			

[2]   Annotations added to original schedule for information of the Chief of Staff.

[3]   Same as #2.

[4]   Same as #2.

[5]   Same as #2.

[6]   Same as #2.

[7]   Same as #2.

[8]   Same as #2.

REVISIED EDITION NUMBER 3   Appx A to

(replacing target list   17/1/9/Ops (First Cdn Army)

issued as Appx A to Revised   84G/TS 76/3/Ops (84 Gp RAF)

Edition No. 2 dated 2 Oct 44)

FIRST CDN ARMY/84 GP RAF   Copy Number

Op "INFATUATE"

TARGET SCHEDULE

for Pre-Planned Air Targets

prior to D-Day. OUTSIDE

Resources of 84 Gp RAF

AA Btys limiting operation of 84 Gp RAF

Target No	Type of Target	Description	Map Reference	Photo Reference	Results and Remarks
W1	Gun posn HAA	Bty 26. 4 gun 105 mm HAA bty. Deep crescent layout. Open emplacements 31-35 yds apart. 3 concrete shelters to WEST. Cam. CP centrally located. 2 SLs one off each flank. Sec Armament: 3 20 mm AA guns. A large RED CROSS is seen in centre of bty posn. May be in cupolas. Estimated max range 19000 yds.	D133237	R4/860 Print 3062	Attacked by hy bombers. Bomber Comd RAF 11 Oct Nos 2 and 3 posns hit. Activity at No. 1 posn. Robable damage to Nos. 2 and 3 guns and range finder. NOT affected by floods. (APIS 21 A Gp 16 Oct.) Nos. 2 and 3 emplacements hit - other installations damaged by large conc of craters fwd of Nos. 2 and 3 guns. NOT flooded. (1 Cdn APIS 24 Oct 44.)[1]

---

[1]   Annotations added to original schedule for information of the Chief of Staff.

1   Report No. 188

Target No	Type of Target	Description	Map Reference	Photo Reference	Results and Remarks
W2	Gun posn HAA	Bty 18. 4 gun 105 mm HAA bty crescent layout. Guns in turrets set in sunken concrete emplacements 35 yds apart. Several large shelters in rear. Cam. CP central in rear connects to FREYA RADAR at 112278. 1 SL SOUTH of bty, another at 111278. Sec armament; 2 20 mm AA guns. Estimated max range 19000 yds.	D119272	R16/1145 Print 3005 R4/788 Print 3102 R4/860 Print 4032	NOT affected by flooding. Radar operating. (1 Cdn APIS 15 Oct.) All round bty flooded, but bty probably active a duckwalk path over saturated area connects to dyke rd. NO bomb damage (1 Cdn APIS 24 Oct 44.)[2]
W3	Gun posn HAA	Bty 21. 4 gun 105 mm HAA bty crescent layout. Open rivetted emplacements 25' diameter spaced 20 yds apart. Cam. CP centrally located. May be in cupolas. Estimated max range 19000 yds.	D090252	R16/1145 Print 4167 R4/798 Print 3002	No 4 gun destroyed by attack 6/7 Oct. Flooding near bty but does NOT affect firing. (APIS 21 A Gp 16 Oct.) Bty on dyke NOT affected by flooding. Crew quarters in rear probably flooded. (1 Cdn APIS 24 Oct 44.)[3]
W4	Gun posn HAA	Bty 19. 3 gun 75 mm HAA bty. Crescent layout. Open emplacements 30' diameter, spaced 83 yds apart, 2 concrete shelters to EAST. Further construction at 084257. Hy cam.	D082262	R4/788 Print 3104 and 3106 R4/860 Print 3077	Three gun bty may possibly be LAA NOT affect by floods. (1 Cdn APIS 24 Oct 44.)[4]
W5	Gun posn AA	Bty 6. 4 gun 94 mm AA bty. Open emplacements 25' apart on top of buried shelters. Several shelters to NE. Sec armament; one 20 mm AA gun at 054370 Estimated max range 17000 yds.	D053374	R16/1145 Print 4025 R4/860 Print 3211	2 emplacements occupied-2 unoccupied. Gun from unoccupied emplacements probably moved to EAST of W16. (1 Cdn APIS 24 Oct 44.)
W33	Gun posn HAA	6 gun HAA bty in deep crescent layout	D128249	R4/860 Print 3027/8	NOT flooded. Some bombs nearby after hy bomber attack 11 Oct. (1 Cdn APIS 15 Oct.) 3 posns damaged. Now probably 3 LAA NOT 6 HAA. (1 Cdn APIS 24 Oct 44.)[5]

[2] Annotations added to original schedule for information of the Chief of Staff.

[3] Same as #2.

[4] Same as #2.

[5] Same as #2

Target No	Type of Target	Description	Map Reference	Photo Reference	Results and Remarks
W34	Gun posn HAA	4 x 105 mm HAA bty. Estimated range 19000 yds.	D175352	Phs to follow (Does not affect operation) [6]	Has been moved up above water level.

Annotations added to original schedule for information of the Chief of Staff.

```
REVISED EDITION NUMBER 3                Appx A to

(replacing target list                  17/1/9/Ops (First Cdn Army)

issued as Appx A to Revised             84G/TS 76/3/Ops (84 Gp RAF)

Edition No. 2 dated 2 Oct 44)           22 Oct 44
```

FIRST CDN ARMY/84 GP RAF   Copy Number

Op "INFATUATE"

TARGET SCHEDULE

for Pre-Planned Air Targets

prior to D-Day. OUTSIDE

Resources of 84 GP RAF

Remaining btys

Target No	Type of Target	Description	Map Reference	Photo Reference	Results and Remarks
W20	Gun posn CD	Bty 15. 4 x 76.2 mm gun tp. Irregular line layout. About 2640 yds inland. Open emplacement 35' sq spaced 16-42 yds apart. OP centrally located. Shelter in rear.	D078300	R/161145 Print 3185	Weight of attack fell on dummy posn nearby. NOT flooded. (1 Cdn APIS 15 Oct)
		(Bty well saturated)[1]			
W18	Gun posn CD	Thought to be a strong pt with possibly 2 lt guns in casemates	D076388	R4/788 Print 3195/6	Probable strong pt with small casemates for two lt guns. NOT flooded NO damage. (1 Cdn APIS 24 Oct 44.)
W24	Gun posn CD	4 gun 150 mm howitzer posn. Estimated max range 14500 yds. Open emplacements.	D094364	R16/1145 Print 4069	

[1]   Annotations added to original schedule for information of the Chief of Staff.

Target No	Type of Target	Description	Map Reference	Photo Reference	Results and Remarks
			(Bty completed flooded.)[2]		
W36	Gun posn FD	4 gun posn (fd). Occupied.	D083299	Photo to follow	
			(Bty area well saturated)[3]		
W37	Gun posn CD	1 x 150 mm gun.	D059379	R4/997 Print 4020/1/12	NO change (1 Cdn APIS 24 Oct 44).[4]
W38	Gun posn CD	4 x 75 mm gun howitzers. In open emplacements. Occupied. Estimated max range 13000 yds.	D036342	Photo to follow	
			(Bty area saturated.)[5]		

[2]   Same as #1.

[3]   Annotations added to original schedule for information of the Chief of Staff.

[4]   Same as #3.

[5]   Same as #3.

REVISED EDITION NUMBER 3   Appx A to

(replacing target list   17/1/9/Ops (First Cdn Army)

issued as Appx A to Revised   84G/TS 76/3/Ops (84 Gp RAF)

Edition No. 2 dated 2 Oct 44)   22 Oct 44

FIRST CDN ARMY/84 GP RAF   Copy Number

Op "INFATUATE"

TARGET SCHEDULE

for Pre-Planned Air Targets

prior to D-Day. OUTSIDE

Resources of 84 GP RAF

Strong pts and concrete emplacements.

Target No	Type of Target	Description	Map Reference	Photo Reference	Results and Remarks
W281	Defs	Strong pt, concrete shelters and emplacements.	D043368	R4/997 Prints 3151/2	NOT flooded - active 20 Oct. (1 Cdn APIS 20 Oct.) NO change. (1 Cdn APIS 24 Oct 44.)[1]
W282	Defs	Strong pt, concrete shelters and emplacements.	D036364	R4/997 Print 3152/3	NOT flooded - active 20 Oct. (1 Cdn APIS 20 Oct.) NO change. (1 Cdn APIS 24 Oct 44.)[2]
W283	Defs	Strong pt, concrete shelters and emplacements.	D030361	R4/997 Print 3153/4	NOT flooded - active 20 Oct. (1 Cdn APIS 20 Oct.) NO change. (1 Cdn APIS 24 Oct 44.)[3]

---

[1]   Annotations added to original schedule for information of the Chief of Staff.

[2]   Same as #1.

[3]   Same as #1.

1   Report No. 188

Target No	Type of Target	Description	Map Reference	Photo Reference	Results and Remarks
W284	Defs	Strong pt, concrete shelters and emplacements.	D022357	R4/997 Print 3155/6	NOT flooded - active 20 Oct. (1 Cdn APIS 20 Oct.) NO change. (1 Cdn APIS 24 Oct 44.)[4]
W285	Defs	Strong pt, concrete emplacements dominating landing beach at short range.	D026331	R4/997 Prints 4015/6	NOT flooded - active 20 Oct. (1 Cdn APIS 20 Oct.) NO change. (1 Cdn APIS 24 Oct 44.)[5]
W286	Defs	Strong pt with concrete emplacements.	D029325	R4/997 Print 4016/7	NOT flooded - active 20 Oct. (1 Cdn APIS 20 Oct.) NO change. (1 Cdn APIS 24 Oct 44.)[6]
W287	Defs	Strong pt with concrete emplacements.	D042312	R4/997 Print 3020/1	NOT flooded - active 20 Oct. (1 Cdn APIS 20 Oct.) NO change. (1 Cdn APIS 24 Oct 44.)[7]
W288	Defs	Strong pt with concrete emplacements and trenches.	D055304	R4/997 Print 4034/5	NOT flooded - active 20 Oct. (1 Cdn APIS 20 Oct.) NO change. (1 Cdn APIS 24 Oct 44.)[8]
W289	Strong pts	Two hy casemates and pillboxes on shoulder of gap.	D019336	R4/1139 Prints 4029/30	

(W.D., "G" Plans, H.Q. First Cdn Army, October 1944:   Approx 21, folios 124-131.)

---

[4]   Annotations added to original schedule for information of the Chief of Staff.

[5]   Same as #4.

[6]   Same as #4.

[7]   Same as #4.

[8]   Same as #4.

OPERATION "INFATUATE"

AIR PLAN

Appendix "A" - Summary of target allocation.

Appendix "B" - Cover and close support - D-Day.

Aim of Operation

1.   The aim of Operation "Infatuate" is to capture the island of WALCHEREN
as part of the plan for clearing the mouth of the SCHEDULE to enable ANTWERP
to be used as a port.

Plan for Assault

2.   The First Canadian Army propose to launch two seaborned assaults on the
island of WALCEREN as follows:

     a.   <u>Infatuate I</u> - an assault by elements of 52 Div on FLUSHING.

     b.   <u>Infatuate II</u> - an assault by "Force T" carrying 4th S.S. Bde to
            land on the breach made by Bomber Command in the dyke at
            WESTKAPELLE.

Flooding

3.   Flooding was a preliminary part of the plan, for the purpose of:

     a.   enabling coastal defences to be taken in rear by water-borne
            forces;

1

Index